Émile de Kératry

The Rise and Fall of the Emperor Maximilian

A narrative of the Mexican Empire, 1861-7: from authentic documents. With the imperial correspondence

Émile de Kératry

The Rise and Fall of the Emperor Maximilian

A narrative of the Mexican Empire, 1861-7: from authentic documents. With the imperial correspondence

ISBN/EAN: 9783337175320

Printed in Europe, USA, Canada, Australia, Japan

Cover: Foto ©ninafisch / pixelio.de

More available books at **www.hansebooks.com**

THE RISE AND FALL

OF

THE EMPEROR MAXIMILIAN.

A NARRATIVE OF

THE MEXICAN EMPIRE, 1861-7.

From Authentic Documents.

WITH THE IMPERIAL CORRESPONDENCE.

BY

COUNT ÉMILE DE KÉRATRY.

TRANSLATED BY ARRANGEMENT UNDER THE INTERNATIONAL CONVENTION

BY

G. H. VENABLES.

LONDON:
SAMPSON LOW, SON, AND MARSTON,
MILTON HOUSE, LUDGATE HILL.
1868.

CONTENTS.

PAGE

INTRODUCTION 1

CHAPTER I.

Alleged Cause of the French Intervention—The Convention of La Soledad—Real Position of Juarez—Commencement of Hostilities—Previous Negotiations with Maximilian—Secret Aim of the French Intervention—Cause of England's Withdrawal—Disappointment and Opposition of General Prim—Napoleon's first 'Idea'—He throws off the Mask—Feeble Character of the French Policy 3

CHAPTER II.

The War begun—The Repulse at Puebla, and its Causes—General Marquez—Condition of Mexico—Arrival of General Forey—His Delays and Mismanagement—Protracted Siege and Capture of Puebla—Triumphal Entry of French into Mexico . . . 19

CHAPTER III.

French Organisation of Mexico—Convocation of a Junta—Unwillingness to join it, and the Cause—Decision for a Monarchy—Offer of the Crown to Maximilian—The Council of Regency—Maximilian's Doubts—Arrival of General Bazaine as Commander-in-Chief—His Difficulties—Juarez and Church Property—Peace restored in Mexico—Arrival of Maximilian—His Virtues, his Faults, and his Fate 28

CHAPTER IV.

Intention of this History—Political Conduct of the French and Mexican Cabinets—Character of Maximilian, and his Earliest

CONTENTS.

Measures—Energy of General Bazaine—Reorganisation of the Mexican Resources—General Bazaine's Explanations—Military Movements—Calumnies against French Officers—Appeal to the Empress—Maximilian's Want of Appreciation of the Indians—Financial Embarrassments—Apathy of Mexican Officials—Success of the French Campaigns 42

CHAPTER V.

Military and Civil Arrangements—Organising Commissions Dissolved—Capture and Escape of Porfirio Diaz—Fresh Military Plans of the Emperor—Their Imprudence and Inexpediency—The Question of Church Property—The American Question—Attitude of the United States, and Recall of their Minister—Treason of Cortina—Revolt breaks out 60

CHAPTER VI.

Marshal Bazaine's Advice on American Matters—It is not Taken—Marshal Bazaine's Marriage, and Dowry to his Bride—Mexicans in the Days of Cortez—Condition of the Indians—Opposition of the Landholders and Officials—Juarez's Hiding-Place. . . 71

CHAPTER VII.

Fatal Decree of October 3—Its real Bearing—Empress Charlotte's Letter—Decay of Mexican Resources—Inaction of Mexican Officials, and consequent Disasters—Extent of French Occupation—Statement of the National Army 86

CHAPTER VIII.

Disasters in the Empire—Dissensions between the Foreign Contingents and Mexican Troops—The Empress Charlotte's Opinion of the French Army—Difficulty in paying the Troops, and consequent Desertions—Maximilian's Project to subdue Yucatan—Its Policy—The two Chances for the Empire—Poverty of the Mexican Troops—Pecuniary Help rendered by Marshal Bazaine—M. de Lacunza's Moving Appeal to Marshal Bazaine—Meeting at the Imperial Palace—Maximilian speaks out—Yankee Intrigues—American Dictation to France—Mr. Seward's Note—Maximilian secretly sacrificed 96

CONTENTS.　　　　　　　　　v

CHAPTER IX.
PAGE

Arrival of Baron Saillard—Despatches from M. Drouyn de Lhuys—Proposals for French Evacuation—French Hypocrisy—Position of Maximilian—M. Almonte sent to the Court of the Tuileries—Proposal for Concentration of the Foreign Contingents—Thwarted by Maximilian's Advisers—Fruitless Bungling 115

CHAPTER X.

Establishment of *Cazadores* and Gendarmes—The Marshal's Plan for Evacuation favourable to Maximilian—Maximilian's wise Measures of Retrenchment—His Confidence, Energy, and Hopes—His Plans explained to Marshal Bazaine—Revolt of Chihuahua and Reoccupation by the French—Maximilian's Letter of Congratulation to Marshal Bazaine—His Disagreement with the Marshal—Mr. Bigelow's Despatch—Left no Hope for Maximilian. 124

CHAPTER XI.

Bad System of Enlistment followed—Energy of the Empress Charlotte—Destruction of Mejia's Division—The Emperor Napoleon's harsh Reply to M. Almonte's Mission—Its Effect on the Mexican Court—Maximilian's Project of Abdication stopped by the Empress—Her Expedition to Europe—Painful Incident—Fresh Imperial Disasters—Maximilian's Idea of Declaring a State of Siege—It is opposed by Marshal Bazaine 142

CHAPTER XII.

Arrival of the Empress Charlotte at Saint Nazaire—Her Journey to Paris—Conversation with M. Drouyn de Lhuys—Her exciting Interview with Napoleon III.—American Despatches as to her Arrival—Maximilian's *Coup d'état*.—The Abbé Fischer—The Emperor's Reactionary Policy—Concentration of French Troops—American Assistance to the Liberal Party 157

CHAPTER XIII.

Reactionary Influence of the new Ministry—Maximilian's injudicious Innovations—Fall of Tampico—Correspondence thereon—Marshal Bazaine's Explanations—Mutiny of the Belgian Contingent—Singular Loss of Belgian Despatches—Bad State of the National Army—Complaints made by the French Commandants of the *Cazadores*—Well-founded Appeal of General Guttierez—Clerical Interference with the Course of Justice 168

CHAPTER XIV.

French Officers in the Mexican Administration—Correspondence on this Subject—Marshal Bazaine's Acquiescence—Disavowed at Paris—Neglect of the Mexican Naval Department—Convention of July 30—Sudden Alteration in the Views of the French Cabinet—The Mission of General Castelnau—Matters getting Worse in Mexico—Maximilian's Plans to ensure his safe Retreat—Marshal Bazaine receives fresh Orders from Paris—Mr. Seward's Despatch—Complaints of the Mexican Ministry rebutted by Marshal Bazaine—Mysterious Aim of General Castelnau's Mission—The Four-fold Drama—Maximilian's Protest 181

CHAPTER XV.

Maximilian prepares for Departure—Last Moments at Chapultepec – Arrival of sad News—The Health of the Empress Charlotte—Maximilian resolves to leave—Cowardly Conduct of the Ministers—Marshal Bazaine's Firmness—Maximilian leaves the Capital—His Three last Wishes—His Journey—Peculiarities in Maximilian's Character. 200

CHAPTER XVI.

Maximilian's Entry into Orizaba—His enthusiastic Reception—Retires into Seclusion—Intrigues of Father Fischer and the Clerical Party—Disaster to the Austrian Contingent—Fall of Oajaca, and increasing Liberal Successes—Maximilian still undecided—His kind Thought for the Austro-Belgian Contingent—M. Eloïn's Letter—Decides Maximilian to renew the Contest . 210

CHAPTER XVII.

General Castelnau proceeds to the Capital—Marshal Bazaine's ambiguous Position—His Difficulties and Error—Dark Views of the French Cabinet—Agitated State of the Country and City of Mexico—Mexican Ingratitude—French Intrigues with Ortega—Attitude of the United States—Campbell and Sherman's Mission to Mexico – Mr. Seward's Instructions to the Envoys—They arrive at Tampico 218

CHAPTER XVIII.

Maximilian's new Resolutions—Generals Marquez and Miramon—Secret Imperial Envoys to Washington—M. Larès' Requests to Marshal Bazaine—Father Fischer's Diplomacy—Maximilian's

PAGE

final Requisitions—The French Representatives deceived—Marquis de Montholon's Letters to Marshal Bazaine—Accordant Views of France and the United States—Letter of Porfirio Diaz—Final Disappointment of the American Envoys . . . 230

CHAPTER XIX.

Conference of Mexican Ministers—Seductive Plans of the Clerical Party— Meditated Campaigns by Marquez and Miramon—Maximilian announces his fresh Resolve—His Manifesto—M. Larès' Letter to the French Representatives—Dissatisfaction in the French Camp—Destruction of the French Schemes—Harsh Measures of the Emperor Napoleon—Recall of the Foreign Legion—Mr. Bigelow's Despatch—Irritation at the Tuileries—The lost Despatch—Hostile Feeling between the French and Mexican Governments—Maximilian returns to the Capital . 246

CHAPTER XX.

French Pecuniary Claims enforced—Forcible Proceedings at Vera Cruz—Customhouse Difficulties in the City of Mexico—Arbitrary Conduct of the French—The Mexican Minister's Protest—Discord in the French Camp—Marshal Bazaine's Painful Position—French Intrigues with the Rebels—Decisive Telegram to General Castelnau—Maximilian's Difficulties increase—His Generous Resolve as to Foreign Soldiers — Letter from the Empress Eugénie—The Clerical Plans fail—Imperial Disasters—Maximilian's Interview with Marshal Bazaine—Plain Statement by the Latter—The Junta in Mexico—Marshal Bazaine attends it—The Marshal's Declaration—The Junta decides for the Empire—Sale of the French Cavalry Horses—Exchange of Prisoners—Honourable Conduct of the Liberals—Appeals to French Honour—The Austrian Farewell 263

CHAPTER XXI.

Withdrawal of French Troops from the Capital—Position of the Rebels—Dissatisfaction of M. Larès at the passive Attitude of the French Army—Marshal Bazaine's vindicatory Letter—Maximilian's final Rupture with the French Authorities—Proposition as to the 'Cross of Guadeloupe'—Interference of Abbé Fischer—His Reproval by the French Authorities—Orders for immediate Embarkation—French Measures for the Protection of the Capital—Destruction of French Munitions of War—Maximilian's

PAGE

Mistrust and Visit to the Citadel—French Flag struck in the City of Mexico—Characters of Mejia and Miramon—General Castelnau's Return—Marshal Bazaine's last Appeal to Maximilian—Its Failure—Marshal Bazaine fortifies Vera Cruz—Marshal Bazaine's Letter to the French Admiral—Final Departure from Vera Cruz of the French Troops—The Marshal's bad Reception in France—Its Cause and Its Injustice 288

CHAPTER XXII.

Termination of the French Intervention in Mexico—Reflections on the Fate of Maximilian—His Illusions and Errors—Retrospect and Final Considerations 305

APPENDIX 308

THE RISE AND FALL

OF

THE EMPEROR MAXIMILIAN.

INTRODUCTION.

THE French expedition to Mexico henceforth to history. The second emperor of that country was shot to death at Queretaro in 1867, as the first had been at Padilla in 1824. Yet both loved their adopted country, and Maximilian brought with him a high-minded conception of his mission.

Just at the time when a solemn debate is resounding within the walls of our Palais Législatif, we may perhaps be permitted to investigate the various causes which have combined in the ruin of this distant enterprise. The present time is all the more favourable to this investigation since the several acts of the Mexican drama—so fertile in catastrophes—date, so to speak, only from yesterday. Besides, it seems to us only just to apportion out and ascribe to each of the actors in this sanguinary tragedy the share of responsibility which duly falls upon him, both in the conception and management of the undertaking, and also in the failure of this unfortunate campaign. Let us then pursue this enquiry, and let us try to do it as impartially as possible.

We must, first of all, admit that the French armed force, both sailors and soldiers, are beside the question in our present enquiry. It was this armed force alone which was found adequate to its mission. The slave of duty, it fulfilled its obligations to the end, and never for a moment swerved from its noble traditions. This fatal expedition will be estimated as but a fresh claim to glory. Rarely has French valour been compelled to testify to its personal prowess in so vast a field as this. If our country could only have been a witness of the thousand deeds of arms which were obscurely done during the last five years in every corner of Mexico, by a handful of men lost, as it were, in its vast expanse, the admiration which would have been inspired by the warlike virtues of her children might have stilled for a time the tumult of opposition and complaint. The brave men left scattered over the path from the Antilles to the Pacific proclaim loudly enough the noble devotion of the expeditionary corps.

It is then in the first 'idea' of the cabinet of the Tuileries—in the instructions which emanated therefrom—in the management of our policy and of our military operations, that we must seek for the information which is indispensable to throw a light upon the sad scene in which the national prestige has been diminished, and the throne set up by the hand of France has crumbled down in blood.

CHAPTER I.

Alleged Cause of the French Intervention—The Convention of La Soledad—Real Position of Juarez—Commencement of Hostilities—Previous Negotiations with Maximilian—Secret Aim of the French Intervention—Cause of England's Withdrawal—Disappointment and Opposition of General Prim—Napoleon's first 'Idea'—He throws off the Mask—Feeble Character of the French Policy.

WHAT was the idea which was dominant at first when the French flag was sent under the walls of Vera Cruz? And, later, what was the real cause of the declaration of war hurled against the President Juarez?

If we are to depend upon the official declarations, we see that the government of the emperor, in virtue of a convention signed November 20, 1861, in conjunction with England and Spain, had determined, by a joint intervention, 'to compel Mexico to fulfil the obligations already solemnly contracted, and to give us a guarantee of a more efficient protection for the persons and property of our respective countrymen.' These are the instructions which were intrusted to Rear-Admiral Jurien de la Gravière, who was invested with the chief command of our military forces sent to Mexico, together with a naval squadron. M. Thouvenel, the minister of foreign affairs, made the following addition to the admiral's instructions:—

'The allied powers decline any intervention in the domestic affairs of the country, and especially any exercise of pressure on the will of the population with regard to their choice of a government.'

In the early part of January, the three plenipotentiaries addressed a collective note to the Mexican government, demanding reparation for all the grievances and wrongs which had been suffered. On February 9, 1862, the allied commissioners informed Doblado, Juarez's minister, that the allied troops would march about the middle of the month to occupy more wholesome quarters in the interior, and invited him to come to an understanding with the Count de Reuss (General Prim).

The army, on landing, had been placed under the orders of the Spanish general Prim. Spain had 7,000 men there, and France about 3,000. England had only landed some marines. On February 13, 1862, the Mexican government and the plenipotentiaries of Spain, England, and France, signed respectively the preliminary convention of La Soledad; the 1st article of this confirmed the authority of Juarez, and the 6th stipulated that the Mexican flag, which had been lowered on the approach of the allied squadrons menacing Vera Cruz, should be again hoisted.

Nearly two months necessarily elapsed before the draft of the treaty found its way back from Europe to the camp of the negotiating parties, who had been obliged to consult their respective governments. Through a very proper exercise of foresight, article 3 of the convention of La Soledad had stipulated that, during the progress of negotiations, the expeditionary corps should occupy the towns of Cordova, Orizaba, and Tehuacan—quarters that were favourable to the health of the soldiers. Doblado, the minister, had made this concession, and Juarez had ratified it. Although it seemed right, from our point of view, looking at the fatal effect of the 'terres chaudes,' especially during the winter season, to imperiously exact this liberty of moving the troops, still the pride of the Mexicans was deeply wounded by the president's concession; they also felt humiliated because the evacuation of their invaded territory had not preceded the preliminaries of reconciliation. But Juarez, more inclined to subtlety than courage, was animated by a real desire to grant the reparations claimed by the allies, and clearly comprehended that he would never obtain the withdrawal of the hostile forces before serious pledges of conciliation had been exchanged. Confiding, however, in our word, the Mexican government had added a condition to the liberty of movement which had been dictated by humane feelings only, and had stipulated that, 'if the negotiations were broken off' (article 4), the allied forces should retire from the positions they had taken up, and should fall back along the road to Vera Cruz, as far as Paso Ancho, before any acts of hostility were committed, and, in this case, that the allied hospitals should remain under the safeguard of the Mexican nation.

The courier, whose return from Europe had been anxiously expected, was at last signaled in the roadstead. It was ascertained that England, rejecting all idea of an expedition into the interior of Mexico, had ratified the signature of Sir C. Wyke, its plenipotentiary. Spain, though expressing a certain reluctance, did not disavow that of General Prim. But France, through the medium of the *Moniteur*, declared boldly that she could not accept the convention of La Soledad, as being 'counter to the national dignity.' This public disavowal, inflicted as it was on an officer who was justly reputed to be jealous of the honour of his flag, excited a painful feeling of astonishment, and had but an untoward effect.

The admiral commenced his retrograde movement

on April 1. The French troops had been occupying Tehuacan; they halted at Cordova, three stages from Paso Ancho, by the side of the Spanish force. But a rupture between the three allied bodies was now imminent, their respective views and interests being so plainly at variance. On April 9, 1862, the rupture was consummated; the cause especially alleged was the presence under our flag of Almonte, and some emigrants, who had arrived in the early part of March, who on account of their monarchical opinions were objects of suspicion both to Juarez and also to the English government. Sir C. Wyke, the British minister, wrote to Earl Russell—' By giving our intervention the appearance of a friendly protectorate, we shall be best able to consolidate a government which represents the intelligent and respectable portion of the nation.'

We will now state that, in 1857, a constitution voted by the general congress had conferred the presidency on General Comonfort, who was illegally deposed from his chair; that Juarez, in virtue of his commission as vice-president, had defended this constitution for six years. The Indian advocate seemed the only one who had not perjured himself! He held the position of chief magistrate in a republic which was convulsed and ruined by civil war. Standing at the head of affairs in a country thoroughly demoralised by the evil passions which sought to overflow it, he might perhaps have been able to do better, but he might also have done much worse. On him has fallen with all its weight the unhappy result of half a century of fanaticism and anarchy, and he has had the courage to bear his burden without giving way. For him at least the word 'country' has not been without signification, and he who would judge him, if he means to judge justly, must turn his back upon Europe and its ideas, and look only at the troubled horizon of Mexico.

The die was cast! The English and Spanish squadrons put to sea again, and the French expeditionary forces (about 6,000 strong) were left alone. They prepared for the offensive by pursuing their backward movement towards the Chiquihuite—an embanked torrent situate almost half-way between the Gulf and Orizaba—the wooded escarpments of which commanding the pass had been armed for the defensive by the Mexicans. Whilst the French commander, faithful to the engagement he had entered into, was making this counter-march, a report was spread that the lives of our sick soldiers who had been left behind in the hospital at Orizaba, under the protection of the enemy, were threatened by the Juarist army. The French commander, yielding to the dread that his defenceless men would be put to death, immediately faced about, and violating, though with reluctance, the promise he had given, began the offensive by making his way by forced marches to Orizaba, without having repassed the strong position of the Chiquihuite.

Such is a brief recapitulation of the events in the first phase of the Mexican expedition. If we consider nothing but the facts which the imperial government laid before the country, it looks as if Napoleon III. had but one aim in view—that of protecting the interests of our countrymen, interests which would have been wronged by the convention of La Soledad, if the latter had been ratified. Surely, France was only generous in protecting with its safeguard those Mexican refugees who wished to tread once more the soil of their country. If we were to believe the official language, the war took its rise from the refusal or illusory concessions opposed by the Mexican president to the legitimate demand for reparation put forward by our minister. Juarez then must remain alone responsible to posterity for the ruin of his people, and for all the blood shed upon Mexican soil, shed, too, in such profusion, but yet powerless to fertilise it!

We will, however, endeavour to seek out the truth which in this matter is so difficult to get at; and now that we have placed the principal actors on the stage, let us enquire what was passing behind the scenes. To the ambiguity of official phraseology, we shall reply by hard facts and incontestable documents.

On January 18, 1861, exactly ten months before the convention was signed by the three powers, whilst Juarez was presiding in his capital, and little thinking of the storm that was gathering in Europe in order to break over his head, *France was conspiring for his fall.* In the little town of Tlalpam, about four leagues from Mexico, General Leonardo Marquez was riveting the first links in the chain of intrigue which already united the cabinet of the Tuileries with the palace of Miramar. On this very night, an Indian courier, bearing a confidential note, entered Mexico. General Marquez wrote to the Licenciado Aquilar, Santa Anna's former minister, to say that the time was come 'for organising a reaction—political, social, and military.' He offered him the presidentship of a directory, and the right of choosing as its members those whom he thought most capable of serving the good cause. The motto '*Dios e Orden*' was proclaimed; it was the signal of revolt against '*Libertad e Independencia*,' which was the republican formula.

At the same time, a body of Mexican refugees, at whose head stood MM. Gutierrez de Estrada, Hidalgo, Almonte, Mgr. La Bastida, and the ex-president Miramon, was agitating in Paris; they profited by the favour in which they stood at the Tuileries, and by their admission to the court, to awaken an august sympathy in behalf of their cause. Moreover, Mgr. La Bastida, Archbishop of Mexico, speaking in the name of his clergy—deprived of their mortmain property by a law issued in 1859 (property amounting to 900 millions of francs)—contended warmly for the same interests at the court of Rome, which was not backward in showing favour to a project the intention of which was to place a prince of the Catholic race of Hapsburg on the throne on which Iturbide once sat.

Some persons maintain that the Mexican empire was one of the results of the peace of Villafranca. Without attaching any great importance to this assertion, it is beyond all doubt that, at the very time when Marquez was organising a revolt, the Mexican refugee party, secretly supported by the French government (in the bosom of which Spanish sympathies prevailed), offered the imperial crown of Mexico to the Archduke Maximilian, who had just renounced all official position in his own country, and held himself ready for any eventuality.

The negotiations between Paris and Miramar lasted about eight months ere the reluctance of the archduke could be overcome. At last, the prince addressed to M. Gutierrez de Estrada, the authorised confidant, a letter written in Spanish, on both sides of a large page. Maximilian declared that he would accept the throne that was offered to him, but only ' on the condition that France and England would support him with their moral and material guarantee, both on land and sea.' M. Gutierrez, who was at Paris, at once forwarded this precious document (*which we have read*) to the Licenciado Aquilar, in order that he might make it known to the members of the plot which was hatching in

Mexico. But the secret was not so well kept but that, in 1862, this late minister of Santa Anna was placed in confinement. Some time after, in default of any sufficient proof of guilt, Doblado signed his warrant of release.

The archduke's acceptance therefore was binding on France as early as the end of 1861, at the very moment when the maritime expedition, concerted by the three powers against the republic, was about to be carried out. In this combination, developed under the veil of secrecy, we shall discover the mysterious aim of the intervention of the French government, which had hoped to have induced the English cabinet to share its views, and to promise its active co-operation in the establishment of the Emperor Maximilian on the throne which had been promised him. The rebel party, recruited mostly among the clerical faction, only waited for the appearance of the tri-coloured flag in Mexican waters before commencing to open the campaign.

The defence of our countrymen, the wish to avenge the outrages they had suffered—outrages which it would be more just to lay to the charge of all Mexico than to Juarez personally—all this was nothing but a pretext, which was intended from the first to be subordinate to the second scheme of the enterprise. But this pretext was appealed to, so as to get the troops landed on the republican territory, and to get foothold there, in expectation of the day when the French government might be freely able to inaugurate its policy in the New World—a policy pregnant with danger, and causing France to contradict completely its professed principle of non-intervention. If any doubts were entertained as to this, they would be soon put an end to by two subsequent events which exercised a great influence on the disastrous issue of the enterprise. We allude to the rupture of the convention of La Soledad, and to the Emperor Napoleon's letter to General Forey.

Why was the convention of La Soledad torn up by France only?

From the very day that England was indirectly initiated into the projects secretly nourished by the French government, she was eager, by signing the convention, to get clear of the Mexican question. It was not till October 1861, after Maximilian had made his demand for the English guarantee, that M. Thouvenel gave directions that the British cabinet should be sounded on this subject, without anything distinct being implied in the overtures which were made. It turned out that these overtures were badly received on the other side of the Channel. Without delay, our minister of foreign affairs, having been several times questioned by the English ambassador, and fearing that he had gone on rather too far, replied very categorically that 'no government would be forced on the Mexican people' (despatch of Lord Cowley to Earl Russell, May 2, 1862). On another occasion, M. Thouvenel, being questioned by Lord Cowley on the subject of the candidature of the Archduke Maximilian, and being asked whether negotiations on the point were pending between France and Austria, replied in the negative. Our minister's statement was as follows:—' Negotiations have been entered on by the Mexicans themselves alone, who have proceeded to Vienna for this purpose.'

In spite of these denials, England thought it prudent to assert the authority of Juarez, and to retire from the business. She cared but little to compromise her responsibility by giving the future emperor a guarantee which she has subsequently proved she is not very prodigal in granting. She was well aware that the guarantee which was demanded of her was almost without limit, and might precipitate her fleet into a conflict with the United States. Even if the British cabinet had been imprudent enough to grant it, the parliament would most certainly have disavowed their act. Thus, Sir C. Wyke, her plenipotentiary, had but one aim, and that was, as is commonly said, to get out of the scrape as well as he could, and, profiting by the joint pressure, to obtain advantageous indemnities which would heal all the wounds of the English claimants. In fact, England has been the one to profit most by the sacrifices we have made, thanks to the deductions made in her favour from the Mexican receipts during the whole time of the expedition.

As to the court of Madrid, General Prim had enticed it into the Mexican expedition, animated as he was by a purely personal ambition. Being allied through his wife to the family of Etcheverria, a member of which was actually in Juarez's council, and keeping up, as he did, an active connection with Mexico, which he knew was always ready for military '*pronunciamientos*,' the Count de Reuss, whose brilliant reputation had already preceded him, pictured for himself, if not a royal diadem, at least a viceroy's coronet, which would once more attach the former Spanish colony to its mother-country. As soon as he was conscious of the state of things which France desired to introduce, and when he heard of the arrival of the reinforcements brought by General de Lorencez, and intended for an expedition into the interior, which he had flattered himself that he should attempt alone, Prim felt that his illusions were at an end, and at once persuaded his government to abandon the project, discountenancing at the same time the French enterprise. His journey to Vichy had given rise in his mind to certain magic hopes; the vanishing away of all these excited, therefore, considerable ill-will, and dictated his famous oration to the Spanish senate, numerous copies of which he took good care to forward to the United States. Prim must surely have forgotten that he had had the honour of commanding the combined expeditionary force! For, in May 1863, whilst the French were being killed under the walls of Puebla, he sent to his uncle, the Juarist minister, under the cover of the British legation, and through the hostile port of Tuxpan, a large number of copies of this very speech, so inimical to the arms of his late allies.

Finally, why was it that the French government *alone* put an end to the compact of La Soledad? Admiral Jurien, our plenipotentiary, who has left behind him in Mexico a beloved name and a high reputation for honour and rectitude, received the affront of a public disavowal when the emperor ' adopted the resolution of withdrawing his full powers from the admiral.' Now, it is certain that the admiral, surrounded as he was by the public esteem, might have gone to Mexico all alone without any fear for his safety, and could have personally arranged with President Juarez all the differences which divided the two governments. Prudence itself dictated this course of action. Was it more desirable to upset the power then existing in virtue of the constitution, under a pretext that it did not enjoy all the power and all the authority that might be expedient? On the other hand, it is beyond doubt that the French plenipotentiary had perfectly reconciled the dignity of his country with the interests of his countrymen.

'The Mexican government,' Doblado had written

in Juarez's name, to the allied commissioners, 'is resolved to make every kind of sacrifice in order to prove to friendly nations that the faithful fulfilment of the engagements it enters into will be, for the future, one of the invariable principles of the liberal administration.'

This declaration, if made in good faith by a stable government, should have been satisfactory. It is true that a reference to the past permitted doubts being entertained as to the execution of these promises. It would, therefore, have been better, at the very outset, when the admiral first left Paris, to have frankly declared war. Negotiations seemed idle, if a refusal to give the time that was requisite for carrying them into effect had been previously determined on, and if they were in anticipation to be declared illusory in consideration of the weakness and presumed bad faith of Juarez.

The admiral acted properly, and the best proof of this is the fact that a few months after this disavowal (against which, however, public opinion had pronounced), the chief of the state himself called to his side Admiral Jurien, who, besides this flattering distinction, was sent a second time to Mexico, hoisting his flag in the iron-clad frigate 'La Normandie.' It is impossible not to be struck with this strange contradiction. But we shall find an explanation of it in the letter written in 1862 to General Forey, at the time when the latter received the command of the corps d'armée intended to avenge the check experienced by General de Lorencez, a check of which we shall speak in due course.

The emperor wrote:—

Fontainebleau, July 3, 1862.

... If, on the contrary, Mexico preserves its independence,

and maintains the integrity of its territory; if, with the assistance of France, a firm government is kept up there, *we, on the other side of the ocean, shall have restored to the Latin race its power and its prestige.* NAPOLEON.

Henceforth, then, the expedition has for its aim the triumph of the Latin race on American soil, in order to oppose the encroachments of the Anglo-Saxon. In this imperial document, the real idea of the emperor is for the first time revealed. It stands in formal contradiction to the instructions given by the French government to its plenipotentiary, and also to the language of its ministers—MM. Billault and Rouher—which, up to that time, asserted from the tribune that the creation of an empire for Maximilian had never been a matter in question, and that the defence of our national interests had been the sole cause of the hostilities against Juarez.

In fact, the redress of the wrongs of our countrymen had been nothing but a mask which it was at last time to take off. The archduke was about to appear upon the scene. The admiral had been disavowed, because, acting as he did in good faith, he very nearly ruined a hidden project of which he had been kept in ignorance. The convention was repudiated by France because the latter would not treat, being in fact unable to do so, bound as it was to Maximilian. Our financial claims were for the time no longer in question. The downfall of Juarez was the only business in hand, and in order to upset the president's chair, it was necessary that the French army should enter Mexico arms in hand.

Thus, from the outset, the intervention of France in Mexico was the result of an ambiguous policy, which proved a constant incubus on the enterprise; and when Juarez consented to engage in this war *à outrance*, signalised and terminated as it was by such terrible reprisals, it was because he recognised from the very first that the tri-coloured flag was but a mask for the imperial banner which followed in the track of the foreigner, and that the existence of the republic was menaced in the very first instance. We may well believe that this unavowed aim was the principal cause of the disguised support which was furnished by the United States to the republican cause from the beginning—a support which sufficed to hold in check, and finally to ruin, the French influence in America. Certain documents, which were found in General Comonfort's baggage, abandoned in the foundry at San Lorenzo, have come under our observation. They leave no doubt whatever as to the co-operation of the United States, and that the latter comprehended that France desired to profit by the war which was internally devastating them, so as to effect a counterbalance to the Anglo-Saxon influence. President Lincoln, whose honesty was so praised in France, wrote to Juarez:—'We are not at open war with France, but reckon on money, cannon, and voluntary enlistments, all of which we shall countenance.' *He kept his word.*

Here, too, one cannot help being painfully impressed by the vacillations of the imperial government, which seemed as if it dared not adopt a decided character in its trans-oceanic policy, and from the commencement to the conclusion of the expedition resorted to little else but half-measures. The idea of placing the Latin race as a bulwark against the encroachments of the Anglo-Saxon, who probably half a century hence will embrace the entire globe by joining hands with the Russians, was certainly an imposing one, and well worthy to tempt a bold heart and a great nation; but only on the condition that the means of its success were a previously assured certainty. It was easy to foresee that in any case of rebuff, the ruin of this idea would accelerate and irretrievably precipitate the downfall of Latin influence in America, and would for ever destroy its prestige, which the Spaniards had done so much to compromise. But if this idea was to triumph, it needed the co-operation of the United States themselves. It is very certain that there was a favourable opportunity in 1862, looking at the secession of the Southern States from those of the North. Then was the time for France to have acted vigorously, and to have obtained allies even in the enemy's camp. Two courses were open, and both were practicable; but here we shall not pretend to decide between them. Either it was necessary at the first onset to decide in good earnest for the cause of the Union, and to restrain the South by a threatening demonstration on the frontier of the Rio Bravo; or, if the belligerent character of the secession party was recognised, it was essential to go the whole length without hesitation, and to consummate the work of separation by declaring openly for the planters of the Southern States, who, fired with the recollections of French glory, waited but the succour of our promise to triumphantly offer a helping hand to our expeditionary force which was marching on Mexico. Through an inconsistency which one can now, on looking back, hardly conceive possible, the imperial policy wandered away from every logical tradition. The belligerent character which had been accorded to the Southern States served only to prolong to no purpose a sanguinary contest; and our government repulsed the reiterated overtures of the Southern proprietors, whom they encouraged, as it were, only yesterday, and finally abandoned to their fate. From that time the Latin cause was lost. The victorious Yankees crossed the Texan frontier *en masse*, and, allured by the hopes of plunder, assumed the form of Juarist guerillas, and overran the Mexican provinces of Nuevo Leon, La Sonora, and Tamaulipas.

CHAPTER II.

The War begun—The Repulse at Puebla, and its Causes—General Marquez—Condition of Mexico—Arrival of General Forey—His Delays and Mismanagement—Protracted Siege and Capture of Puebla—Triumphal Entry of French into Mexico.

NOW commences the *second phase* of the French expedition. Now we leave the domain of diplomacy and politics to enter upon the field of war. Here also mistakes were made, and they were followed by disastrous consequences. After the rupture of the convention of La Soledad, the French troops, reinforced by 3,500 men brought by General de Lorencez, commenced hostilities. The line of the Chiquihuite had not been repassed, as the convention of La Soledad had stipulated. This violation of the promise which had been given formed but an unhappy beginning, and produced a deplorable effect. A civilised people, who made it their boast that they were about to teach a nation which was almost barbarous a respect for justice and for plighted faith, commenced by thus treading under foot a solemn promise. It was a double error. Besides diminishing the prestige of our force, we became the first to open the door of treason. Moreover, the Mexicans imagined, and vied with one another in repeating in their bragging language, that the French had been afraid to give up to them the pass of the Chiquihuite, 'a formidable position that we should not have been able to pass a second time if it had been defended by the noble sons of Cortes.' To anyone who knew anything about it it was plain that they were under an illusion. The way through the pass was armed with a few cast-iron cannon and some guns of position, which were difficult to manœuvre; they enfiladed but badly the winding-road which opened up from the sea, and the pass might be easily turned by means of the neighbouring heights; so it is a matter of certainty that the resistance would not have been of long duration. But, at all events, it would have been preferable to suffer some loss, even at the risk of delaying the succour to the sick men left at Orizaba, than to allow it to be thought that we had broken our word. Good right, on this occasion too, seemed to be on the Mexican side, who did not fail to make the most of our neglect of treaties among the population generally.

We shall not attempt here to describe the military operations commenced under such unhappy auspices, which resulted in such a painful issue, on May 5, 1862, under the walls of Puebla; but we must say that our government committed a series of errors which attest a complete ignorance on their part of the country in which they were waging war, as well as a strange forgetfulness of the feeling in our own country which had given rise to the allied invasion.

General de Lorencez was commissioned to open a campaign of this sort at the head of a force which was ridiculous for its insufficiency. The responsibility of his non-success is to be justly traced back to the government, who had neglected to follow out the rules of the simplest foresight. The laurels so rapidly gathered in China by a few fortunate battalions had no doubt caused them to hope for a fresh harvest of glory in Mexico. It needed all the heroism that a handful of men could show, that the check experienced under the forts of Guadelupe and Loreto did not result in a complete disaster, and impartial history will loudly declare that General de Lorencez's retreat across thirty leagues of troubled country, inundated as it was, and affording every facility for ambuscade—intimidating by the bold bearing of his little column Carbajal's numerous cavalry which crowned the *cerros*, without daring to come down, and bringing back his wounded and stores safe to Orizaba, stands at the head of all noble feats of arms. Two mistakes were made by the military authorities, who had misunderstood the great principles of the war. In the first place, they were bound to see how matters stood before they placed themselves at the entrance of Puebla, into which they thought they could enter as into a friendly city; but it received them, when they were a short distance off, with a running fire; subsequently, it was a measure of necessity that they should make themselves sure, in a military point of view, of Borrego, which commanded the town of Orizaba, in which they had to seek a refuge after the retreat.

But the defeat at Puebla was principally caused by the complete ignorance which M. Saligny, who was armed with extensive powers, and marched with the army, showed as to all that concerned the place and its inhabitants. The general, deceived by the assertions of an ill-informed diplomacy, pushed straight on, convinced that the streets of Puebla were adorned with triumphal arches in honour of our soldier-liberators. The disappointment was a cruel one, and it ought to have been foreseen. Could the refugee party, who had for years been growing old as exiles from their country, be expected to give the necessary information? Besides, we had taken for our ally General Marquez, well known in Mexico for his cruelty, who, in obedience to the orders of President Miramon, and in opposition to the authority of Juarez, was guilty of having broken open, by means of his soldiers, the official seal and treasure-coffers of the English legation, in order to take away seven millions of francs which were therein deposited; he was guilty, too, of having shot the wounded, both our countrymen and foreigners, who were lying in the hospitals at Tacubaya. His flag went before ours, and it was saluted by the country as it well deserved. Marquez had invited the invasion. Was it thus that we should have offered ourselves as liberators to the Mexicans, who were full of hatred to Marquez—an energetic soldier certainly, but who combined with his military qualities the instincts of an executioner? The late siege of Mexico, which this general was defending about three weeks ago, was marked by excesses which, as the unfortunate Maximilian himself confessed, were a dishonour to the imperial cause. But we henceforth suffered the consequences of our errors. General Marquez was naturally our indispensable ally, as it was he who, since 1861, had held in his hands the threads of the Franco-Mexican intrigue.

Mexico is like a country cursed by God; there the words 'my country' excite no vibration of sympathy. It is divided into two parties, the *clerical* and the *liberal party*, without reckoning the bands of every colour who plunder the towns and hold travellers to ransom in the name of God and liberty. There are, doubtless, in both parties honourable individuals, who groan over the civil wars and decadence of their country. Whilst five millions of Indians were working and suffering, the clerical party desired to retain the property they had acquired at the expense of the general prosperity; and the liberals wished to enrich themselves and to attain to honours. Both parties were to blame; but the liberals, faithful to the constitution, have not incurred the shame of having betrayed their native land to a foreigner. Allow even that this is the sole merit of President Juarez, still it is from this that he derives his power. It is with this power that France has had to deal; and it is this merit which will give to Juarez, when before the tribunal of history, the benefit of extenuating circumstances.

Whilst General de Lorencez, shut up in Orizaba during the winter of 1862, was suffering a thousand privations, and was resisting with his little force all the efforts of the enemy, General Forey set sail for Vera Cruz with 30,000 fresh troops. On the arrival of the new expeditionary force, General de Lorencez returned to France, carrying with him the sincere regrets of his soldiers. The commander-in-chief, at the beginning of October, fixed his head-quarters at Orizaba.

Everyone hoped to come to blows with the enemy at once, and the campaign might thus have soon come to an end. November, December, January, and February were the months which were most favourable to military operations on the lofty plateaus which divide Orizaba from Mexico. Although 5,000 combatants had failed in the undertaking, a force of 35,000 men, full of enthusiasm, and eager to avenge an unexpected check, ought to have easily taken Puebla (an unfortified town), and also the forts belonging to it, which, for want of time, had not been rendered formidable by any defensive works. The fleet, to the lot of which had fallen the difficult and thankless task of conveying the troops and warlike stores, had been found inadequate to bringing the necessary stock of provisions. It was therefore essential that the little corps of General Lorencez, which was well acquainted with the resources and localities of the district, should have ascended without delay on to the plateau of San Andres, which was rich in maize and cattle. The regiments which had just disembarked should have closely followed, and would thus have escaped the unhealthy action of the 'hot grounds.' A constant supply of food would have been thus assured for the various columns converging on Puebla by the routes of Tehuacan, Palmar, and Perote. The French army would have entered Mexico, as it were, at a bound, without any great loss, and without plundering, or allowing others to plunder, the country, to which the sudden war must have already proved sufficiently hurtful.

All the anticipations of the army, which was impatient to begin operations, were destined to be deceived. General Forey's proceedings were so slow that he gave the Juarists time to prepare their defence, to raise the Indians *en masse*, to muster the contingents which were farthest removed from the centre of the territory, to ravage for their own benefit the *haciendas* on the high plateaus, to burn the provisions which they could not carry away, and, finally, to shelter Puebla behind a double barrier of ramparts and cannon.

Five long months were thus spent in marches and counter-marches full of fatigue, until in April 1863 the French army advanced, but at a slow pace, impoverishing the country by its prolonged stay, and redoubling the confidence of the liberals by the excess of its precautions.

Thus, when we ascended the Cumbres, the enemy had cleared everything off before our columns on the plateau of Anahuac. The country was devastated, and almost barren. The hot climate had decimated our forces, and it was necessary to ask the United

States and Havannah to supply the corn requisite both for man and beast. Considerable sums of money were devoted by the commissariat to the purchase of mules, which they sought for far and wide, whilst at that very time they abounded at our outposts; and a portion of a large quantity of oats, imported from New York, remained, for want of means of transport to the plains, standing on the quays at Vera Cruz, and inundated by sea water, until the time came when, finding them quite useless, it was decided to reship them to France, where they arrived considerably damaged. A plan for remounting our soldiers was also attempted at Tampico, and each horse brought back to Vera Cruz by our African troopers, after estimating all the expenses, cost, on an average, 25,000 francs. It is true that the operation also cost us a gunboat, 'La France,' which was lost on the bar of the river. Such were the fruits of procrastination.

At last the *ville des anges* appeared before our eyes as a sort of promised land. It was thought necessary to commence a siege in all due form. The same system which had hitherto prevailed in the management of military operations was applied to the investment of the town. All idea of an assault was scouted, which certainly might have been attempted against the Mexicans if some entrenchments had been thrown up to aid the approach, and if the attack had been made at first on the town only, and the forts of Guadelupe and Loreto had been left to fall through famine. Subsequently, the capture of the Penitencier gave us for an instant the key of the town, for the assailants had pushed on as far as the *quadres*, from which they could easily have reached the cathedral, which served as a residence for General Ortega. The besieged, driven to close quarters, gave way, and fell into panic-stricken confusion. The command was given to retire, and to abandon the positions already taken, the maintenance of which appeared too much out of order or too perilous. And, after this sanguinary evening, the French were compelled to be content with attacking and capturing blocks of houses every night in succession, which were dearly bought, and were then lost and taken again; proceeding in this methodical way, and being stopped at some prearranged limit, as if to check the enthusiasm of the troops, they thus clearly indicated to the enemies the point that would be attacked the next day, always allowing them eighteen hours' respite to double their lines of barricade, and to pierce loop-holes, through which, sheltered and invisible, they could shoot down our soldiers, advancing full-fronted in the darkness.

Thanks to this system—condemned by all military men distinguished for their experience—this dreadful siege lasted three days longer than that of Saragossa; and but for the fortunate attack on the fort of Totimehuacan, causing the fall of the town, preparations must have been made to undergo the rains of winter in front of the entrenchments of Puebla. The *cerro* San Juan, where the French head-quarters were fixed, had been already covered with wooden barracks and mud huts intended for the troops. The inadequacy of our cannon was not noticed until after the siege had commenced, and it became necessary to send the Commandant Bruat to procure rifled guns of large calibre from the fleet.

After the capitulation of Puebla, the march on Mexico would certainly have been put off but for the interposition of the generals of division. This mere wantonness would have had the effect of causing another siege, for Mexico was surrounded with works which they were beginning to arm. Being attacked suddenly, the capital made no resistance.

If General Forey, by the rapidity of his movements, had avoided the siege of Puebla, the aspect of things in Mexico might perhaps have changed. In consequence of our delay, the spirit of resistance had been developed in the republic, and there had been time to gain over all the provinces which subsequently pronounced for the presidential authority. The state-capitals, which became so many hot-beds of insurrection, would have remained tranquil for want of any mutual concert between them, and France, entering Mexico dominantly at the beginning of 1863, would have been at perfect liberty to openly ally herself to the Southern Secessionists, who would have thereby gained ground.

In spite of the flowers and fireworks which were scattered in the path of General Forey on his entering Mexico, the enthusiasm was only factitious. The point that ought to have been the first thing to strike an observant commander was the fact that Juarez had not been expelled by the population of the capital. The chief of the state had yielded to force, but without compromise. In his retreat, he took with him the republican power, but he never allowed it to slip from his hands. He was brought down, but he never abdicated. He had all the pertinacity of a sense of right. This was for five years the secret of the old Indian's power, either in inactivity or in resistance, as he fell back from village to village, and never met with either traitor or assassin on his road.

CHAPTER III.

French Organisation of Mexico—Convocation of a Junta—Unwillingness to join it, and the Cause—Decision for a Monarchy—Offer of the Crown to Maximilian—The Council of Regency—Maximilian's Doubts—Arrival of General Bazaine as Commander-in-Chief—His Difficulties—Juarez and Church Property—Peace restored in Mexico—Arrival of Maximilian—His Virtues, his Faults, and his Fate.

THE *third phase* of the expedition begins with the entry of the French force into the capital of Mexico (July 1863). It comprises two entirely distinct periods, during which the two French commanders-in-chief who succeeded one another respectively followed out a diametrically opposite course of action. This want of harmony in the views of the military and political authorities was the necessary consequence of a programme the object of which had been at first concealed; it was, too, the cause of dangerous and unwise measures, and of sudden changes, which excited the mistrust even of that portion of public opinion which was most favourable to intervention. The sacred fire of our army began even to burn dully; for its good sense was not long in error as to the value of men and things, which it had been the better able to judge of as it advanced farther into the interior of the country.

To our military movements, to which Mexico had been assigned as the glorious goal, now succeeded the political organisation of the country, the regular government of which had disappeared before our flag. This task fell upon General Forey, with the co-operation of the French minister, M. Dubois de Saligny. The moment was now come for tearing away the last veil. At the invitation of M. de Saligny, after an interview at the legation, Almonte, General Marquez, and the Licenciado Aquilar, announced at the first outset the candidature of the Archduke Maximilian under the patronage of the clerical party. A 'junta' of 'notables' was convoked in the capital by General Forey to choose the form of the future government. Their suffrages were to decide the destinies of Mexico. The notables were summoned to deliberate in peace under the shadow of our flag.

The principal personages in the capital showed no marked eagerness to attend the junta. French promises inspired too scanty a confidence. It must be confessed that our former course of procedure had not been calculated to encourage them to openly compromise themselves by joining a meeting on leaving which they might have their names inscribed on 'the lists of Scylla.' During the marches and counter-marches in which our columns had been occupied before they encamped before Puebla, the labour of victualling and mounting the troops had led our arms into all the richest centres of population. Thus it was that San Andres and Tehuacan were visited, and that a landing had been made even at Tampico, and the inhabitants and the neighbouring villages had been invited to supply grain and animals. The Mexicans of these towns consented to the transactions only on the promise that the French troops should not evacuate their cities—henceforth doomed to suffer from the vengeance of the liberals—or that a sufficient garrison should be left in them. And then some morning they woke up to find themselves abandoned, or to hear of the sudden departure of our columns. They were compelled to fly, or to remain at the mercy of the Juarists, who either shot or hanged them. Thus an unhappy renown had gone before us in Mexico. Besides, the *haciendas* of the 'notables' themselves, scattered as they were over the neighbouring provinces, would, in case of the faithlessness of their owners, become the prey of an enemy ready enough to exercise their vengeance. Now, we were quite unable to give them any efficient protection.

Nevertheless, in spite of non-attendances which were to be regretted, a phantom* of a junta was got together, held a meeting, and voted, accompanied by the sound of the cannon, which proclaimed the birth of the empire. The Licenciado Aquilar read a remarkable report, full of good intentions, deciding for a monarchy, and proposing to offer the crown to the Archduke Maximilian. A commission, of which the author of the report was nominated a member, was appointed to proceed to the chateau of Miramar, passing through Paris and Rome, and to be the bearers of the requisite documents and an imperial sceptre.

This page of history was but little worthy of the country whose name is connected with it; France owed another homage to universal suffrage. One ought to have taken a part in this episode of the intervention in order to estimate it at its true value. This memorable meeting of the junta will ever be a deplorable example of an outrage against truth. Not but that a portion of the assembly, anxious for safety and quiet, had not really cast its eyes on a prince whose virtues could not fail to be a great stimulus for Mexico, but the assembly as a whole had neither authority nor character sufficient to enable it to pledge the whole

---

* We had to pay for the apparel of some of the 'notables,' just as we had to pay for flowers which were thrown under the feet of the French on their entry into Mexico.

country. What had become of the declarations made to Lord Cowley by our minister of foreign affairs?—' No government will be forced on the Mexican people!'

Whilst the commissioners, encouraged by the cabinet of the Tuileries, were at Miramar endeavouring to overcome the hesitation of the brother of the Emperor of Austria, in whose mind the siege of Puebla and the coolness of England had given rise to just forebodings, General Forey was making a last appeal for peace to the rebel Mexicans, who still held the country districts. Unfortunately, yielding to clerical influence, he published a *bando*, which was both impolitic and also barbarous and cruel. This *bando* pronounced that the property of all the liberals who did not lay down their arms would be confiscated. This was the means of giving to Juarez the right of reprisal. To the honour of the French government, this decree was disavowed at Paris, and was annulled at Mexico. Whilst the definitive acceptance of the archduke was in suspense, a council of regency was established in the capital; it was composed of three Mexicans— Almonte, General Salas, and the Archbishop of Mexico. Almonte acted as president; this selection was a happy one, although in former times he had shown himself to be an ardent republican.

In spite of the persuasions of our government, who were impatient to establish order, Maximilian was too high-spirited to yield to an appeal so fraught with precipitation as was that of the junta. M. Drouyn de Lhuys, who had succeeded M. de Thouvenel in the ministry of foreign affairs, was compelled, on August 17, 1863, to write as follows to the commander-in-chief (although the imperial policy had from the very first named the city of Mexico as the limit of our military operations):—' We can only consider the votes of the assembly at Mexico as a first indication of the inclination of the country —— '

This was the signal for a new campaign, intended ' *to collect the suffrages of the provincial towns.*' It was felt that too much haste had been used, without having sufficiently taken account of the public spirit, and above all of the delicacy of the future sovereign, who required a sincere suffrage. Once more then, in spite of all the promises made at the French tribune, without any kind of foresight, we were about to plunge into new contingencies, and to commence a third series of costly sacrifices. We were no longer ' masters of the situation ;' we were bound to follow the slippery path on which we had entered. Now, however, was the time to reflect on the state of matters, and notwithstanding the repugnance of M. Rouher, the time, too, to treat with the conquered Juarez, if we ourselves wished to come off as conquerors.

In the month of October 1863, General Bazaine took the command-in-chief out of the hands of General Forey, who had been promoted to be marshal, and had been recalled to France; he also assumed the functions which had devolved on M. de Saligny, who did not long delay in following the captor of Puebla.

General Bazaine assumed the reins of office at a critical time. The Juarist contingents were forming again in the interior, and were getting dangerous; bandits infested the roads and the environs of the capital; the inclinations of General Forey towards the clerical party had alienated those honest liberals who were ready to rally round him' in the hope that a generous inspiration had been kindled by France to put an end to discord; that, when once the honour of her arms had been satisfied, the public rights would not remain unrecognised; and that without any distinction of parties, every man that was willing would be called upon to give his advice freely as to public matters. The clergy, on the other hand, had announced that Maximilian had engaged with the pope to reinstate them in their mortmain property, and had thus given alarm to the numerous holders, both Mexicans and foreigners, of the realty which had been sold. The Archbishop of Mexico, a member of the council of regency, contributed no little by his intrigues and restless character to give authority to these unhappy reports.

The religious question was the real knotty point in Mexico, which, for six years past, had arrayed the inhabitants in arms one against the other. The ecclesiastical property was so considerable that it represented a value of about a thousand million of francs. This immense capital belonged legitimately in part to the church; but undue means and abuses of authority had had much to do with this accumulation of wealth so contrary to the ideas of self-denial. Juarez's government, whilst obeying the spirit of progress which rejects mortmain endowments, had fallen into the grave error of not acting with sufficient moderation—of not leaving for the benevolent, charitable, and educational institutions those resources which were requisite for their maintenance—of stripping the church of all the pomps of worship, and of not providing, from the very outset, by means of a concordat, for the proper position of the clergy; besides all this, the sales of the ecclesiastical lands had been conducted in a scandalous manner, and it was important both for the interests of the treasury and for the dignity of the state that a revision of the contracts should be effected. On these grounds of conciliation, the new commander-in-chief, who wisely saw the danger there would be in attempting to re-

D

trieve the past by any larger measure, undertook to rally round him all well-disposed men. This line of conduct had all the better chance of success as General Bazaine, on succeeding to the command, was preceded by a reputation for bravery which had its influence even over the Mexicans, who besides were not indifferent to his good humour, so full both of heartiness and polish. The latter, too, felt flattered at hearing the French commander-in-chief speak the Spanish language, which he had learnt during the last Spanish war.

Some *coups de main*, vigorously carried out against the plundering bands which infested the country, soon restored confidence in Mexico and the neighbouring towns. They augured well for the quick despatch, after the rains, of the expedition which was being prepared for the purpose of driving away the Juarists from the interior, and of thus allowing the central provinces to choose a new government. Unfortunately, the council of regency already exhibited the spectacle of a sad division, to which it was highly necessary that the general should put an end, so as not to leave behind him the elements of discord whilst he was engaged in military operations. The dissolution of the regency now became a question; but the idea was rejected by the general himself, who felt that this act of vigour might throw discredit on the origin of Maximilian's title to power, and would infallibly be made the most of by the partisans of Juarez. The president of the council of regency, a wise and disinterested man, and devoted to his country, the aspirations of which he had ill understood, because he attributed to it virtues of which it was incapable, followed in the path traced out by General Bazaine. Salas, the second member of the council, an inoffensive old man, followed him in it like his shadow. But the Archbishop of Mexico, who had been able to gain the confidence of the Tuileries, made up his mind to thwart every salutary decision, and yet managed to colour all his acts of systematic opposition with the softest hues. The general, making use of the same tactics, and with Almonte's acquiescence, without any exposure or violence, gave him to understand with clever politeness, that he had ceased *de facto* to belong to the council of regency. Mexico only found it out by the disappearance of the guard of honour which had been appropriated to the archiepiscopal palace.

When the untoward influence of Mgr. Bastida was once removed, in the beginning of November 1863, our army, which had been dispersed beforehand with the view of making an encircling movement, received the order to move in several convergent directions. The Juarist generals Uraga, Doblado, Negrete, and Comonfort, had re-formed corps d'armée for the defence of the republic. In six weeks the enemy was overthrown by the rapidity of our march. The Franco-Mexican flag fluttered on all the plateaus from Morelia to San Luis, towns which Marquez and Mejia won brilliantly for the future crown; from Mexico to Guadalajara, into which General Bazaine, after six weeks' marching in a straight line, entered without striking a blow. The laurels of San Lorenzo were yet green; everywhere the enemy gave way at his approach. This was a campaign entirely of speed, and, according to general opinion, happily planned and promptly terminated. All the towns of the interior, in which we at first met with a most frigid reception (except at Leon), gradually decided in favour of the archduke (whose very name some were ignorant of); they did so with the same readiness with which they would have espoused the cause of anyone whom we had supported with a similar display of force. In the month of February 1864, General Bazaine, accompanied by his escort only, returned at night to the capital, which was surprised by his sudden arrival. His presence there was quite necessary to counterbalance the intrigues of the archbishop and the clerical party, who, during his absence, had thought proper to excommunicate the French army. The prelate got out of the scrape by publicly giving them his benediction.

Never since 1821, the date of its independence, had Mexico, from the Atlantic to the Pacific Ocean, enjoyed a calm equal to that which it experienced during the four months which followed this campaign in the interior. There had been a moment of reaction which was favourable to the ideas of order and comfort which the French army brought with them. Maximilian could not have chosen a more propitious moment to inaugurate his reign, when he finally determined to turn a deaf ear to the advice of his own family. General Bazaine did much for Maximilian's crown.

On May 28, 1864, the new sovereigns landed at Vera Cruz, to the great relief of the cabinet of the Tuileries, which had feared for the moment that, in consequence of the opposition of the archduke, it would see the structure crumble away which it had so laboriously raised. It is well known that the sovereigns were but badly received there. It was natural that this commercial town, accustomed as it was to the large profits derived from the plunder of the custom-house, should see with grief the inauguration of a new era of morality and honesty. Isolated as was their landing, the sovereigns made their entry into Mexico followed by a whole race, which formed a brilliant cortege. These were the real body of the people, who would have saved and upheld the emperor if he had only known and appreciated them.

By order of the clergy, who flattered themselves that the visit of Maximilian to the capital of the Holy See would ensure the success of their unjust claims, the Indians rose *en masse*; they were already devoted to the cause, but still were intent and eager to hear from the imperial lips a promise of liberty, and of a reestablishment of their rights. They went back again in despair to their miserable *ranchos*.

On Maximilian's arrival, an active imperialist party, sincere and full of enthusiasm, was freely and spontaneously formed, captivated as they were by the personal charms of their majesties. There was then a time when the empire, in spite of the difficulty and peril which the task promised, had a good chance for a great future. It was an unexpected hour for Mexico; but neither the prince nor his subjects knew how to take advantage of it. Despite the efforts of a wife abounding in illusions, which were subsequently to be so painfully deceived and so grievously punished, whose name, however, will ever leave a shining track in the history of that unfortunate country, Maximilian, who dared not do as he would, committed numerous errors, because with his chivalric and undecided character he persisted in fancying that he was seated on an European throne. Under his easy rule every bad passion, with its accompanying appetites, again got the upper hand. He forgot that treason circulates in the very blood of Mexico. The Mexicans needed a Louis XI. or a Cromwell, who would unflinchingly pursue his set course, thinking of the country's good, without caring for individuals. He could not expect to conquer his kingdom with a bulletin of laws as his weapon; he should, on the contrary, have been always in the saddle, sword in hand. It was necessary to speak to their eyes before he attempted to appeal to their hearts. The empire withered away for want of concentration, because he wanted to undertake everything at once. One may civilise a hundred square leagues, whither the arm of industry and the comforts of security may be easily summoned; but one cannot civilise deserts exposed to every wind that blows. Thus the French army spent itself gloriously in this immensity of space, without profiting the crown, the prosperity of which it longed to see, if it were only from feelings of patriotism, leading them to hope for some return for the grievous sacrifices of men and money which had been swallowed up in this Mexican gulf. For Juarez, it is to be expected, will sink with Mexico into the abyss which the intervention has lastingly dug out between the two parties. Perhaps, if it had been left to itself, and to its own instincts of self-preservation, Mexico, being still in its infancy, might have been able to purify and regenerate itself in the school of misfortune. France itself was not made in a day. How many centuries have been required, since Charlemagne, for shaking off barbarism and fanaticism, and for finally organising a nation, and how many commotions has it cost? We are all too forgetful of history.

Public opinion was painfully excited by the discord which broke out during the last year between the imperial authority of Mexico and the French commander. There is but little reason to wonder at it, if it is true that the instructions emanating from Paris, and going a year back, directed that an almost compulsory abdication was to be obtained from Maximilian. But we cannot allow ourselves to put faith in such a report, which, if true, would be so painful. Nevertheless, it must be confessed that our government failed in its engagements by withdrawing its troops all at once, and before the fixed time had elapsed, in consequence of the threats of the United States; they thus left Maximilian suddenly disarmed. Our government committed an error in promising any prolongation of its intervention, which was to have ceased after our occupation of Mexico; but it committed another error in not keeping its word. In spite of this, the marshal would have deserved well of Europe if he had adopted on his own responsibility a measure of exceptional determination, which might perhaps have raised a clamour, but would have been justified by reason and humanity. When Maximilian, half distracted, came to Orizaba on his return to Europe, thus obeying the suppliant appeal of the now undeceived empress, he threw himself back into the mêlée because the clerical party offered him their fallacious succour in the shape of soldiers and money. At this momentous juncture, when the noble-minded prince was allowing his honour to force him over the precipice which lay open before him and manifest enough to all eyes, it would have been generous to have carried away even by force the companion of our evil fortunes and to have restored him (even against his will) to his fatherland, and to a princess well worthy of the respect due to great misfortune. A lamentable catastrophe would have been thus averted both from Juarez and Europe, a catastrophe which has thrilled through every human fibre, so as almost to put to silence the sober voice of cool reason. A sad conclusion to this great drama, every page of which is written in blood! On June 19, at seven o'clock in the morning, on the *cerro de la campana* which hangs over Queretaro, Maximilian fell before the bullets which at the same time struck down his generals: Miramon, the former president of the republic, and Mejia, the only general in Mexico who ever died faithful to his party. It was exactly ten years before that Colonel Mejia had entered Queretaro in triumph.

Marquez, who was defending Mexico, capitulated on the 21st. 'On June 27,' announced the *Moniteur* itself, 'Vera Cruz was occupied without disorder, and the foreign troops were able to embark without interference.' The liberals then did not commit the excesses which were feared, and, in three months, the authority of Juarez, who was considered powerless, had been again asserted on every point of Mexican territory. It must now be acknowledged that this fugitive government had at its disposal a majority of public opinion, for it was able to get together an army directly our soldiers ceased to take a part in the conflict. This fact, apart from all other grounds of complaint, would be a sufficient condemnation of this prolonged expedition, which the French press, had it but been free, would have certainly checked, if not prevented.

Maximilian fell under the stroke of the decree of October 1865, which he had signed and issued against every man taken with arms in his hand; a decree which was repugnant to his generous nature, and was but one of the fatal progenies of the civil war. In virtue of this terrible decree, the regular generals, Arteaga and Salazar, had been executed. Violence invites reprisals! The heart cannot fail to be wrung by the distressing thought that the condemned and royal prince had not the consolation of exchanging a last look with his august spouse; but the last adieus of the Juarist generals were not less touching. Let a sacred pity spread the same funeral veil over the three graves in which repose the victims of undoubtedly noble sentiments. Maximilian has expiated by his blood his confidence in the assistance of our government, and his useless though sincere devotion to his adopted people. Arteaga and Salazar died like soldiers fighting against the invasion of their native soil. Juarez certainly let slip a grand opportunity of astonishing Europe by an act of clemency—the sure characteristic of the strong—which would have been the means of conciliating all the courts of Europe; but it is very certain that this act of clemency would have failed to save Maximilian's life, and would have cost Juarez his. Anyone who is acquainted with the country, and knows how its savage passions were then wrought up to a paroxysm of fury, will not for an instant doubt this.

CHAPTER IV.

Intention of this History—Political Conduct of the French and Mexican Cabinets—Character of Maximilian, and his Earliest Measures—Energy of General Bazaine—Reorganisation of the Mexican Resources—General Bazaine's Explanations—Military Movements—Calumnies against French Officers—Appeal to the Empress—Maximilian's Want of Appreciation of the Indians—Financial Embarrassments—Apathy of Mexican Officials—Success of the French Campaigns.

BEING in possession of the documents relative to the last year of the reign of the Emperor of Mexico, we shall now proceed to trace out its history, and, by the help of facts, we shall put to silence all adverse comments. His sense of discipline would repel the idea that the marshal of France, partly honoured with the confidence of the emperor up to the time of the evacuation, whose acts during the last part of the period called forth a thousand expressions of approbation in various quarters, would have executed any orders but those which emanated directly from the sovereign. It was therefore most important to the dignity of our government to show, by publications of a more serious nature than the words of M. Rouher, that, in the hope perhaps of hurriedly reorganising a new state of things, and with the intention of preventing the complete disorder which must follow our evacuation, they had not plotted the downfall of Maximilian, as they had before plotted his elevation. Since it has thought proper to keep silence, we desire to tell the truth.

The principal aim of this historical study is to divide out and assign to each of the actors in the sanguinary drama that we call 'the French intervention' his due share of responsibility. That portion which concerns Maximilian, which will be developed in this new consideration of past events, will explain, before the tribunal of history, the faults and the misfortunes of that unhappy sovereign. Looking to the numerous documents before us of unquestionable authenticity, two principal points will, from the very outset of the imperial reign, make their appearance through the veil we are about to tear away, and will dilate on the Mexican horizon up to the fatal end. On one side will be revealed the instability, the indecision, and the blindness of Maximilian, animated though he was by the most generous sentiments, which he willingly ratified with his royal blood, after having been deceived by the sudden desertion of our government; and, on the other side, will shine forth the rough freedom, the continuous loyalty, and the co-operating devotion which was shown to the second Emperor of Mexico by the French military commander.

In order to understand fully the march of events which signalised the period of the Mexican intervention from 1866 to 1867, it will not be without interest to cast back a brief glance on the political conduct of the French and Mexican cabinets.

From the day on which the French government invited Maximilian to ascend the throne which the famous junta of notables had raised for him under the ægis of our flag, the Emperor Napoleon, who flattered himself that he had attained his first end—*the regeneration of Mexico through the influence of the Latin race*—considered that the proper time had now come for demanding the reparations due to the interests of our countrymen. For this purpose, after the acceptance of the throne by the archduke, which took place on April 10, 1864, the treaty of Miramar was concluded, 'intended both to settle past events and also to put us in possession of the advantages acquired by our arms. By this convention, France was bound to maintain a military force in Mexico on certain settled conditions. The new sovereign engaged in return to pay, at the times and in the way pointed out, the expenses of this occupation; he engaged also to reimburse us the cost of the expedition, and to indemnify the French whose wrongs had provoked it.'

The official programme was therefore a plain one, and devoid of all ambiguity; and Maximilian comprehended beforehand the whole import of it. He was going to reign in Mexico, and to govern it with the assistance of France; and in return for this protection, he promised to honour all the engagements he had made to our country. The Emperor Napoleon, in reward for military sacrifices past and future, obtained the right of carrying out the reimbursement of the indemnities stipulated by the treaty of Miramar, and also, after three months' notice, of calling for a *bona fide* examination of the debts due to our countrymen —and all this while proving his moderation. He ought, therefore, to have reckoned on the co-operation of the young prince whose ambition, excited and countenanced by his arms, had longed for and had found a crown.

In spite of the unsteadiness of his disposition, Maximilian possessed a self-willed temper. Even during the time of the regency at Mexico, he himself, from his palace at Miramar, put things in train as far as he thought necessary to prepare for his accession to the throne. Scarcely had he provisionally accepted the crown (October 3, 1863) ere he effectively took possession of it, although at so great distance; even at this epoch he sent precise instructions to M. Almonte, the president of the regency; subsequently also, after having nominated him lieutenant-governor of the empire on the occasion of signing the treaty of Miramar, he continued to acquaint him with his views; and it must be confessed that at the very outset the latter betrayed, if not actual hostility, at least a great carelessness for French interests; for during the six weeks which elapsed between Maximilian's definitive acceptance of the crown and his landing in Mexico (May 29, 1864), the Marquis de Montholon, French minister at Mexico, who had been commissioned to press the regent to turn his attention to the settlement of the French claims, had to contend with the following evasive reply from M. Almonte:—'I can do nothing; it is necessary for me to take my orders from his majesty, who is at Miramar, and to consult M. Gutierrez de Estrada, who is at Rome.' It was strange that the Mexican cabinet, which had for a long time derived all its suggestions from Europe, had as yet settled nothing even preliminarily on the subject of so urgent a question, which had already been maturely debated between the two sovereigns, which also kept in suspense the interests of so many persons.

No sooner had the emperor trod the soil of his new country than, oblivious of all gratitude (a fault too often attributable to princes), he set aside nearly all the personages belonging to the so-called conservative or clerical party who had assisted the intervention, and seemed bent upon constituting a ministry from elements hostile to the French name, and calling themselves the national party. He was persuaded that it would appear good policy in the eyes of his people to repudiate from the very outset a too great community of action with our government. Thus it was that the fighting party which had kept the field, and had been the first to hoist the imperial flag, was decimated by many most ungracious dismissals. The colonel of gendarmerie, La Peña, of Tulancingo, who had rendered both valuable and dangerous services, was slighted, and also the chiefs Galvez and Arguyes. The foremost generals were gradually set aside and overwhelmed with discredit; the dismissal even of the faithful Mejia himself was contemplated, he who subsequently remained the only true friend in misfortune. The army, the *préfectures*, and the *gardes rurales*, were recruited with treacherous men, who secretly plotted treason, and neutralised the efforts of our troops from the very commencement of operations.

General Bazaine, however, keeping strictly to his military duties, had lost no time, and had in no way relaxed the measures which were favourable to the new régime, for the success of which he had been ten months preparing. Persevering in the labours begun by Marshal Forey, who, on the arrival of our regiments at Mexico, had directed the re-establishment of the arsenal and of the cannon foundry at Chapultepec, he took the greatest care in fortifying the capital and its approaches; he had also extended these same defensive measures to the capitals of the states of the interior, which had been occupied by our forces and the Mexican troops. On his arrival in the first city of the republic, he found the artillery service completely disorganised; the working stock was dilapidated, and not in working order; the magazines had been given up to plunder, the arsenal was without a tool, the machinery partly taken to pieces, and partly given up to certain individuals in settlement of their claims against the government. The implements of the foundry had disappeared, and the percussion-cap manufactory was not in a condition to make any.

Four hundred French workmen had in a few months reorganised and set to full work the factories at Molino del Rey, which supplied munitions, arms, and stores to various fortified places, and also to the movable columns operating with the army. During the winter, 1863-64, fifty pieces of ordnance were placed on the fortifications of Mexico. Fifteen thousand muskets, brought in from every corner of the subdued territory, were distributed to the Mexican troops, as well as to all the great centres of population which were desirous of arming in defence of their homes against the partisan bands. Mejia's and Marquez's two divisions, the cadres of which had been weeded out and strengthened, had taken the field with soldiers well paid, newly clothed, and regularly equipped. One of Maximilian's first acts was to commission General Bazaine, in whom he had the highest confidence, to reconstruct the whole military system, which he was anxious to bring into conformity with the real wants and the supposed resources of the empire. This was a difficult task, requiring an unremitting and concentrated energy of order, if any durable success was to be ensured. The general, desirous of responding frankly to the emperor's appeal, acquainted him that very day with the military arrangements which he was making for the pacification of the country; but, at the same time, he spoke to him in plain terms, which could leave him no grounds for doubt as to the real character of the French intervention. Several towns, either through their political prefects or their leading men, had begged Maximilian to grant them the permanent protection of French garrisons. It was a matter of duty to warn the sovereign at the very beginning against tendencies of this kind, which, if they were encouraged, would increase the supineness of the population and their merely local selfishness. If they felt assured of their security under our flag, they would get accustomed to a mischievous state of tutelage, which would certainly result in scattering our army over every part of the territory, and in preventing it from operating opportunely as a compact force. The only efficient system for raising and maintaining the energies of the inhabitants was traversing the country by movable columns, which, radiating in every direction, would afford protection to the towns and to the *haciendas*, would furnish them with arms, and would even help them in arranging their means of defence. The following was the plan the commander-in-chief adopted:—

Mexico, July 4, 1864.

Sire,—I have the honour of informing your majesty that I think the time has now come for despatching movable columns to traverse the mountainous country between Tulancingo, Zacuatilpan, Llanos de Apam, Perote, and Jalapa, extending on the north as far as Huexutla, and on the east to Tampico.

The sierras into which this mountainous range is divided are difficult of access, but contain some tolerably important centres of population. Numerous bands are infesting the sierras, capturing the inhabitants for sake of ransom, impeding the communications, and spreading disorder and uneasiness, thereby keeping up a state of anarchy. My intention would be to send from Mexico a light French column of about 600 men of all arms, another weaker column from Pachuca, and lastly, from Jalapa and Perote, a third column of mixed troops.

These movable columns, traversing the sierra in every direction, will repel the insurgents, and thus, giving time to the inhabitants to arm and organise for their defence, will have the effect of exciting their too easily depressed energies.

But it will not be possible to appoint permanent French garrisons. It is now a suitable time to explain to your majesty the hurtful tendency which the whole population manifest, of never thinking themselves in safety except behind the shelter of our bayonets. Whenever our troops have visited any locality, and have stayed there some time, induced either by the exigencies of war, or by a wish to assist the inhabitants in organising themselves, or in establishing defensive works, building a redoubt, &c., I have had to contend against the incessant demands of the local authorities, who declared that the departure of our troops would be the signal for cruel reprisals on the part of the enemy, which the inhabitants had no means of resisting.

I cannot accede to all these demands, because it is impossible to allow the army to be scattered, and thus deprive it of its cohesion, which is its principal strength; especially also because it has appeared to me to be indispensable that the population generally should habituate itself to reckon on its own means of defence, and should not lull itself into a false security, due only to the presence of our soldiers.

Your majesty has already received numerous requests for French garrisons. The political prefects, and the chief commandants themselves, have represented to the emperor the necessity for making this or that military operation within the circle of their own individual sphere of action, each one looking only to that portion of territory under his immediate charge.

But the commander-in-chief alone holds the threads of this complicated web, and he alone can judge not only of the opportune moment for undertaking any operation, but also as to the expedient mode for combining all the movements so as to arrive at a definite result without fear of danger in any direction.

I have thought it my duty to warn your majesty against these tendencies, due, as they are, to a sentiment of exaggerated zeal and merely local egotism, and also against the timidity of the population generally, who will not fail to send both addresses and delegates, with a view of obtaining French garrisons.

The examples of Tulancingo, Chapa de Nota, and some other towns which have been fortified by our instrumentality, and are now entrenched and organised for defence, prove that, with good will and energy, the inhabitants themselves ought to be able to defend the towns of their territory. I shall take every pains to develope these two sentiments, and to inspire with self-confidence the inhabitants of the towns and *haciendas*. I shall furnish them with arms, and shall help them in organising their means of defence; but it will be impossible for me to leave them garrisons.

The duty of the movable columns is to take the place of these garrisons. Their effect is even more powerful, and military spirit and discipline will thus suffer no injury.

BAZAINE.

The emperor approved of this plan, which was the result of experience; and the light columns were despatched across the turbulent districts extending from Tulancingo to La Huasteca, up to the banks of the Panuco, a mountainous and woody range of country, with ravines, abrupt declivities and steep bluffs, and known as *sierras*.

The reorganisation of the Mexican army was now actively taken in hand. It was, at this time, massed in two great divisions—that of General Marquez, operating in the Michoacan, at the south of Mexico; and General Mejia's division, which had taken up its position in the north, in the city of San Luis, which it had boldly captured from the liberal army after a sanguinary conflict. For some months, a permanent board had been revising the commissions of officers of all ranks. Looking at the redundance in the list of the staff and officers generally, this measure was highly necessary; it raised, however, a tempest of opposition, and was the cause of inevitable defections, because a large number of generals and colonels had illegitimately conferred on themselves these titles, merely with a view of heading bands recruited for the purposes of rapine on the main roads. At this time, half of the Franco-Mexican army was also moving towards the north. The French head-quarters, impatient to assert Maximilian's authority, had given orders to undertake a serious campaign, with a view of driving back to the American frontier Juarez and his government, who were now installed in the capital of Nuevo Leon, about two hundred leagues from Mexico. Although always pursued, and always conquered, the president of the Mexican republic remained unshaken, and resolved never to let slip his lawful rights.

As a reward for their services, certain generals in our army found themselves calumniated to the sovereign, and the ministers, jealous of our well-merited influence, made themselves the mouthpieces in high quarters of the impassioned complaints emanating from certain hostile political prefects, who had taken care to nominate themselves in the provinces, so as to reserve a chance of safety for the future. In the month of September 1864, the charges which had been brought to the ears of the Empress Charlotte, whose ardent temper would probably be affected by them, redoubled the prevailing acrimony. The commander-in-chief, on being apprised of the matter, did not hesitate to address himself to the empress herself, and loyally denounced the intrigues of these high functionaries, as being both injurious to the dignity of the crown and to our reputation.

Mexico, September 24, 1864.

To Her Majesty the Empress.

Madam,—The commander-in-chief again calls her majesty's attention to the complaints which he has several times been compelled to make against the exaggerated, not to say untrue, reports, made by functionaries high in the administration.

The military commandants act only under the direction of the commander-in-chief. The measures complained of, the fines imposed on the people at large, and even on individuals, have all been carried out by order and on established rules, and with a set purpose which cannot be disclaimed by the authorities.

This agitation, maintained by party spirit, is sanctioned to some extent by events to be regretted in every respect, and the responsibility of which can only be attributed to agents whose incapacity or weakness may be pointed out without exercising any too great severity.

The late events at San Angel, where armed bandits have just seized, in the very centre of the town, the arms and stores which had been placed at random in an unguarded house, abundantly prove that the civil authorities are not on the watch, but that they lull themselves into a deplorable sense of security, even if they are not guilty of a corrupt complicity.

The people themselves, whose zeal and devotion are so praised by certain functionaries, are wanting in energy at the moment of action, and this may be certainly laid to the deficiency in promptitude and initiative spirit of those who, by their position, ought to have persuaded them to resistance, even if they had not urged them by their example.

. The latest news that I have received from Zacuatilpan depict this town as abandoned by its inhabitants, who were making their escape, as also were the brigands, pursued by a handful of our soldiers.

This state of things is much to be regretted, and I cannot too much impress upon your majesty that a circular should be addressed to the people, and widely circulated among them, to persuade everyone to remain at their homes to defend their hearths, or at all events not to abandon them. . . .

With the deepest respect, madam, &c.
BAZAINE.

It was proved by documents that our military commandants had only acted according to the orders that they had regularly received, and that their conduct could not be otherwise than approved of. Unfortunately, the fidelity of the imperialist authorities did not come up to the rectitude of the French officers. Even where the former were not accomplices of the enemy, they slumbered in a strange security, allowing, as at San Angel, the rebels to carry away from towns close to Mexico the arms and stores which had been entrusted to them, which, however, they had forgotten to distribute for the purposes of defence.

Maximilian did not appear to be roused by these vexatious indications. He had come from Miramar with a budget of laws ready prepared, which he called 'his statutes,' and being thoroughly imbued with preconceived ideas, he worked at his desk unceasingly, issuing excellent decrees, which became waste-paper in the hands of his ministers; summoning and presiding at numerous French commissions, the efforts of which were pre-condemned to inutility for want of one vigorous guiding hand. For the emperor, who was not armed for the strife with a sufficiently sustained energy, looked at every question from a theoretical point of view, without pertinaciously forcing his way to a practical result. He forgot the temperament and habits of his subjects, and remembered only the character of European officials. He did not comprehend that he ought to be both the *head* and the *arm* of the nation. Nevertheless he did not want for advice and even for remonstrance.

From the very first, the emperor did not perceive that the only condition on which the Indian race could be called upon to form the regenerating leaven of his people was that they should be made free of ' péonage,' and also that they should have a share of the soil abandoned by the neglect of the state. Nevertheless, the throne boasted a valiant champion in General Mejia, who was an Indian, like Juarez himself, and like the famous Porfirio Diaz, the future defender of Oajaca. Ought not these people to have met with some consideration from the crown? Yet the head-quarters authorities were compelled to appeal to the authority of the emperor as to the persecutions to which certain members of this caste so worthy of interest were subjected by the Mexican authorities.

Mexico, November 16, 1864.

Sire,—I was visited yesterday by a certain Manuel Medel, sub-prefect and ex-commandant of Tepeji de la Seda, who has just been dismissed by M. Pardo, political prefect of the department of Puebla. I only know Manuel Medel by the reputation for honesty and energy which he bears in the country. His excellency Marshal Forey thought right to nominate him as a chevalier of the Legion of Honour on account of the vigorous resistance he offered to the Juarists. Medel is a true-born Indian, of the energetic type and somewhat timid manners peculiar to this race. He professes the utmost devotion to the empire and the very best intentions, referring back to what he has already done as an evidence in favour of his principles.

I am not aware what motives M. Pardo can have had for dismissing him, and I must refer it to your majesty, who will, I am sure, listen to a servant who is the only Indian of the civil service wearing the insignia of the Legion of Honour, and may thus be able to convince yourself of the truth, and to appreciate the facts in their real light. . . .   BAZAINE.

This act, done in the name of the emperor, cooled the devotion of many a one.

The subject of finances began to be a question of life or death for the infant empire. At the time when he first trod the Mexican soil, Maximilian ought to have surveyed in all its aspects this monster which was to destroy him. But he brought with him some great misconceptions as to the financial power of his adopted country, and as to its mineral resources. He had fancied that the mere appearance of the French flag floating over the distant central towns would be sufficient to re-establish the circulation of capital; and from his palace at Chapultepec, where he was about to sink large sums in the restoration of the building, and in making a road to connect it with the capital, he failed to notice that his own troops, both in the north and south, were beginning to fall short of their pay, and were ready to mutiny in the face of the enemy.

Six months had elapsed since the inauguration of his reign, when the emperor received a French note, dated at the end of November 1864, which called his attention to certain delays which were prejudicial to the interests of his empire. At his desire, a complete financial staff had been sent out from France. After a conference, to which Maximilian had summoned his minister of war and his secretary of state for finance to meet Marshal Bazaine, in order to consult on the necessary measures, the above staff was portioned out through the country. Our authorities had forwarded these financial agents, as soon as they arrived in Mexico, to their respective destinations, where they were to carry out their duties of supervision and control; at the same time, circulars were distributed in the departments addressed to the military chiefs, who were directed to assist them. On the other hand, the minister of finance had formally promised to send without delay similar instructions to the directors of the public *haciendas* in the provinces of the empire which were then subject. When they reached their posts, the French officials were politely repudiated by the local administrations. No arrangement whatever had been settled, as is shown by the marshal's letter to the emperor:—

Mexico, September 30, 1864.

Sire,—Your majesty having authorised me in a conference with which I was honoured, to meet the minister of war and the under secretary of state for finance, to agree on the instructions which should be forwarded to the chief commandants and agents of the Mexican government, as to the financial agents at present in Mexico being sent out into the seaports and principal towns of the interior, I made my arrangements immediately, and have transmitted my directions and circulars, and have dismissed the agents to their respective destinations.

I acquainted M. the under secretary of state that the French officials had left. I sent him a copy of the instructions given to them, and to the chief commandants, who were called on to assist them in their mission, and I also insisted that M. the under secretary of state should send instructions of a similar character to mine to the directors of the public *haciendas* in the several departments of the empire.

His reply to me was that this question was still under consideration, and that no resolution on it had yet been come to!

I fear that the French financial agents will find themselves in a false position, and that, for want of some arrangement, and not being provided with commissions in due form, they will be unable to accomplish the duties of supervision and control which they have been called upon to fulfil.

I have the honour of submitting these observations to your majesty's consideration, and to point out to you this delay, which will certainly be prejudicial to the financial interests of the country. BAZAINE.

Thus were the wisest measures paralysed by the inertness of the royal advisers. Whilst the emperor's orders, so feebly administered, were quietly lying in the portfolios, valuable time was being wasted. The depredations at the custom-houses were not repressed, and the taxes did not find their way into the public treasury. Maximilian would have had better success if he had personally superintended the execution of his orders. Could he not have presented himself at those more important points, where difficulties were every day being revealed to him by our military reports? The presence of a sovereign is always eloquent, and warms the feelings of the masses. Was it not by this system that Alexander conquered Asia in three years, and impressed on the whole country a character that it has never lost since that grand era? But the German system, with all its deliberate inaction, was the prevailing one here. But it is only just to confess that the Mexican climate had already affected the constitution of the emperor, and in these latitudes the state of health reacts cruelly on the mental faculties.

In the departments, the political prefects chosen out of the midst of the national party neutralised all the efforts of our movable columns. Besides these injurious tendencies, against which Maximilian, misled, as he was, by the suggestions of those round him, but feebly contended, the ministry, managed by M. Eloïn, a Belgian attached to the suite of the Empress Charlotte, furnished fresh proofs every day of its ill-will in everything that concerned French interests. In spite of the repeated entreaties of the Marquis de Montholon, the commission which had been formed at Mexico to discuss and estimate the demands of our claimants found itself incessantly impeded by planned occurrences. Apart from the pressure brought to bear on him by his advisers, Maximilian would doubtless have fulfilled his engagements; but he met with encouragement to his resistance even from Paris itself, through the stimulus of M. Hidalgo, whose recriminations were not without influence at the court of the Tuileries, thanks to a certain august intervention. We must also state that the French requirements, not without reason, appeared to Maximilian to be exaggerated, and in part not well founded, so far as regarded the portion relating to the usurious bonds of Jecker, the Swiss, who had been naturalised as a Frenchman after the outset of the intervention.

There had been a point in litigation for about five months. Our minister in Mexico demanded, but did not obtain, *interest* on those claims which were to be subject to revision. If this revision was an equitable one, it was also just to compensate by interest for the delay in the settlement thereby caused; and it would hardly be desired that our countrymen should be worse treated as regards the legal rate than the ordinary creditors of the state. It was not until December 9, 1864, that M. Ramirez, minister of foreign affairs, wrote to the Marquis de Montholon—' That his sovereign, *although convinced that justice was entirely on his side, had, to avoid disturbing the good understanding with the Emperor of the French,* given orders by the packet to M. Hidalgo, his minister at Paris, to admit that, for the future, interest was guaranteed on the claims which were subject to revision.'

About the same time the news of the pacification of the central provinces, effected by our arms, reached head-quarters. The military situation in the districts traversed by the Franco-Mexican army appeared to be excellent. In the north, General de Castagny, at the head of a French division, General Mejia, followed by his Mexican force, and the French contra-guerillas, advanced in a parallel line over a breadth of one hundred and fifty leagues of country, and a simultaneous march drove back the enemy to the United States frontier. In the other direction, General Douay, in conjunction with Marquez, had effected a brilliant line of march as far as Colima, a state capital situated on the edge of the Pacific; and Colonel de Pothier, taking Arteaga's army in the rear, had hurled the latter across the Rio Grande. In every direction, warlike stores and field-pieces thrown into the *barrancas** remained in the hands of the French, whilst

---

* Deep ravines hollowed out by the tropical rains.

our fleet was successfully assisting the operations by effecting landings on the two coasts, of the Gulf and of the Ocean. But the Mexican arms, when left to themselves, appeared to be less fortunate. General Vicario, who occupied the southern road to the Pacific, although he had been warned twenty days beforehand by the commander-in-chief that General Douay's movements on his right would inevitably have the effect of turning back on him a portion of the enemy's forces, had taken no defensive measures, and found himself forced to beat a retreat. In order to protect the town of Cuernavaca, left uncovered by the imperialist reverse, and to relieve the country, already becoming demoralised, Marshal Bazaine lost no time in sending a column to the endangered districts.

CHAPTER V.

Military and Civil Arrangements—Organising Commissions Dissolved—Capture and Escape of Porfirio Diaz—Fresh Military Plans of the Emperor—Their Imprudence and Inexpediency—The Question of Church Property—The American Question—Attitude of the United States, and Recall of their Minister—Treason of Cortina—Revolt breaks out.

AT the beginning of the year 1865, the French commander had abundantly performed the task which the Emperor of Mexico (since his landing, May 29, 1864) had entrusted to his zeal and activity. The country was pacified, and peace was now reappearing. The national army had been reorganised on the basis of the schemes which each of our military chiefs, following his own special views, had elaborated and proposed. The whole territory had been divided into nine military departments, each with its constituted and regular staff. All the confirmatory documents were placed in the imperial hands. Besides, a list of the political and administrative *employés*, conscientiously framed by our heads of columns, permitted an effective control to be exercised over all the individuals who were called on to take a part in the various branches of the services. On January 26, the emperor signed the military code of laws, and two months after, now that things had been set in train by the French officers, he released our head-quarters staff from its duties by a letter couched in the following cordial terms:—

Mexico, March 26, 1865.

My dear marshal,—On July 7 of last year, I entrusted to your distinguished and able management the task of elaborating a scheme for the reorganisation of the Mexican army. The documents which your excellency has from time to time forwarded to me have proved most useful in the formation of a code of military laws, which I signed on January 26 of this year.

I thank your excellency for the devoted co-operation which you have afforded me in this matter, and for the fresh services which you have thereby rendered to the country.

The commission, and sub-commissions, of which you were the president, will be dissolved, and the recently reorganised ministry of war, by means of the regulations put in force, will be able to deal with the questions which have not yet been settled. Your affectionate

MAXIMILIAN.

Henceforth, the minister of war had to deal personally with the questions which remained to be decided. Maximilian, who had fancied that his own council were capable of directing the affairs which the ministers had endeavoured to get into their own hands with the sole desire of diminishing the French authority, was not long ere he discovered that disorder was again beginning to creep into the machinery of the military service. Important operations even were endangered by this confusion. Contingents which had been appointed to march on Oajaca had not even left their quarters at Mexico.

It must be here borne in mind that Marshal Bazaine, by an energetic siege, had just shut up the Juarist general Porfirio Diaz in the town of Oajaca, and had forced him to capitulate with the whole of his army. This liberal chief, who had valiantly upheld his cause sword in hand, had a right to be treated as a prisoner of war, and with all the respect due to the vanquished. Marshal Forey, in asserting in the French senate that he deserved to be shot, made a mistake; for Porfirio Diaz, the regular chief of a state, the capital of which it was his duty to defend, deserved only to be strictly confined, or rather to be banished to the Antilles, since his territory had never yet been trod either by the French or imperial armies. Measures of violence, which mistake the true character of an enemy, only provoke terrible reprisals.

Porfirio was conducted to Puebla as a prisoner by the French army, and was confined in the fort of Guadalupe, from which escape was impossible. By order of the emperor, he was placed under the guard of the Austrians, who, after having brought him back into the city, allowed him to escape. Porfirio, still faithful to Juarez, again took the field, and was subsequently the means of overturning the imperial throne. But it must be confessed that, after the fights at Miahuatlan and La Carbonera, he treated the French prisoners in a proper way, and also gave the Austrians who remained in his hands after the fall of Oajaca every facility of exchange. Everything leads to the belief that the emperor himself, moved by a generous but imprudent feeling, was privy to his escape.

It was soon perceptible that the minister of war took upon himself to move troops, and to give orders directly to the generals, without consulting or even informing our head-quarters, and tacitly abolished the flying-guard placed to secure the communications on the road from Mexico to Vera Cruz, thus giving free course to a system of brigandage which now made fresh victims.

After a month of Mexican management, the emperor, now undeceived, adopted the course of entrusting the supervision of his army to better hands. A French general* was placed at his disposal, but he was re-

* This general, being recalled to France, waited in vain for Maximilian's decision, and was ultimately compelled to leave after a month's useless delay.

THE EMPEROR'S MILITARY PLAN. 63

moved by the influence of M. Eloïn. On May 5, 1865, the emperor made up his mind to invest the Austrian general Count de Thun with this post of command. This took place during his stay at the *hacienda* of Jalapilla. He himself there settled on the plan for a fresh military organisation, and summoned to Puebla a portion of the troops stationed at Toluca, Ario, Jalapa, Morelia, and Mexico, in order to form a brigade.

Hacienda de Jalapilla, May 5, 1865.

My dear marshal,—Sharing, as I do, the opinion of your excellency that the organisation of the army must be rapidly proceeded with, and being unable to find a French or Mexican general who either would or could undertake it, I have made up my mind to entrust the task to General Count de Thun.

The first arrangement to be made is to bring together the forces necessary to form a brigade. I request that your excellency will give orders that the under-named corps proceed to Puebla, the place that I have chosen for its organisation:—

- The Bataillon de l'Empereur, stationed at Toluca;
- The 3rd Battalion of the line, stationed at Ario;
- The company of engineers, stationed at Ario;
- The portions of battalions stationed at Jalapa and at Morelia;
- The Régiment de Cavalerie de l'Impératrice; all the detachments scattered in different places being united.

I have selected these troops as being those the least required for the time in the places which they occupy.

After all I have observed on my journey, and reflecting seriously on military matters, I adopt the opinion of the necessity of a prompt and effective organisation of the gendarmerie.

In the first place, we want an active chief, thoroughly acquainted with the admirable arrangements of the French gendarmerie, and then a short list of officers and sub-officers, who would ably assist their chief in an organisation so new and therefore so difficult for this country.

I think that it will be necessary to commence by embodying a not very numerous force, which will occupy the capital, and will form the nucleus of a progressive organisation.

MAXIMILIAN.

This letter of May 5, by which Maximilian gave the order to remove the troops from the town of Morelia and its environs, proves that the sovereign acted of his own accord, and that the marshal, as chief of his army, was not in an independent position. It also effectually impugns a military statement emanating from Maximilian at this time, and reproduced in a recent publication, entitled 'The Court of Rome and the Emperor Maximilian':—

'The town of Morelia is surrounded by the enemy,' say these imperial notes; . . . 'the most perilous point is to ensure the safety of the large towns. . . . The public treasury is ruined; the poor country must pay the French troops.'

It is difficult to explain the view thus taken of the country. The French army, as well as the fleet, can attest that at this very epoch they occupied all the chief cities of the states, and the principal ports of Mexico. We are not aware that they ever yielded up a place to the liberals as conquerors. One city alone, the capital of the state of Guanajato, had been confided to the care of the Mexican arms, because it was protected on all four sides by a cordon of fortified places under our charge, which acted as barriers against the advance of the enemy. On the other hand, Oajaca had just succumbed to the brilliant siege and attack directed by Marshal Bazaine in person.

As to the treasury being 'ruined' by the payment of our troops, the unfortunate sovereign had no right to complain of the sums which Mexico paid to France; for when he placed on his brows the crown which he had so imprudently accepted, he voluntarily signed article 10 of the treaty of Miramar, which stipulated that the yearly expense of every French soldier should amount to a thousand francs, which Mexico would pay.

But the truth must be told. The imperial notes, which were intended for certain public journals in Europe, were often worded in the secretary's office in a way that, by giving a more gloomy view of matters, would exercise an indirect pressure on public opinion and on the French cabinet; the latter being too much inclined to diminish prematurely its military force, as subsequent events have proved.

It must be observed that these military modifications in the distribution of the forces, which were repeated time after time by the Emperor Maximilian, were but little calculated to give solidity to the troops, who were amazed at constantly having to obey fresh chiefs.

Moreover, the mixture of the Austro-Belgian auxiliary contingents with the national troops was a mistake; for the latter looked upon them with mistrust, and were too much reminded of the foreign extraction of their sovereign; Puebla, too, was exactly like an Austrian camp. Maximilian was likewise in the wrong in establishing, in addition to the ministry of war, a military cabinet—an institution he had derived from his own country—and also in decreeing the formation of a military section comprising the Austro-Belgian troops exclusively, and under *direct* management. These innovations only tended to weaken the unity of command, and to deprive the marshal—the sole commander-in-chief in virtue of article 6 of the treaty of Miramar (an article which the emperor had need subsequently to appeal to)—of a portion of the authority so necessary to rapidity of action in a country so vast and so disturbed as Mexico was. At about the same date, Maximilian entertained the happy idea of establishing a corps of *gendarmerie* on the French model, intended to occupy the capital and its environs, and to be extended by degrees to the other military divisions. To help in its formation, he appealed to the officers and sub-officers of the expeditionary corps, who did not delay in responding. A French lieutenant-colonel received the command; but he soon had to give way to a Dutch colonel, named Tindal, who was appointed to this post by the sovereign's desire.

General de Thun, who was invested with the highest confidence, soon sought to shake off the French direction. These tendencies were, however, inevitable, if we take into account the national susceptibilities which were called into action. It must be confessed, on the other hand, that his position presented great difficulties; for the Austrian general met with no co-operation from his subordinates in the ministerial body, and the Mexican officers hindered his readiness of will by their natural inertness.

Although Maximilian fell into errors, resulting especially from his indecision and his fickleness of temper, as well as from his ignorance of the Mexican character, the impartiality of history will pronounce that his imprudent ambition had accepted a very heavy task, alike momentous both within and without the empire; and we are justified in asking if anyone else, filling his position, would have proved either more capable or more fortunate?

Two important foreign questions, to which the new reign was necessarily the heir, weighed heavily on domestic matters in Mexico. In the first place, the settlement of the mortmain endowments still remained in suspense. The court of Rome had not yet consented to declare its sentiments, and appeared still less inclined to do so, as the emperor had repudiated the clerical party, to whom he owed his crown. This sudden change of policy had but little inclined the pope to make any concessions. For the Holy See, in assisting an Austrian archduke to place himself on an old Spanish throne, had expected that it would bring back these distant lands into the bosom of the Church. On the other hand, the holders of the clerical property professed that they were anxious for a settlement favourable to their interests, although, to a great extent, their right of property had originated in fraud. They therefore employed every means they could to hurry the steps of the emperor in the path which would lead him to a rupture with the 'Saint-Père.' The organs of the liberal press, especially at Puebla, stirred up with unseasonable violence a question which required all the more caution as the papal nuncio was then expected for the purpose of negotiation.

And there was also the American question, which was just as replete with danger. The late events in the United States, and the threatening movements of the Juarist general Negrete on the northern frontier of the empire, constituted a peril affecting the security of the crown. It was well known that the partisans of Juarez were bestirring themselves, and were only waiting for the cessation of hostilities between the Northern and Southern States in order to bring serious difficulties on Maximilian. Through the intrigues of Romero, the accredited representative of the president of the Mexican republic, public enlistment-offices had been opened in the principal cities of the Union; and the press appealed to the adventurers, and urged them to cross the frontier.

Then it was that Maximilian, in the hope of baffling the filibusters, and of putting an end to the system of American volunteering, made up his mind, without consulting the French authorities, to endeavour to obtain the support or at least the neutrality of the cabinet at Washington by means of certain secret measures. In order to carry out this purpose, he despatched M. Arroyo with directions to attempt certain overtures. It may be recollected what kind of reception was reserved for this mysterious ambassador, who was politely bowed out by the republican cabinet. It really is a cause for astonishment that Maximilian, subject as he was to evil influence, should have yielded to such a temptation. Was not the *status quo*, with its concealed filibusterism, a hundred times preferable to a loss of influence which could not fail to become public and disquiet those who were still in doubt as to the real sentiments of the United States? The Emperor of Mexico had very quickly forgotten the following important document, which could hardly have escaped his examination, the form as well as the matter of which were equally unfriendly to the French cabinet:—

From Mr. Seward to Mr. Dayton, Minister of the United States at Paris.

Washington, April 7, 1864.

Sir,—I send you a copy of a resolution passed unanimously by the house of representatives, on the 4th of this month. It asserts the opposition of this body *to any recognition of a monarchy in Mexico.*

After all I have written you with so much candour for the information of France, it is scarcely necessary for me to say that this resolution honestly represents *the unanimous feeling of the people* of the United States with regard to Mexico.

W. H. Seward.

Thus spoke the Federals, at the very time when Richmond resounded with the victories of General Lee, and when the Confederates seemed menacing President Lincoln. The question of principle was clearly laid down. There was yet time for them to have shrunk from bidding an eternal adieu to the gardens of Miramar, and to the beloved billows of the Adriatic! Some weeks later, when the imperial family were sailing on the waters of the Havannah, in the direction of Vera Cruz, they crossed the track of a vessel which was carrying away the American representative recalled from Mexico by his government.

From Mr. Seward to Mr. Dayton.

Department of State, Washington, May 21, 1864.

We beg to inform you that Mr. Corwin, our minister plenipotentiary to Mexico, is now at Havannah, en route for the United States, where he returns on *leave of absence.*

W. H. SEWARD.

Notwithstanding the French intervention, Mr. Corwin had remained in Mexico, and only went away on the arrival of the new sovereigns. Such a position could give little hope of a reconciliation, especially after the disastrous overthrow of the Southerners. The simplest prudence and a regard for his own dignity should have forbidden any application by M. Arroyo to the White House.

The French army had already done its utmost to repulse the attacks of the filibusters. Colonel Jeanningros immediately strengthened the fortress of Monterey, and, by means of earthworks thrown up round Cadeyreta, protected the district with a considerable force in case of an American invasion being attempted. Higher up, General Brincourt watched the upper part of the river frontier ready for any eventuality. Unfortunately, General Cortina, who commanded a party of troops ranged *en échelon* on the lower portion of the Rio Bravo, and was already notorious for his treachery, suddenly declared himself against the empire, and endeavoured to deliver up the valuable port of Matamoros into the hands of Negrete, with whom he had agreed for a large sum of money. What blindness, in spite of repeated warning, could have urged Maximilian six months before to pardon Cortina, a merely irregular general, and a thief, as cowardly as he was unruly, at the time when he was blockaded in Matamoros, without hope of escape, and was compelled to surrender after many extortions? Then, again, why should he have been promoted on the same day to the rank of regular general, and given an active command on the frontier, and in the very town he had just plundered without remorse? Maximilian believed he was acting with good policy, and that he would thus appease the other non-contents. Negrete immediately attacked Matamoros, but his contingent was obliged to be disbanded owing to the landing at Bagdad of our naval forces, who came to the help of Mejia, who occupied the place.

The signal of revolt was given. The imperial government had directed that the department of Tamaulipas, so laboriously conquered by the French contra-guerillas, should be given over to one of its brigades. Two months afterwards this province was again entirely lost, and Monterey, the capital of Nuevo Leon, which the Mexican authorities, in spite of all the recommendations from our head-quarters, had neglected to put in a proper state of defence, also succumbed under the attacks of the rebel party. During the month of May, the marshal was obliged to resume the offensive at all the points invaded, and to capture them afresh.

CHAPTER VI.

Marshal Bazaine's Advice on American Matters—It is not Taken—Marshal Bazaine's Marriage, and Dowry to his Bride—Mexicans in the Days of Cortez—Condition of the Indians—Opposition of the Landholders and Officials—Juarez's Hiding-Place.

ALL these internal commotions might yet have been appeased if the court of Mexico had only dared in good time to nip the evil in the bud, that is, to shield itself from the filibusters by turning them into its subjects and defenders. Thus, too, it would have thwarted the manœuvres of Mr. Seward. A favourable opportunity for an attempt of this sort had just presented itself. At the end of May 1865, the Confederate General Slaughter, who commanded at Brownsville, on the opposite bank of the Rio Bravo, hearing of the disasters of the Southerners, hesitated whether he should lay down his arms, or whether he should cross the Mexican frontier with his 25,000 partisans, who seemed disposed to ask shelter from the emperor on the condition of obtaining grants of land in the north-west departments. This invasion of colonists would have been a piece of good luck for Mexico; for these groups of squatters, located like an advance-guard along the river frontier, might one day have the effect of arresting any Yankee invasion from the side of Texas. Negotiations were opened on this point; there was no time to be lost in placing themselves in a position to face certain threatening contingencies. The sending to Matamoros of an imperial commissioner furnished with special powers could not at this moment awaken the jealousies of the Northern States, which in their desire of conquering the secessionists would have seen with pleasure General Slaughter's cessation of hostilities, and Lincoln would probably have shut his eyes to the passage of 25,000 Confederates into the neighbouring territory as Mexican subjects. The marshal hastened to call Maximilian's attention to this question of such deep importance to the future of the monarchy.

Mexico, May 29, 1865.

Sire,—The late events in the United States and General Negrete's movements on the northern frontier of the empire make it my duty to lay before your majesty the actual state of things, as I understand them, and to invite your earnest attention to certain contingencies, which, without constituting any imminent source of danger, are still of deep importance.

It is now beyond all doubt that the agents of the Juarist party are endeavouring to throw upon the Mexican empire all the difficulties and trouble which the cessation of hostilities between the Northern and Southern States renders inevitable.

The public enlistments which have been organised in the principal towns of the Union, and the appeals which the American press are making for emigrants to Mexico, abundantly prove the intrigues of a party which holds Mexican nationality so cheap, and show that the sympathies of the American people, whose adventurous spirit is unhappily too well known, are all in favour of this party.

Your majesty has nothing to dread for the present. All my preparations are ready for repulsing any bands of filibusters which may attempt to invade the south of the empire.

The abortive attempt of General Negrete, which can only be explained by the hope that he had of being supported by these armed bands, has ended in nothing. It has only proved that the pretended allegiance of certain persons, amongst others, that of Cortina, was entirely fictitious, and that the odious part taken by the latter renders him for ever unworthy of your majesty's clemency.

It has been shown that the want of energy in other commanders made them unworthy of the confidence reposed in them, *and, finally, it has convinced me that my orders relating to the preparations for the defence of the towns held by the Mexican army have not been executed.*

Monterey has actually been captured by means of its defenders, because none of my recommendations were followed by them.

The retreat of Negrete, caused by the opposition that he encountered at Matamoros, and by the landing of the French troops at Bagdad, plainly shows how little confidence that Juarist chief had in his soldiers, and authorises the suppositions which I have had the honour of suggesting above. . . .

The marshal then enumerated the orders which he had given, recounting to his majesty in detail the movements which he had directed, the works which were in hand, and the marches which had been concerted to recapture the town of Monterey, and to reconquer the state of Tamaulipas, and to scatter or blockade the rebels; he then entered on the question regarding the Confederates:—

. . . I have the honour of repeating to your majesty that all my arrangements are made for meeting the former contingencies.

It is possible that, when the Confederate general Slaughter, who is in command at Brownsville, hears of the disasters of his party, and the capture by the Federals of President Jefferson Davis, he may lay down his arms, like the other Southern generals; but it is also not improbable that the proximity of the Mexican territory may induce him to come across to the right bank of the river, and to take refuge with his disarmed corps in a friendly country.

International law fully authorises an asylum being given under these conditions to a conquered army. After the preliminary disarming of the Southern force, would it not be possible to form between Monterey and the Saltillo, on the lands belonging to the state in this district, groups of colonists, who would in this case constitute a line of defence against the irruptions of the filibusters? . . .

The marshal did not conceal either the inconvenience or the danger of a measure of this sort; but it was important to obtain American allies. Amidst the perplexing embarrassments which the universal apathy of the Mèxicans could not unravel, it became a necessity to act. He discerned so thoroughly the state of matters, and knew so well the necessity of considering the susceptibilities of Yankee pride as regarded monarchy, that he went on to say:—

. . . I point out this contingency to your majesty that you may be pleased to give the instructions you consider most fitting to meet the events.

It appears to me to be a matter of urgent necessity that an imperial commissioner should be sent to Matamoros, and I will take the liberty of observing to your majesty that a *civil* commissioner, provided with political powers, appears to me to be more fit to fulfil a mission in this quarter than a military one would be, since General Mejia has acquired a certain influence there in this respect.

The news of an asylum being granted to General Slaughter's army might excite the irritable temper of the Yankees to produce fresh and serious difficulties.

I scarcely notice the contingency of any desperate resistance being made by the remains of the Southern forces in Texas; the issue could be neither doubtful nor delayed.

Nevertheless, as every event must be provided against, I think that this latter state of things would be most dangerous for the northern frontier of Mexico. The American armies invading Texas would be formidable neighbours to the empire, and would increase the necessity for your majesty having an agent at Matamoros on whose devotion you could fully rely.

The commander-in-chief concluded by stating that he was prepared against every emergency, but he begged the emperor not to neglect measures which would be salutary in the future. For, although the French army were then masters of every position, the Mexican army would be called upon to succeed to it. The marshal also calculated on the defection of some of the imperialists.

... There is no time to be lost in placing yourself in a complete position to meet every contingency, and I venture to solicit your majesty to forgive my persistency for the sake of the motives which dictate it. BAZAINE.

The future immigrants demanded to be received as citizens, on their accepting all the legal conditions; they engaged to disband themselves before their admission, and their arms were not to be restored to them until they were subsequently needed for the defence of their homes against the free Indians. Their secret agent, whom we do not wish to name for fear of compromising him, repaired to Mexico, and, in accordance with the imperial decision, prepared either to treat for their admission into the empire or to announce their surrender to the United States. A kind of half-measure was proposed by the cabinet of Mexico; it was urged that the 25,000 Confederates should be looked upon in the first place as *prisoners of war*. The partisans were deeply dissatisfied, and negotiations were suddenly broken off by the capture of Jefferson Davis. Now that the United States were completely triumphant, there was nothing more to be hoped for from them, and on this occasion, too, a chance of success was lost.

To whichever party in the United States victory leaned, Maximilian was well aware that it would be dangerous for his policy if he did not secure for himself, without delay, this Confederate corps; for he had been informed that, in the early part of the month of February, a conference had taken place at Hampton

Roads in the James River, between the rebel plenipotentiaries and President Lincoln. In this interview, which was described as being of a cordial nature, Stephens, in the name of President Jefferson Davis, now hard-pressed, had demanded the temporary recognition of a Southern Confederation, until a favourable time arrived for the reconstruction of the Union. Waiting this, the South, in conjunction with the North, pledged themselves to effect the triumph of the ' Monroe doctrine,' by freeing Mexico from the French occupation, and by wresting Canada from the English rule. The Confederates proposed in this way to avenge themselves for the overthrow of the secret hopes which had been encouraged from the very outset of the contest by the cabinet of the Tuileries, which had accorded to them the belligerent character, and had after all abandoned them. The Mexican dynasty had therefore a powerful motive for neutralising this hostile movement by at once coming to an understanding with Slaughter's soldiers.

This check was felt by our head-quarters authorities, who had flattered themselves on the accession of this considerable reinforcement, so necessary to complete the pacification of the country now in danger. Everything was imperilled that was left in Mexican hands. The marshal, in the meantime, did not hesitate to point out freely to the emperor the necessity that existed for granting extensive powers of command, which, in the first instance, must be exercised by French generals. He also apprised him in writing as to the urgency of the situation. He begged of him not to neglect any precaution. We had already established a line of telegraph from Vera Cruz to Mexico. It was also important that the north should be connected with the capital by a telegraphic line, which should reach at least as far as San Luis; and in order that there should be no delay in its construction, the French officers and soldiers were directed to lay it down as they marched. Notwithstanding the distance, this line was not long in getting to work as soon as the wires and appliances arrived.

In spite of reverses and defections, in spite of the numberless bothers in the Austro-Belgian army inseparable from the contact of so many heterogeneous military elements, and in spite of palace intrigues, perfect harmony prevailed at this time between their Mexican majesties and the marshal. Maximilian, who did justice to the loyalty and powerful help rendered him by our commander, and felt that from the latter alone he derived all his power either of constructing or organising, had had no little share in promoting the union of the marshal with a Mexican family of Spanish origin, powerful more from its connections than from its property, now in danger. The family of La Peña had indeed furnished, both to the army and the magistracy, distinguished generals and honoured advocates. In 1833, General Pedrazza, the uncle of the future 'maréchale,' had been raised to the dignity of president of the republic, and her aunt was chosen as maid-of-honour by the Empress Iturbide.

Following the example of the sultan, who generously rewarded the Duc de Malakoff after the fall of Sebastopol, the imperial family settled a rich dowry on the *maréchale* on the occasion of her marriage, desiring thus to manifest their high sense of gratitude to the French army, by honouring it in the person of its chief. The imperial letter, deposited in the archives of Mexico, and annexed to the deed of gift, was thus expressed:—*

---

* This domain, now in the power of the republican authorities, has been of no value to Madame Bazaine; the Emperor Maximilian generously

Mexico, June 26, 1865.

My dear Marshal Bazaine,—Desiring to give a proof of my personal friendship, as well as of my gratitude for the services you have rendered to our country, we take advantage of the occasion of your marriage, and confer on the Maréchale Bazaine the palace of Buena-Vista, including the gardens and furniture; with the condition that, when you return to Europe, or if from any other cause you do not wish to retain the said palace, the nation shall again resume the property; and in this case the government binds itself to pay to the Maréchale Bazaine as dowry the sum of a hundred thousand piastres.—Your most affectionate MAXIMILIAN.
CASTILLO. ALMONTE.

It is well known that some weeks after his solemn entry into Mexico, Maximilian addressed to his minister, M. Velasquez de Leon, a remarkable financial and administrative programme, embracing the various branches of the two services. This manifesto contains the germs of the sovereign's intentions, who certainly came to Mexico with a high-minded sense of his regenerative mission. The taxes, the custom-house, the loans, the railroads and telegraphic lines, the public works, the postal service, the unity of weights and measures, the control of the public funds, were all discussed with great intelligence, and the formation of the necessary commissions was directed. With regard to colonisation, the royal will was expressed as follows:—' After having adopted a base for the ordinary taxes, the commission will take in hand the sales of waste lands. The extent and the value of these lands cannot be determined for want of correct information. *In the present*

---

offered, at the time of the evacuation, to pay her the 500,000 francs for her separate fortune; but his offer was naturally declined by a marshal of France, who had already refused to receive from the imperial munificence, expressed through M. Lacunza, the president of the council, the title of Duke of Mexico, and a rich property situated in the Zongolica.

state of things, the colonisation of the country by industrious families cannot yet be undertaken or encouraged. The commission will submit to us the arrangement and scheme which appear best fitted to collect the elements of exact information.'

In writing these instructions, Maximilian forgot that under his sceptre there were about six millions of Indians, a sober and industrious race, who, before they were reduced to slavery by a victorious aristocracy, astonished Cortez by their civilisation, not less magnificent than the court of Montezuma. The Spanish conqueror sent to Charles V. a vessel laden with the most wonderful productions of Mexican art which had evaded the first plundering of his soldiers. 'Their feather-paintings, their ornaments chased in gold and silver, and their utensils,' he wrote to his sovereign, 'are marvellous.' It is true that these simple-minded people had hitherto despised the precious metals as money, as they used in their barter nothing but the small almonds of the cacao. Robertson's description of them from the manuscripts of Cortez and Herrara is eloquent enough. 'The improved state of government among the Mexicans is conspicuous, not only in points essential to the being of a well-ordered society, but in several regulations of inferior consequence with respect to police. The institution, which I have already mentioned, of public couriers, stationed at proper intervals, to convey intelligence from one part of the empire to the other, was a refinement in police not introduced into any kingdom of Europe at that period. The structure of the capital city in a lake, with artificial dykes, and causeways of great length, which served as avenues to it from different quarters, erected in the water, with no less ingenuity than labour, seems to be an idea that could not have occurred to any but a civilised people. The same observation may be applied to the structure of the aqueducts, or conduits, by which they conveyed a stream of fresh water from a considerable distance into the city, along one of the causeways. The appointment of a number of persons to clean the streets, to light them by fires kindled in different places, and to patrol as watchmen during the night, discovers a degree of attention which even polished nations are late in acquiring.'

We think that Mexico would perhaps have been the gainer by going back to its 'iron age.' Be that as it may, did not the posterity of these so-called barbarians deserve a better fate than that which bound them as serfs to the soil, and condemned them to the duties of beasts of burden? These were the people who formed the brilliant cortege which welcomed the emperor and empress when they ascended the road from Orizaba to Mexico; they had exhumed all their old ornaments, the relics of bygone splendour, in order to do honour to the descendant of Charles V.

Maximilian, who might have made amends for the crime of his royal ancestor, committed the error, when he dismissed them from the capital, of not sending away to their homes as freemen these victims to the conquests of the sixteenth century. It would have been a princely mode of inaugurating his reign.

It was not until the end of September 1865 that, thinking better of it, he issued a decree which pronounced the emancipation of the Indian peons as well as the extinction of their past debts; debts often both usurious and disgraceful, which inflicted bondage on the babe yet unborn. This liberal and humane measure will ever remain to the honour of Maximilian—it ought to have sufficed to disarm his judges at Queretaro. Unfortunately, the measure was an incomplete one; it was but a half-measure, arising out of the state of things which the sovereign had caused, desirous of pleasing the two extreme parties. By this decree of emancipation the *peons* were not rendered proprietors of the soil. And yet in what better hands than those of the enfranchised *peons* could the state have entrusted 'those waste lands' spoken of in the imperial manifesto to the minister Velasquez, when his majesty regretted that, '*for want of an accurate estimation of the extent and value of these lands, they could not be handed over to industrious families?*' The Mexican commission constituted for more than a year, but constituted in vain, had not been able to foresee that it would not do to enfranchise a whole race of labourers without giving them at the same time the requisite field of labour. The Mexican government thus lost (as it had already lost Slaughter's 25,000 soldiers, all labourers or artisans) some millions of vigorous colonists, possessing to a high degree the love of marriage and family ties. They were forced to beg their daily bread, if the proprietors of the *haciendas* did not engage them on their farms. Now, the *hacenderos*, being deprived by this decree both of the payment of their claims and of the strong arms of their *peons*, were discontented, and refused to employ the services of those Indians who wished to profit by their legal liberation. Thus it was that the old condition of bondage for the *peon* fatally revived; in the fear of seeing his family perish of hunger, he, of his own accord, resumed his chain.

On the other hand, the clergy had become the personal enemies of the crown; they, too, countenanced the discontent of the *hacenderos*, being anxious to recover their evil influence over the *peons*, whose emancipation would tend to diminish their fanaticism and pious offerings. The clerical party, however, did not seek to hide their hostile feelings, which had only increased since the coronation of Maximilian, and the manifestation of his bias towards the liberal party. The unconcealed expression of it broke forth in the following letter from Mgr. La Bastida, Archbishop of Mexico. This historical document seems to us too important not to be recorded here for the exoneration of Maximilian, whose intentions were calumniated so early as four months after the sceptre was offered to him at Miramar.

A clandestine pamphlet, characterising *the generals who were conducting the intervention as the most inveterate enemies of religion and order*, had been circulated in Mexico, and had been seized by the police. The military commandant of the place protested that the prelates had always been treated with the utmost respect and veneration, and denounced these manœuvres to the archbishop, who replied:—

Mgr. La Bastida to General Baron Neigre.

... It is a proved fact that we have all protested against *those two individuals** *who have pretended to be a government*, and that we have declared categorically that the Church has now to put up with the same attacks against its immunities and rights as those which it suffered from during Juarez's government; and that it has never been persecuted with greater animosity. Pelagio Antonio,
Archbishop of Mexico.

This violent language augured but badly for the future. Thus beset both in the great centres of action as well as in the *haciendas*, how could the chief

---

* General Almonte and General Salas, who composed the regency, from which General Bazaine had been compelled (before the arrival of the emperor) to remove the archbishop, on account of his intrigues and systematic hostility.

of the state have any hope of appeasing the conflicting passions? All his most pregnant ideas which existed in germ in the imperial programme became abortive for want of agents capable of developing them honestly; and this was the case, in spite of the unceasing cooperation of the French functionaries, to whom, however, the court of Mexico did not fail to give due credit. It will be recollected that the head-quarters authorities, in November 1864, boldly called attention to the carelessness of the directors of the public *haciendas*, with respect to the financial staff which was summoned from Europe to assist the Mexican government. At the end of July 1865, a fresh pressing note was brought before the emperor himself, attesting that the public *haciendas* had only recognised in the French agents most insignificant powers, which would not permit them to exercise any useful control on the receipt of the public monies, and the employment of the same by the local administrations; the latter opposing the same resistance to any foreign interference as that which M. Langlois, the successor to M. Corta, met with in the capital. This state councillor had been sent from France at Maximilian's request, to clean out the ' Augean stables,' in which the customs' duties and the taxes were plundered even by the principal servants of the crown. The same watchword prevailed everywhere in the ranks of the Mexican administration.

Another pretext for disturbance did not a little contribute to retard the success of the expeditionary corps, the members of which vied with one another in activity, without taking account either of losses or fatigue, and without allowing themselves to be rebuffed by any kind of obstacle. The reorganisation of a nation can only be effected by hard labour, and a thousand local and individual sacrifices. The territorial alterations, which had been rendered necessary by the creation of great military commands, had deeply wounded the spirit of routine in the large landed proprietors, and had interfered with the habits of the clerical party, by displacing their centres of action. A portion of the malcontent *hacenderos*, without venturing to declare openly against the empire, afforded help to the rebellion, and rendered hospitality and paid money to the guerillas; they remounted their cavalry, and took care of their wounded or tired horses, which were again claimed by the guerillas when they were fit for service.

In the course of this year (1865), the French fleet and army had exerted themselves so vigorously from the Gulf to the Pacific that a force of less than 29,000 combatants had managed to visit and to encourage every port and all the state capitals except those of Guerrero and Chiapas. We have already proved that this scattering of the military forces, although it was advised by Maximilian and the empress, was a serious imprudence, and was likely to create dangers for the future. It would have been much better to have made gradual extensions of a *peaceful* rule as resources allowed, encouraging every interest, and enlarging bit by bit a solidly constructed circle, than, as was the case, to spread out at the first onset over vast solitudes thinly sprinkled with small centres of population; for it might easily be foreseen that ere long it would be necessary to abandon them, giving rise to all the horrors of war which always accompany a retreat. Nevertheless, our columns, crossing the prairies, had invaded the capital of Chihuahua, the last stronghold of the president of the republic, and the news was spread in the empire that Juarez had deserted the Mexican soil. The fugitive had fled from Chihuahua to Paso del Norte, a little town, the houses of which stand in a line along the bank of the Rio Grande. A hundred yards on the other side of the river the United States territory begins. It may be easily understood that, in a position like this, President Juarez (whose capture, however, would in no way have modified the resistance of the liberals) felt himself entirely safe from our troops. If a horseman came in sight, he had only to cross the river, and afterwards return when the danger had disappeared. Thus, for nearly eighteen months, Juarez lived on the Rio Grande, with the full understanding of the Washington cabinet. Was it possible to guard the whole course of a river running down from this point to the Gulf, so as to prevent his admission into their territory?

CHAPTER VII.

Fatal Decree of October 3 — Its real Bearing — Empress Charlotte's Letter — Decay of Mexican Resources — Inaction of Mexican Officials, and consequent Disasters — Extent of French Occupation — Statement of the National Army.

NOW comes on to the stage the famous decree of October 3, 1865, which has cost so many tears. It is deeply important to establish its real origin, as well as its exact import. We must, first of all, say that there is cause for painful surprise that the ministers who countersigned this decree, and subsequently abandoned Maximilian in order to take refuge in France, have not as yet raised their voice to defend the memory of the sovereign who himself conceived and signed this fatal *bando*; for in full council, and from the very lips of the emperor, they had learnt *the truth*.

As soon as the news that Juarez had crossed the frontier at Paso del Norte reached Mexico, there was great joy at the palace. The army then held all the strong positions. The disappearance of the republican chief afforded a hope of an abatement of hostilities on the part of the so-called liberal party, now driven into a corner and left without a head. Maximilian, who believed that he was the *bonâ fide* choice of a people wearied out with disorder and turmoil, felt a pride in his regenerating character, and flattered himself that the Juarists were completely overthrown, and that by paying honour to the vanquished party, he should deal a decisive blow against the rebellion, which would henceforth be countenanced by none but bands of brigands. He then brought before his council the project of offering Juarez the presidency of the supreme court, and his own sincere desire of rallying round him all the illustrious men in the country.

As a means of opening negotiations, he drew up the decree of October 3. At the beginning of this decree, he laid it down that the republican cause had lost its last support, and the preambles were a homage paid to the character of Juarez. As to the decree itself, it certainly was only directed, *in the intention of the emperor*, against those persons whose only aim was to shelter their brigandage under the republican flag. This fatal decree, the original minutes of which may be consulted, was written entirely by Maximilian's own hand, although he had a secretary at his side. All the ministers who countenanced the idea affixed their signatures to it. The marshal alone did not sign it. Before investing it with any official character, Maximilian thought it right to consult the marshal. The answer returned from our head-quarters was that, in the first place, the preamble so flattering to the president (who was opposed by France as an enemy) appeared to be directed against the intervention; also, that, apart from this painful interpretation, the decree itself was useless, as courts-martial were acting which had the guarantee of the cognisance of the French officers; besides, that it was impolitic, because it rendered Mexicans amenable to Mexicans, and that all the odium in it would fall upon the person of the sovereign, whose most precious attribute was the right of mercy and pardon. The emperor, with the entire approbation of his five ministers, persisted in his original idea—that of attaching Juarez by this public declaration emanating from the throne,—and took no notice of the above remonstrance. At the last moment, the commander-in-chief, whose duty it was as head of the two armies to execute the decree, asked and obtained the addition of an article fining any *hacenderos* convicted of having taken care of and concealed the arms and horses of the rebels.

This decree of October 3, which was about to rekindle the civil war by gratifying private malice, was the suicide of the monarchy, led away, as it was, by chivalrous illusions and by the traditions of civilised countries. Juarez, who had never abdicated his rights, repulsed any overture of reconciliation, and the ostracism directed against the 'outlawed republicans' caused a great sensation in the United States, where it stirred up anger against a prince and princess who were, in fact, generous to an extreme. For, many a time, outbursts of feeling on the part of the imperial family, whose good faith it was easy to beguile, had injuriously curbed the justice of our courts-martial. Such is the history of this fatal day's work, which must no longer continue to be a stain on the memory of the noble victim of Queretaro.

There was a moment, at the birth-time of the empire, when a part of the population, as much from weariness of disorder as from spontaneous sympathy for the new sovereigns, was inclined to make an earnest trial of a monarchy. This precious moment vanished away, ere the crown, for want of an initiative spirit, knew how to profit by it. The following letter, written by the Empress Charlotte, an intelligent and large-hearted princess, who had taken an active part in the direction both of political and military affairs, shows clearly that too little value was set upon the Indian element, and also manifests the decided feeling of the crown not to allow the Mexican treasury to be ruined, in the conviction that the French finances would provide for everything. This letter proves also that palace intrigues, hostile to the French officers, had been fermenting round the throne since the beginning of the monarchy.

Mexico, September 16, 1864.

General,—My opinion is asked on the subject of the enclosed letter, but, as it has to do with generals, I want in the first place to know *your* opinion. For my part, I believe it is nothing but an intrigue which proves the very contrary of that which is sought to be shown.

Be kind enough to give me the requisite information, and send me the paper after you have read it, for M. Velasquez wishes me to give him an answer to-morrow.

It will fall upon you to deal with various questions with which we are occupied in the council. The most important is the pacification of the Sierra. The prefect of Talancingo has some ideas about it which are not bad. It seems to me that by sending some detachments to a fixed post, and some others to make expeditions, good results will be produced. Only in this case, I would ask you to give me notice, so that the civil authorities may arrange measures to co-operate with yours in helping on the undertaking.

If it were possible to arrange beforehand certain movements, keeping them in the meantime as secret as possible, I think it would produce great results, and the passage of the troops might be followed by some kind of organisation.

As for the Indians who are desirous to defend themselves against the *Plateados*, you must tell me if you think that it is necessary to provide them with arms. This sort of thing begins to get too frequent, and as for money, the government have resolved not to give any to anyone.—Believe, general, &c., CHARLOTTE.

I hope that you know all about the army for the 16th, and also that it will be reviewed as soon as I return to the palace, and before the reception of the authorities. You did not give me any memorandum as to it on Sunday.

In two months the reorganisation of the Mexican army, laboriously carried out by the French authorities, was again endangered by the government itself. As to the political and departmental management, it appeared in a deplorable state. The ministerial delays, extending even to personal questions and the forwarding of orders, had allowed even the best-disposed districts to fall back into their original apathy. The difficulty was to choose men who were capable of inspiring confidence. No stimulus seemed to excite them, and patriotism had not yet woke up. No one among the imperial party gave any thought to save the commonwealth in spite of the noble example of personal self-denial set by the imperial family. Wherever the French were numerous, they came in contact with authorities who were either unfavourably disposed or unprovided with proper instructions. In a word, all the trouble fell on our officers, who found themselves compelled, in the interests of the country, to gradually make preparations against every contingency. Disgusted also at seeing functionaries slumbering in disgraceful carelessness, or discrediting and discouraging publicly those of their countrymen, who still clung to the empire as a means of safety, our officers ended by taking in hand the most trifling business in the various localities where they were carrying on their military duties. The fear was lest everything should drift away down the flood of insurrection which had taken its source from the American frontier, and was now rolling down from north to south.

It will not do to impute to Maximilian the responsibility of all the decay through which the empire was about to succumb; money, the sinews of war, was already deficient. As the French government had resolved, at the cost of enormous sacrifices, opposed by public opinion, to found a firm dynasty in Mexico, was it not wrong in having paid to its ally only forty millions out of two enormous loans—loans by which it had realised, through its own receivers-general, the sum of five hundred millions lent by imprudent subscribers who had been allured and then deceived? Was it not from the very outset a mere ushering into the world a still-born kingdom? Our minister of foreign affairs was kept too well informed, by the reports emanating from our head-quarters, to be able to deceive himself as to the real situation of Mexico. Yet, with a policy full of inconsistency, the cabinet of the Tuileries allowed its work to crumble away from the first beginning, by refusing to it the resources which were indispensable. At the end of 1865, the Mexican treasury was getting very low, and the bad financial administration stimulated an increase of the *deficit*, which, however, could never have been made up by the strictest control; for the receipts, even if they had been regularly collected, would not have exceeded ninety millions of francs, whilst, without noticing the sinking fund, the expenses swallowed up one hundred and fifty millions at least. Never, however, was the want of money more stringently manifested.

Certain military positions on the shores of the Pacific were no longer tenable. Among other places, the climate of Acapulco had exercised so deadly an influence on the French force who defended this port that the commandant, D'Assas, was compelled to propose the formation of a battalion recruited on the coast of Tehuantepec among the natives, who were accustomed to the tropical sky. Further away, Parras justly demanded reinforcements; for this industrious place had given an example, alas too rare, of energy and self-sacrifice which, if it had been generally followed, would have saved the empire. The inhabitants of this town had voluntarily taxed themselves to the amount of about eighteen thousand piastres, to raise a troop of 400 men; and this was done at the instigation of an energetic prefect. They now found themselves at the end of their resources, and their soldiers were consequently disbanded, leaving the inhabitants exposed to the reprisals of the liberals. The minister of war, not being well informed, questioned the authenticity of this disquieting news which had reached the emperor. The evidence was, however, too strong when the cries of distress sent up from this part of the territory made their way to Mexico.

The marshal, seeing the full necessity of protecting these towns on the Pacific, as important places both in a military and commercial point of view, ordered our fleet (whose devotion was put to a cruel test in these dangerous waters) to provision Manzanillo, so that our men-of-war might be able to take advantage of their voyages along the coast from Manzanillo to Acapulco, to bring food, meat, and medicines to the garrison. As to Parras, the head-quarters authorities, being desirous of relieving the population, caused four free companies to be raised, and consented that their pay should be guaranteed by the French treasury, as an advance. No opportunity was lost of helping any of the energetic inhabitants. But there was a just limit which our commander-in-chief was not entitled to pass. For, unless he betrayed his duties as a Frenchman, he was obliged to regard the safety of his soldiers as well as the wishes of the imperial family. Now, article 2 of the treaty of Miramar, which Maximilian had signed in full knowledge of the facts, stipulated that, after the throne had been taken possession of, ' our expeditionary corps should be reduced to an *effectif* of 25,000 combatants, including the foreign legion.' Moreover, this number was to be still further reduced in proportion as the Mexican troops became organised.

In contradiction to this double clause, the French army had always been above the number of 28,000 men, notwithstanding the return to Europe of the brigade of General Lhériller. Besides, this brigade, which only consisted of about 4,000 fighting men, was succeeded by the Austrian legion, 8,000 bayonets strong; the forces were thus increased, instead of being diminished. But yet the marshal could not, even with this force, occupy effectively an extent of about eighteen hundred leagues, and thus abandon weak French detachments to all the hazards of desertion and want. These, however, were the tactics to which the Emperor Maximilian was inclined, whose tendencies to scattering the military forces did not cease to show themselves; to have yielded to them would have been to overlook the share of responsibility which would fall on our head-quarters in case of any check.

The city of La Paz, the capital of Lower California, is situated about 500 leagues from Mexico, and any communication with this distant point presented very great difficulties. Nevertheless, it was occupied in 1865 by the interventionary forces, who only left after they had assisted in the political and military organisation of the country. This city, after the departure of our forces, again pronounced in favour of the Juarists. When Maximilian heard the news, he wrote as follows to the commander-in-chief:—

Mexico, December 17, 1865.

Marshal,—I have just learned that a counter-revolution has broken out at La Paz, and that the imperial authorities have been obliged to leave. This revolt has been effected by about a hundred men.

Although the political importance of Lower California may be inconsiderable, this counter-revolution will produce the very worst effect on public opinion both in the United States and in Europe, by giving rise to the idea that, so far from pacifying the country, we are, on the contrary, losing territory.

I therefore desire to know if it will not be possible to send to La Paz a French company whose presence in the port will suffice to re-establish order and preserve this province to the empire.—Your very affectionate

MAXIMILIAN.

How could we leave an isolated company, at such a great distance from the centre of action, at a time when the French were already occupying Acapulco, Guaymas, and Mazatlan on the Pacific, and Matamoros, Tampico, Vera Cruz, Alvarado, Sisal, and Campeachy on the Gulf, all dangerous and unhealthy posts, where even the Mexican troops did not stay for long? It must be understood also that, although financial resources began to diminish to an extent which caused anxiety, the Mexican minister of war could not plead as an excuse for the insurrectionary movements, which were now assuming a decided shape, that he was in want of soldiers to oppose to the rebels; the fact was that he either left the troops unemployed or did not know how to employ them effectively. Tranquillity was insured in every place which saw the gleam of the French bayonet. A glance at the official and veracious list of the forces which the empire had at its disposal at this time—critical by the curtailment of our expeditionary corps—will suffice to prove their adequacy.

On December 31, 1865, the Mexican army reckoned in its ranks—without mentioning a considerable and well-furnished body of artillery—of the national troops (including regulars and the temporary and municipal troops), 35,650 foot soldiers, horsemen, and artillerymen, with 11,073 horses. Of foreign troops—Belgians, 1,324; Austrians, 6,545, with 1,409 horses. This makes 12,482 horses, and an effective military force of 43,520 men.

A force like the above, assisted by the French, was capable, as we have seen, of ensuring the triumph of the empire if only its managers had remained on good terms with one another and full of energy. But, to use the just language of the minister of state—'*God had not ordained it.*'

CHAPTER VIII.

Disasters in the Empire—Dissensions between the Foreign Contingents and Mexican Troops — The Empress Charlotte's Opinion of the French Army — Difficulty in paying the Troops, and consequent Desertions—Maximilian's Project to subdue Yucatan—Its Impolicy—The two Chances for the Empire—Poverty of the Mexican Troops—Pecuniary Help rendered by Marshal Bazaine—M. de Lacunza's Moving Appeal to Marshal Bazaine—Meeting at the Imperial Palace—Maximilian speaks out—Yankee Intrigues—American Dictation to France—Mr. Seward's Note—Maximilian secretly sacrificed.

WE are now entering upon the period of those disastrous events which gradually crushed down the Mexican empire. A just idea may, we hope, have been formed as to the errors which caused them. The following pages, describing step by step the long agony of an empire, will surprise by the recital of sudden events, of solemn promises trodden under foot, of strange and unexpected political changes, through which the policy of the French and Mexican courts (soon to be at variance) will finally shatter itself to pieces against the arrogant threats of the United States.

The year 1866 began under sad auspices. In the early part of January, disaffection began to show itself on all sides in the very heart of the empire. The breath of rebellion had passed over all the high plateaus. Bands of *guerilleros* were devastating Tamaulipas, Nuevo Leon, and Zacatecas, the states bordering on the Union. Pachuca had risen at the very gates of the capital, and Michoacan had raised the standard of revolt. '*Long live the Northern Intervention!*'—this was the insurgents' rallying cry; they claimed the assistance of the great republic, in order to drive the allies of that republic into the sea. The title of ally applied to the Austrians and Belgians as well as to the French. These foreign contingents were not only detested by the malcontents, but had also sown disunion round the throne. Serious disagreements had sprung up between them and the Mexicans, who refused to obey the European officers. Art. 5 of the treaty of Miramar had, in fact, stipulated '*that in case of expeditions with French and Mexican troops combined, the chief command of these troops shall belong to the French general.*' But the Belgians and Austrians had only been summoned to Mexico as troops in the pay of the Mexican treasury, and were consequently subject to the military institutions of the country they were about to serve, thus losing all character of distinctive nationality. In case, therefore, of any combination of troops, the Mexican officers were justified in only accepting orders from Austrians or Belgians of a rank superior to their own. On the other hand, the Belgians complained of having been deceived, and asserted that they had only come as armed colonists intended to cultivate and to defend the land, but not to act as regular soldiers; this misunderstanding had already promoted desertions from their ranks. These northerners, whatever might be their military qualities, were not adapted for a climate such as this, and their powers of action suffered from their temperament not being fit for a partisan war. Besides, the employment of mercenaries is always dangerous and impolitic. The following remark of the Empress Charlotte well describes the state of things:—' The Austrians and Belgians are all very well in quiet times; but when a storm comes, there is nothing like the *red trowsers.*' The unfortunate princess rendered a just homage to the French blood, to which she was akin through the Orleans family.

We must add that Maximilian received numerous complaints from his generals, asserting that their contingents were without horses and arms. Mejia stated that it was very difficult to keep soldiers to their duty who received no pay. The minister of war had informed the emperor (whose displeasure was great) that he had begged the French head-quarters to escort with one of their battalions the *conducta* from Monterey, intended to carry the means of payment for Mejia's division at Matamoros, and that the marshal had not thought fit to afford his co-operation. This accusation against the French commander, who was unceasing in his efforts for the good of the service, called forth genuine surprise. Maximilian was, however, able to convince himself that the matter in question had not been an escort for money intended for the Mexicans, but only as to a commercial convoy, the sending off of which had been delayed by military exigencies. Besides, the ships of the squadron, constantly sailing between Vera Cruz and Matamoros, offered every facility for maritime transport in less than sixty hours, whilst the journey by land would require some weeks, and a uselessly dangerous array of forces; the roads leading to Tamaulipas from Queretaro, San Luis, and Monterey, being infested by the guerillas commanded by Cortina and Carbajal, and helped by bands of Americans.

In situations where the French troops protected the northern frontier, the Americans still hesitated to violate the Mexican territory; but this state of things was a very awkward one, and any aggressive demonstration by our battalions on the Rio Grande or the Rio Bravo might have brought on an immediate conflict with the United States, which by the formal instructions of our government we were to avoid. Besides, the scattered state of the expeditionary force had not permitted any movement of this sort so far from the centre of Mexico. It was necessary in the first place to put down the insurrection in the departments close to the capital, and our commander had to hurry off reinforcements to pacify Michoacan.

These sad events tore down the veil by which, up to this time, the ministers had flattered themselves that they could hide the truth from Maximilian, in spite of the warnings given by the marshal.

Some days before, the commander-in-chief had been forced to draw the attention of the emperor to the frequent military *pronunciamientos*, which bid fair to threaten the very existence of the army.

They are facts which your majesty can explain [said he, stigmatising these desertions] since you are aware that a large number of the authorities have betrayed the government, and that the *gardes rurales* have been organised in such a way that it really appears as if they had been constituted with the sole idea of furnishing resources to the rebels.

. . . First of all, it is necessary *to get rid of perfidious agents, and to ensure the payment of the troops in preference to the other civil service expenditure*, which can wait.

The embellishment of the city of Mexico and of the imperial palace at Chapultepec absorbed considerable sums, although the financial position of the country should have claimed this money for more practical purposes. Nevertheless, at the note of alarm proceeding from our head-quarters, Maximilian trembled.

He had just felt the first shocks which were agitating his throne, and on January 6, 1866, he wrote the following lines, which well depict the state of his mind, and the commencement of his sufferings:—'I know that

I have accepted a singularly difficult task, but my courage is equal to supporting the burden, and I will go on to the end.' What a painful contrast to the calmness of the following letter, which he wrote to the marshal only five weeks before:—

Mexico, December 2, 1865.

My dear Marshal,—The time has now arrived both to govern and to act. I have reckoned on your help to give me some minutes as to the prefects, the imperial commissioners, and the Mexican generals. MAXIMILIAN.

What! had a reign of eighteen months been completely wasted? The necessity of action had not made itself felt until now. The imperial correspondence is full of these strange contradictions. Whilst the departments were rising in revolt, and the want of troops was showing itself by great disasters in many parts of the territory, Maximilian again dreamt of another distant expedition, and stripped, as is proved by the following order, the province of Oajaca, where Porfirio Diaz was about to rekindle the civil war.

... It must not be forgotten that Franco has organised 2,200 good troops, and that if they come under the orders of General de Thun, it seems natural to require them to contribute in great part to the expedition from Tabasco and Tlapacoyan; for it is not necessary to keep so numerous a force in the state of Oajaca. MAXIMILIAN.

Maximilian cherished the idea of conquering a new province, at a time when the old ones were being wrested away from his crown. And Yucatan, a most unhealthy country, and the refuge of many rebel native tribes, had never been in proper subjection to the old presidential authority.

If eighteen months' experience and various harsh lessons had only inspired Maximilian with wisdom, he ought to have understood that he would be unable to unite under the imperial sceptre this scattered cluster of vast provinces, almost unknown one to the other, for want of ways of communication favourable to trade. History taught him that the sacrifices made by the states farthest from the centre and separated from the capital by vast deserts, had resulted only from a desire to defend their independence against foreigners, and from no real sympathy with Mexico or with Juarez, from whom they had but little favour or assistance to hope for. Every state capital had its own administration and its own individual interests. Since the war of independence, Mexico (not to speak of the reign of Iturbide, the first emperor, shot in 1823) had been more of a *federation* than a *republic*. Moreover, if the military efforts of the crown had failed when the troops were regularly paid, and when a civil war was rending the interior of the United States, what could be hoped for in the future, now that the national treasury, forced to provide for the defence of eighteen hundred leagues of territory, was avowedly exhausted, and the victorious Yankees no longer concealed the hostility of their sentiments? Only two chances of safety were left to the tottering monarchy: one would have been, instead of pretending to reign over an imaginary kingdom exposed on every side, to concentrate all his active forces in the richest and most populous central states, to carefully preserve his communications for export and import with both seas, and then to wait for better times before he tried to regain territory. The other plan would have been, to return to the constitution of 1857, and to proclaim the seventeen states free and independent under the ægis of a sovereign ruler. This federal organisation would have been the only measure to calm the easily offended susceptibilities of the American Union.

In the early part of February 1866, the situation of the empire was most critical. The state treasury was completely exhausted, and the Mexican army was calling loudly for its pay. When the French officers remained two months under the walls of Puebla without touching any pay, and when our soldiers also have occasionally waited for the arrival of their money, their bivouac was none the less gay, thanks to our magnificent administrative organisation, which so fully provides for every necessity in a campaign.

But when money was deficient, the Mexican troops would have died of hunger if they had not turned into bands of marauders. The commander-in-chief knew too well the military elements of the Mexican army not to fear that treason and confusion would immediately follow pillage; and he judged it to be his duty to take the best means he could to prevent it. For the sake of the imperial throne, which now seemed ready to break up, he assumed the responsibility of authorising the French paymaster-general to make an advance of five millions, which were required for the subsistence of the imperialists.

We have selected the following letter from the emperor, out of many others, as worthy of being quoted, because it exactly points out the nature of the relations existing at this period between our headquarters and the court of Mexico, now tried by misfortune:—

Palais de Mexico, February 5, 1866.

My dear Marshal,—I have just learnt the valuable service which you have rendered to my government, by coming to its help at the time of a difficult financial crisis.

Be pleased to receive my most sincere thanks for the discretion and kindness which you have exercised in this delicate matter, which, to me, doubles the value of the service.—Your very affectionate MAXIMILIAN.

This service* to the Mexican crown was not well received at Paris, and Marshal Bazaine did not meet with the approval of the cabinet of the Tuileries. He received instructions not to consent to any further advance to the Mexican treasury. The downfall of the empire was no longer a matter of doubt—its last agony was commencing.

The marshal, however, could not turn a deaf ear to the moving supplications of the Mexican government; for its last appeal was truly heartrending. M. de Lacunza, the president of the council, a man devoted to his country, and one of her most enlightened citizens, begged for the help of France, in a letter too appealing to be passed over without notice. This document, full of revelations as to the policy of the French cabinet, marks the epoch of one of the downward steps of the unhappy empire, which was called into being by our hand, and now tottered over the precipice dug away for it by our intervention.

To His Excellency Marshal Bazaine.

Mexico, April 28, 1866.

Most esteemed Marshal,—I had the honour yesterday of paying you a visit, and you are aware that its principal object was to point out to your excellency the indubitable necessity of your continuing the advances to the Mexican treasury which have been made these last few months. I now desire to reiterate to your excellency my most urgent entreaties on this subject, and also to make known to you the circumstances in which we now stand, and the result we must look forward to, if we do not at once get out of the difficulty.

As it is but a short time since I undertook the direction of foreign affairs, I can speak of things as they really are, as I am in no way responsible for them ; these things are no novelty to your excellency, who knows them well ; but a free and candid

---

* The *Corps Législatif* sanctioned this payment.

representation of them will induce you to say, 'This man tells the truth.'

The military state of things, in a financial point of view, is well known to your excellency. In the north, Mejia's division is scarcely able to live even by eating up the meagre resources of the place in which it is stationed, by making almost forced loans, and also by drawing considerable sums from Vera Cruz.

Also in the north, the troops commanded by Quiroga have no food of any consequence, and this chief is compelled to enforce the payment of taxes a whole year in advance, and also to exact loans, so that the citizens of the places where his troops are stationed are obliged to emigrate in order to avoid these molestations.

In the south, the troops which are under Franco's orders cannot leave Oajaca to meet the enemies which menace them because the daily pay of the soldiers is not secured, and also because there is no forage for the horses.

In the centre of the empire, Florentino Lopez* has been compelled by like causes to lose much time before leaving San Luis.

The Austro-Belgian troops are owed more than half a million of piastres, and before your excellency caused them to be paid out of the French treasury, they had spent their last *centime*, and consumed all the available provisions in the towns they occupy.

It is useless to prolong this sad picture of the poverty of our resources in a military point of view; your excellency is well aware of it, and I have been compelled to reply to the sovereign, when I have been requested to help pecuniarily various Mexican corps, that there were not the means of doing it.

What is going on in the central pay-office at Mexico? Various bills have been drawn upon it amounting to about 300,000 piastres, which have not been paid, and for which there is no hope of payment; there are urgent requisitions to which we can pay no attention; there are, finally, the troops forming the garrison to whom *their pay has been owing for nearly two months*.

Your instructions express that you are not to make advances

---

* The general who died at Matehuala.

to Mexico. These instructions are in direct contradiction to the friendly intentions and the very policy of the emperor.

Is there any remedy for this state of things? Certainly, there is one, and it is not of my suggestion; it is M. Langlais who has mentioned it—he who possessed the full confidence of France, and most assuredly well deserved it.

What, then, is this remedy? It consists of a new financial system by which the expenses will be diminished and the revenue increased. The scheme of this system is already decided on, and is almost drawn up; it is also to some extent put in practice.

All the expenses have been reduced to the lowest possible figure, commencing with the emperor's civil list; his majesty is content with only a third of the amount assigned to the Emperor Iturbide, nearly half a century ago. As your excellency is well aware, we are arranging the new system which is to prevail with regard to the public revenue, from which system we expect a considerable augmentation of our resources, and we are preparing the new taxes, a portion of which is already put in force, as, for example, in the maritime customs.

But it is not in man's power either to delay or hasten the march of time, and this is a principal element in every kind of useful progress. If they are to produce their effect, the new plans, which I have every confidence will not delude our hopes, inevitably need a certain space of time for putting them in practice.

During this period of transition, what, are we to depend upon? We cannot trust, for a time, to our own new resources, and it is necessary that France should provide what is immediately required. This also is a truth which was admitted and acted on by M. Langlais.

After his much regretted death, this material help was for a time interrupted, and the government had to submit to the dictation of the capitalists to whom it was compelled to apply. Your excellency is not ignorant of what took place; transactions which were ruinous in every way, made, as they were, under the pressure of necessity, put the government in possession of resources *which lasted eight days*, and discredited it for a much longer time, by obliging it to employ for repayment a portion of the customs-funds, with which the foreign loans ought to have been paid.

This is the result produced by the withdrawal of the French co-operation before the appointed time.

I will say a few words more as to these *results*. Your excellency will understand that a powerful argument is contained in the fact that a large portion of the Mexican nation accepted the French intervention, and likewise accepted and is now supporting the empire, *in spite of their republican principles, which are those they were brought up in;* for with the idea of the intervention and the empire was connected that of good faith, order, and impartiality of government, and, consequently, that of the independence of the Latin race in the New World. This, at least, has been the way in which the grand conception of the Emperor Napoleon has been understood here.

Up to the present time, the emperor and the intervention have played a satisfactory part. The disorder in the financial department (which we are now considering) had disappeared, the payments were punctual, the revenue was no longer exposed to the speculations of stock-jobbery, and the loans subscribed in Europe were contracted in due form. If, after having exhausted the resources produced by these loans (as is the case), the emperor finds himself unable any longer to meet expenses, and is compelled to enter upon the old path of disorder, all the good effected by the new system will be undone, and the hopes which had been founded on it will become at least problematical. The final result may be obtained, but the fresh sacrifices and expenses that it will require will be prolonged and multiplied to an extent that no one can now foresee.

The alternative for your excellency is: either to impose a slight burden on the French treasury, in order to accomplish a work undertaken by the Emperor Napoleon himself, which is a work both grand in idea and useful in itself; or, to refuse to do it, and, consequently, to throw upon this very same treasury the necessity of a far more profuse outlay and more costly sacrifices.

The enterprise cannot be abandoned; will your excellency terminate it at a small expense? or will you leave to your government the task of concluding it at the cost of immense sacrifices?

This is the plain question which is submitted to your excellency by your sincere friend and most affectionate

J. M. A. DE LACUNZA.

Two days after the receipt of this document, which well attests what Maximilian must have suffered, there was a council held at the imperial palace. The commander-in-chief, M. Dano, and M. de Maintenant (the inspector of finances delegated to Mexico by France) had been summoned to it. The emperor was surrounded by all his ministers. The scene was full of sadness. M. Lacunza demanded boldly a monthly advance of five millions from our treasury. The representatives of our government, in virtue of the formal instructions they had received, had urged that his demand should not be entertained. Then the emperor, breaking into the discussion, cried out :—

'Doing away with all detail, the question may be summed up in very few words—*it is either the bankruptcy of the empire or the hope of saving it.* If the personages who represent France at this meeting are not willing to take the responsibility of spending a few millions, they must take that of having allowed bankruptcy to intervene, which assuredly would not be the desire of the Emperor Napoleon, who has always shown himself to be the friend of the Mexican empire.'

The marshal conceded one-half of the advance requested by Maximilian. We have seen before what sort of reception awaited this step taken by the commander-in-chief. How was it that the Emperor Napoleon's letters to Maximilian, constantly containing direct promises of effective co-operation, were always preceded or followed by orders from the ministers forbidding the French agents to make any financial advances? How was it that the marshal's actions did not meet with approval? This last act of the French policy, publicly putting an end to the period of our financial sacrifices, produced a great effect, both in Mexico and also in the Old and New Worlds generally; for this refusal of subsidies was but the precursor of the withdrawal of our expeditionary corps. The government of Napoleon III. was beginning now to reap the fruits of its adventurous policy. Henceforth, the aim of the Washington cabinet was the humiliation of our national self-respect by the overthrow of the Mexican throne. The inmates of the White House had not forgotten that France had once granted belligerent rights to the Southern rebels, anxious as she was to inaugurate a military dictatorship, the future head of which, the celebrated Confederate general, had commenced negotiations with Mexico itself.

Now that the Yankees had triumphed over the Secessionists, they were resolved to make our country as well as Maximilian pay dearly for the part they had taken in the intervention in the neighbouring republic. It must be confessed that the time selected by Mr. Seward, the obstinate secretary of state at Washington, was not ill chosen. Public opinion in France, which had been led away for a time by the pompous statements of our ministers, bound to allure subscribers to the two Mexican loans,* had gradually become enlightened as to the real state of matters, both military and political, in the new empire. Although every transatlantic courier brought to Saint-Nazaire the news of

---

* It will not be without interest to point out here that, notwithstanding these loans were warmly recommended in Mexico, not a family, nor a commercial house in that country, would subscribe to them: in a word, not a single bond could be placed in Mexico, even among the imperial party. The Mexicans were 'wiser in their generation' than our too credulous countrymen.

fresh successes won by our arms, it was also known through private correspondence that the Juarists, countenanced by the privity of the United States, and by the approach of threatening complications in Europe, were not discouraged by the reverses inflicted upon them by our soldiers, and were reconquering without difficulty those portions of the territory which were entrusted for defence to the imperial forces alone.

On the other hand, our government, who were now uneasy as to the eventualities of the German conflict, felt unwilling to be deprived of the help of 30,000 seasoned men, now engaged on the other side of the ocean; a force which it had the intention (we are justified in believing) to maintain in Mexico for an indeterminate period. Besides, it was annoyed in domestic matters by the utterances from the tribune and the notices of the press, which incessantly demanded that an end should be put to this fruitless enterprise. Then it was that the United States, through the medium of Mr. Seward, spoke out dictatorially to the cabinet of the Tuileries. In 1864, this minister had confined himself to asserting to M. Drouyn de Lhuys 'that the unanimous feeling of the American people was opposed to the recognition of a monarchy in Mexico.' Now, become bolder, he challenges directly the French intervention itself, and gives France to understand that the prolongation of an armed occupation might become pregnant with danger.

On December 6, 1865, a note emanating from the state department at Washington had been sent to the Marquis de Montholon, the French minister; it explained, *à propos* of Mexico, the political views of the United States with regard to the American continent. This note, when communicated to the palace of the Tuileries, and there considered, caused considerable sensation. On January 9, 1866, our ministry of foreign affairs sent to its representative a reply to Mr. Seward's communication. The French government announced 'that it was disposed to hasten as much as possible the recall of its troops from Mexico.' Seven days afterwards, the packet conveyed to Mexico M. le Baron Saillard, furnished with confidential instructions.

Not content with this first victory, President Johnson directed that another and still more pressing diplomatic note should be sent to the French legation; it was dated February 12. After having assumed as settled that the recall of our troops was laid down as a principle, it demanded the fixture of an exact date, which would quiet the susceptibilities of his fellow-citizens. Maximilian was, as we see, abruptly sacrificed, and found himself henceforth at the mercy of the United States, which now ruled the French policy on the continent of America. This second diplomatic document, in fifteen pages of which Mr. Seward discussed with inexorable logic all M. Drouyn de Lhuys' dilatory arguments, left no room either for intentional or unintentional delays; and the purport as well as the form of it are so curious a study, if read in the light of the events about to be detailed, that we must here quote some instructive passages of it. The light that will be reflected from them will illumine the whole scene of action.

Note from Mr. Seward to the Marquis de Montholon, the French Minister.

Washington, February 12, 1866.

Sir,—I had the honour, on December 6, of addressing to you, *for the information of the emperor*, a written communication on the subject of Mexican affairs, so far as they are affected by the presence of the French armed force in that country.

... M. Drouyn de Lhuys assures us that the French government is disposed to hasten, as soon as possible, the recall of its troops from Mexico. We welcome this notification as a promise that our government shall be henceforth spared the apprehensions and anxieties which I dwelt upon in the communication which M. Drouyn de Lhuys has had under his consideration.

... It is my duty, however, to maintain that, whatever may have been the intentions, the aim, and the motives of France, the means adopted by a certain class of Mexicans for overturning the republican government of their country, and for availing themselves of the French intervention to establish an imperial monarchy on the ruins of the above government, have been, in the eyes of the United States, without any authorisation on the part of the Mexican people, and have been carried out contrary to its will and its opinion.

... The United States have not seen any satisfactory proof that the people of Mexico have had a voice in the matter, or that *they* have established or accepted the self-styled empire which is asserted to have been established in their capital. As I have remarked on former occasions, the United States are of opinion that no popular assent can be either freely obtained or legitimately accepted at any time, in the presence of the French army of invasion. The withdrawal of the French forces appears to them a necessary measure to allow Mexico to resort to a manifestation of this nature. Doubtless the Emperor of the French is authorised to define the point of view under which it is his duty to pledge this country to a certain state of things. That under which I present it is, however, that which the Union has adopted. The Union, therefore, only recognises, and can only continue to recognise, the former republic in Mexico, and cannot, under any circumstances, consent to enter into any arrangement which would directly or indirectly imply relations with the prince installed at Mexico, or a recognition of him.

... We are thus brought to the isolated question which formed the subject of my communication of December 6, namely, the expediency of the settlement of a question the prolongation of which must constantly impair the harmony and friendship which have always prevailed between the United

States and France. The United States content themselves with explaining to France the exigencies of a situation so embarrassing to Mexico, and with expressing the hope that some means will be discovered compatible both with the interests and dignity of France, and also with the principles and interests of the United States, of *putting an end to this state of things without injurious delay.*

We adhere to our assertion that the war in question has become a political war between France and the Mexican republic, injurious and dangerous both to the United States and to the republican cause, and looking at it under this aspect and in this character only, we demand that it should come to an end.

We look upon the emperor as having announced to us his immediate intention of putting an end to the service of his army in Mexico, and of keeping faithfully, *without any stipulation or condition on our part*, to the principle of non-intervention, as to which he is henceforth agreed with the United States.

. . . To these explanations, I will only add that, in the opinion of the president, *France has no reason whatever for delaying for an instant* the promised withdrawal of her military forces from Mexico.

. . . Looking simply at the point on which our attention has always been fixed, namely, our release from the Mexican embarrassment without disturbing our friendly relations with France, we shall be gratified *when the emperor gives us*, by means either of your esteemed correspondence or in any other way, *definitive information as to the date* at which we may reckon that the French military operations in Mexico will cease. W. R. SEWARD.

The rudeness of this message was at least strange; but it was the inevitable consequence of our policy of intervention. Our respective characters were for the future inverted: the Union now gave orders. Before, France had spoken boldly, in April 1864, saying through M. Drouyn de Lhuys to Mr. Dayton, the American representative at Paris—' Do you bring us peace or war?'—in reply to the resolution of Congress unanimously voting against the establishment of a monarchy in Mexico.

The series of humiliations was now begun, and at the end of 1865 Maximilian was secretly sacrificed. This prince, whose imprudent ambition had impelled him to the shores of Vera Cruz, was about to fall a victim to the weakness of our Government in allowing its conduct to be dictated by American arrogance. Indeed, before rushing into such perilous contingencies, might not this attitude of the United States have been easily foreseen? Our statesmen needed no such rare perspicuity to have discovered the dark shadow of the Northern Republic looming up on the horizon over the Rio Bravo frontier, and only biding its time to make its appearance on the scene. If they were about so resignedly to adopt the resolution of giving way, a resolution which prudence certainly would dictate in a business so far from the mother-country, was it acting generously to lead on the archduke to his certain ruin? On the other hand, a too sudden withdrawal would wound the national pride of our own troops; for it could hardly be expected that our regiments could evacuate in succession, almost sword in hand, the towns which they had occupied, without their looking forward with emotion to the reprisals which the inhabitants would have to undergo from the victorious Liberals; and without groaning over their retreat before the American bravado. This was, we shall say boldly, the way to introduce our soldiers to a bad warlike school, in which the spirit of discussing the acts of their commander, compelled as he was to yield to an humiliating policy, must infallibly have weakened the discipline of our army, so prompt to be roused by anything which seems to them ambiguous.

It may, therefore, be well understood what a difficult part to play had now fallen on our commander-in-chief, having to decide between accomplishing the orders of his sovereign—in which a soldier cannot fail without forfeiting his honour—and witnessing the sad spectacle of the ruin of a throne through the sudden and frightened change in French policy, now hurrying on the destruction of its own handiwork. The marshal did not conceal from himself that he was about to tread a path bristling with obstacles and full of sadness, in which a feeling of duty and the security of the expeditionary corps (justly discontented at its passive attitude) had to be reconciled with all the consideration due to a prince borne down by great misfortune and embittered by our sudden desertion.

CHAPTER IX.

Arrival of Baron Saillard—Despatches from M. Drouyn de Lhuys—Proposals for French Evacuation—French Hypocrisy—Position of Maximilian—M. Almonte sent to the Court of the Tuileries—Proposal for Concentration of the Foreign Contingents—Thwarted by Maximilian's Advisers—Fruitless Bungling.

AT the time when Mr. Seward delivered his long diplomatic note to the French minister, the Baron Saillard, sent on a mission to Mexico by the French cabinet, was landing at Vera Cruz. The same courier brought two despatches from M. Drouyn de Lhuys to M. Dano, one dated January 14, the other January 15, 1866. In the first, he set forth 'that our present situation in Mexico could not be prolonged, and that circumstances compel us to take a decided step in this respect, which the emperor desires me to communicate to his representative.' Our minister of foreign affairs limited himself to affirming 'that the court of Mexico, in spite of the rectitude of its intentions, avowedly found it impossible to fulfil the conditions of the treaty of Miramar.' By putting it in these terms, the entire responsibility of our evacuation was unfairly thrown upon Maximilian, who was left in ignorance of the fact that the Mexican question had now become an *American* one. M. Drouyn de Lhuys ended his first despatch as follows :—

To M. Dano, French Minister at Mexico.
Paris, January 14, 1866.
. . . It is necessary that our occupation should have a fixed limit, and we must prepare for its termination without delay.

The emperor desires you, sir, to settle it, in conjunction with his august ally, after a loyal discussion has taken place in which Marshal Bazaine is naturally called on to join, in order to determine on the means of guaranteeing, as far as possible, the interests of the Mexican government, the safety of our creditors, and the claims of our countrymen. His majesty's wish is that the evacuation should commence towards next autumn.

You will please read this despatch to his excellency the minister of foreign affairs, and hand him a copy of it. I charge M. Baron Saillard to add such verbal explanations as may be necessary, and to bring me as soon as possible the reply, in which you will acquaint me with the definitive arrangements which are resolved on.

Drouyn de Lhuys.

The second despatch, of a more intimate character, aimed to establish that our government intended to get quit of the obligations it contracted in the treaty of Miramar, taking advantage of the power afforded it by the non-execution by Mexico of a reciprocal convention, since the treasury of the latter was empty, and it was no longer able to pay the troops maintained in its territory. The French cabinet added that these difficulties were nothing new, and that we had endeavoured to meet them on various occasions *by facilitating loans which had placed considerable sums at the disposal of Mexico.* This was carrying a forgetfulness of the facts rather too far, as these enormous loans had only placed in Maximilian's hand the comparatively small sum of about forty millions, without reckoning the eight millions which the new sovereign had personally received on taking possession of his throne. With, as it were, bitter irony, this despatch, so strange in its contradictions, while arguing from the inability of the Mexican crown to meet its engagements, seemed to take a pleasure in asserting that the sympathies and hopes of the population were in favour of Maximilian. In conclusion, our government tried even to colour the withdrawal of its troops with a desire of being better able to serve the interests of that throne which it was about to leave to ruin, or, rather, the fall of which it was, as we shall soon prove, about to precipitate.

To M. Dano, French Minister at Paris.

Paris, January 15, 1866.

... This state of things leads me to ask if the interests of the Emperor Maximilian, when thoroughly understood, do not entirely chime in with the necessities to which we are bound to yield. Among all the reproaches which are thrown out by domestic malcontents and foreign enemies, the most dangerous for a government which is in course of establishment is certainly that of being maintained only by a foreign power. No doubt, the suffrage of the Mexicans has given a reply to this imputation; but nevertheless it exists, and it is easily to be understood that it might prove useful to the cause of the empire to deprive its adversaries of this weapon.

Now that various considerations compel us to confront the termination of our military occupation, the emperor's government, *in its solicitude for the glorious work which it has begun*, and in its sympathy for the Emperor Maximilian, feels bound to acquaint itself exactly with the financial position of Mexico. *The situation is a serious one, but is not desperate.* With energy and courage, with a firm and unswerving will, the Mexican empire may triumph over every obstacle in its path; but success can only be attained on these terms. This is the conviction we have arrived at from an attentive and conscientious examination of its obligations and its resources, and you will strive to impress it upon the minds of the Emperor Maximilian and of his government.

DROUYN DE LHUYS.

Can it be pretended that M. Rouher was ignorant of the truth when, from the elevation of the tribune in our Corps Législatif, he drew those pleasant pictures of the Mexican landscape which had been already so brilliantly sketched out by M. Corta? The French cabinet were surely very late in perceiving '*that the most dangerous reproach for a government which is in a course of establishment is that of being maintained only by a foreign power.*' Did not the history of France itself contain all the precepts necessary on this point?

The mission of Baron Saillard, so completely unexpected, brought unutterable trouble into the imperial palace. Maximilian, without realising whence the blow came, had to face the disastrous consequences of this sudden abandonment on the part of France. When he had obtained a complete mastery over his just resentment, which he did not disguise, he distinctly repudiated the propositions which had been laid before him in the name of Napoleon III. Scarcely a month elapsed before fresh and more precise instructions, worded again under American dictation, were sent out to M. Dano. Could it then be supposed at Paris that the Emperor Maximilian, whom they had not even cared to sound on the subject, would passively consent to tear up the treaty of Miramar, or rather, had the government made up their minds to come in direct collision with all the opposition of the prince? The latter idea seems to us the more likely. They had hastened doggedly to cast aside all the modifying measures which so violent a question seemed to require. The despatch of February 16 sufficiently testifies to the sentiments of the court of the Tuileries, impatient to cut the Gordian knot which connected it with the New World.

To M. Dano, French Minister at Paris.

Paris, February 16, 1866.

Sir,—At the time I am writing this despatch, Baron Saillard must have arrived at Mexico. The instructions of the emperor's government are therefore known to you.

... His majesty's desire, as you know, is that the evacuation should commence towards next autumn, and that it should be accomplished as soon as possible. You will have to come to an understanding with Marshal Bazaine to settle as to the course of it, in conjunction with the Emperor Maximilian.

I cannot here enter into the various considerations which must weigh in the conduct of this operation; some of them, of a purely military and technical character, are essentially cognisable only by the marshal commanding in chief; others, of a more political kind, must be left to your mutual consideration, enlightened by the perfect knowledge which you possess of local circumstances and the necessities which they impose.

... These points being arranged, and French interests being thus protected, the emperor's government will not the less continue to *testify in an effective manner* to all the sympathy which his majesty feels towards the person of the sovereign of Mexico, and the noble task to which he has devoted himself. *You will be pleased to assure the Emperor Maximilian of this in his majesty's name.* DROUYN DE LHUYS.

The 'Yellow Book' is not, as we see, uninteresting to refer to. Maximilian was, therefore, placed in a perfect *cul-de-sac*. It must be understood that article 2 of the treaty of Miramar,—worded as follows, 'The French troops shall evacuate Mexico in proportion as his majesty the Emperor of Mexico shall be able to organise troops to replace them'—would confer on France the strict right of diminishing its forces, inasmuch as Maximilian had had for eighteen months both the time and the means for organising a part of his army, if he had not been hindered by his generals and officials. But although it might be desirable as a salutary measure to leave the Mexican nation to rely gradually on its own powers, it did not follow that the evacuation, *commenced in autumn*, should be completed with such fatal precipitation. The point that especially rendered, and at first sight must render, the discussion an irritating, one was the fact that the cabinet of the Tuileries made use of the treaty of Miramar so far as suited its own purpose, and at the same time determined to get rid of the obligations which it had accepted through this convention, which bound the two parties to it. At the end of February, the Baron Saillard, without finishing his mission, set sail for Europe.

By the renewed urgency of our diplomatists, the court of Mexico was not long in perceiving that its cause was being seriously compromised at Paris. It thought that sending an ambassador devoted to the cause, who could explain freely to its august ally all its hopes and fears, would be the means of doing away with, or at least modifying, the resolutions which had been arrived at. M. Almonte, the former regent, received the order to be bearer of an imperial missive to the palace of the Tuileries. Whilst he was awaiting the result of these negotiations, the sovereign of Mexico turned all his attention towards the foreign legion and the Austro-Belgian brigade, the only European elements which would be left after the evacuation to form the buttresses of the imperial edifice. The proper organisation of these forces became of the highest importance for the future, and even for the safety of the crown.

The convention of Miramar, by article 3, had stipulated 'that the foreign legion in the service of France, composed of 8,000 men, should remain for six years in Mexico after all the other French troops had been recalled' (in conformity with article 2). 'After this time, the said legion was to pass into the service and the pay of the Mexican government. The latter government reserved to itself the power of abridging the duration of the employment in Mexico of this foreign corps.'

Looking forward to the future, our head-quarters in 1865 had busied themselves in the special formation of this force, and had taken the greatest care in the choice of the military elements which were to compose it. The legion was not long before it became formidable, and, at the beginning of the year 1866, it already reckoned six battalions, two squadrons, two batteries of artillery, and a company of engineers. It formed a new and firm support for Maximilian in addition to his army, the effective force of which, as we have seen, reached a total of 36,000 men, and about 12,000 horses.

The Austro-Belgian brigade was managed in a similar way to the foreign legion; its cost, however, was almost double that of the French corps. Nevertheless, as its existence was important and its dismissal for want of pay would have been the signal for a general disbanding of the Mexican army, the French government thought it right that our treasury should provide for the expenses of the Belgians and the Austrians. For the sake of the better management of these two contingents which our commissariat had to maintain and control, it was proposed to Maximilian to unite the foreign legion and the Austro-Belgian brigade in one division, both corps being called upon to follow the same fortunes under the same flag. This division was to be commanded by a French general. A combination of this sort was a happy one: it put a stop to any cause for a conflict of authority between the foreign and native officers. Moreover, these European elements, become consolidated by close companionship, would acquire a cohesive force which, in difficult times, would have enabled Maximilian to march victoriously throughout all Mexico. The French general was selected; our acquired rights did not permit us to place our legion under the orders of Austrians who were themselves bound to obey the Mexican officers.

To this double proposition, so favourable to the interests of the crown, Maximilian replied to the commander-in-chief as follows:—

Mexico, April 3, 1866.

My dear Marshal,—I reply as under to your kind letter of the 30th ultimo. It is very pleasing to me to know that, during the temporary duration of the present financial state of the country, the French treasury undertakes to supply the wants of my Austro-Belgian legion. I see in this a fresh proof of the sympathy of the government for the Mexican cause.

As regards the union of the French foreign legion and the Austro-Belgian brigade in one division, under the orders of a French general, *I consent to the measure so far as the legal grounds and the special national circumstances of these two corps will permit*, and provided that their total effective force is not less than 15,000 men. I am anxious therefore to see negotiations opened on the subject.

My intention is that this matter should be discussed by a commission, and I beg that you will acquaint me with the names of the members whom you point out for it.—Your very affectionate MAXIMILIAN.

This reply of the emperor, who thus again allowed another element of power for his throne to escape him, was nothing but a disguised refusal of the military combination submitted to his consideration. The premeditated expressions, 'as far as the legal grounds and special national circumstances of these two *corps*,' opened a wide field for interpretations and ambiguities. Nevertheless, a general of our army, distinguished by his energetic qualities, was placed at the disposal of the court of Mexico. The commission often met, but its deliberations soon manifested those influences which had already hampered the imperial resolutions. The

Belgian and Austrian commissioners demanded for their soldiers an independent discipline, and the right of command for that one of the chiefs who had the largest effective force under his orders. In a word, the effect was to get rid of all French superintendence, and thus to expose them, as events proved, to serious disasters. The end of the matter was that the Austrian general, de Thûn, who, disgusted with having to deal with the Mexican army, had resigned his powers, was called to command these foreign troops, and Maximilian again requested our head-quarters to assume the chief direction of his army. How much time was lost in fruitless bungling!

CHAPTER X.

Establishment of *Cazadores* and Gendarmes—The Marshal's Plan for Evacuation favourable to Maximilian—Maximilian's wise Measures of Retrenchment—His Confidence, Energy, and Hopes—His Plans explained to Marshal Bazaine—Revolt of Chihuahua and Reoccupation by the French—Maximilian's Letter of Congratulation to Marshal Bazaine—His Disagreement with the Marshal—Mr. Bigelow's Despatch—Left no Hope for Maximilian.

THE only co-operation which the marshal was able to afford to the imperial government consisted in the proper management of the war; for article 6 of the treaty of Miramar formally prohibited his intervening in any branch of the Mexican administration. Maximilian reigned in full independence, and, whatever might be the condition of domestic affairs, the responsibility rested on the ministers of the crown, though it is true that they had already begun to release themselves of it.

The head-quarters authorities, whose duty it was to strive against these tendencies, and to keep strictly to their own functions, exerted themselves, at the appeal of the imperial family, to lay down the basis of a new military formation which would double the forces of the foreign legion and the Austro-Belgian brigade. The commander-in-chief took upon himself to demand from his government authority to form nine battalions of Mexican *cazadores* (chasseurs), and to introduce into them a French list of officers, as offering a further guarantee to the court of Mexico.

In a few months, nine battalions of *cazadores*, of ten companies each, making up an average of 400 effectives for each battalion, were installed in the principal towns, for the defence of which they were permanently assigned, so as to be able to keep up their numbers by a local recruitment. Being clothed, equipped, and paid by our treasury, their duty was to patrol their districts, and as partisan companies to lend assistance to the *gardes rurales.* Instructors and agents taken from our ranks were added to this new force, in which certainly the French element prevailed, being represented by 66 officers, 130 sub-officers, and 1,502 private soldiers who had been drawn from the expeditionary corps. The remainder was made up of Indians and Mexicans. Two legions of gendarmerie also were organised at Mexico and Guadalajara, the two capital cities of the empire. The gendarmes, who were principally recruited among the Belgians and Austrians, were distributed in small parties along the high-roads, where they were sheltered in fortified barracks. Their duty was to guard the great line of communication between Vera Cruz and the city of Mexico.

At the same time the marshal, in conformity with the instructions of Napoleon III., forwarded to Paris his plan for a gradual evacuation. Using the latitude which was allowed him by his government, and anxious as far as possible to act for the interests of the new monarchy, he proposed to divide the departure of the French forces into three periods, each coming at a fixed time; so that the withdrawal would be commenced in November 1866, and would be concluded during the autumn of 1867. He thus ensured to the empire twenty months more of French protection. He was fortunate enough to find that this new and important proposition was favourably received at the palace of the Tuileries; but the promises made at Paris were not to be long respected by the French cabinet.

Without allowing his difficulties to dishearten him, Maximilian, in whom the dreams of poetry too often eclipsed the feelings of a sovereign, set courageously to work. His hopes being revived by the formation of the *cazadores*, the emperor made up his mind to cut into the very heart of the military question, by the dismissal of dangerous officers, and by the reduction of the national forces at all those points where they remained at the expense of the treasury, without being of any service to the country. The following letter, which he addressed to his minister of war, shows that now, being made wise by experience, and left to his own ideas, he endeavoured for a time to follow a path full of wisdom :—

Cuernavaca, May 11, 1866.

My dear Minister Garcia,—We return you the draft of the project which you sent us as to the new organisation of the army, the basis of which appears to be generally good.

Nevertheless, you will take care to communicate previously with Marshal Bazaine, so as to make sure that no corps is suppressed which plays any important part in the plan of his military operations.

With regard to the delicate business of suppressing a certain part of our organised forces, you will take all the necessary precautions so as not to discourage the officers at the first outset, and thereby cause them to go and swell the ranks of the malcontents.

It will likewise be proper that you should settle the mode to be adopted in carrying out this reduction, by fixing a date, at which each commandant of a corps, a battery, company, &c. should draw up, assisted by the nearest military authority, a list of the effective force under his command, of their clothing, arms, &c.; and it will be also requisite to point out some one who is to take possession of everything that belongs both to embodied and disbanded forces.

You will devote all your attention to the best plan to be followed in dispersing the small corps, which, by reason of their defective discipline and the ignorance of their commandants, might revolt at the moment when they received the order to disband.

Before making public the arrangement which will reduce our existing forces, you will carefully study as to what parts of the territory are occupied by troops whose withdrawal would expose the countries which they protect to the attacks of the enemy, in order to arrange immediately for the defence of these localities by fresh troops.

In a word, the great object of your attention will be to prevent the inconvenience which measures so important must bring with them.

When the disbanding and disarming of the unnecessary forces are once accomplished, the superior and other officers who are in excess will proceed provisionally to the depôt, until their respective claims shall have been examined either for a pension or discharge.—Your very affectionate

MAXIMILIAN.

In these instructions we find the decided and concise style, and the good sense, of the former admiral of the Austrian marine, who had prepared the laurels won for the glory of his country at Lissa. If he had been aided by his own party, and if he had *not* been fatally deserted by France in obedience to the voice of the United States, Maximilian would perhaps have triumphed over every obstacle. But our head-quarters were almost his only support. The latter hastened to grant to the emperor the help of any of our officers whom he desired to have as coadjutors. M. Friant, the commissary of stores, gave peculiar satisfaction to the court of Mexico, who thought highly of his services. The emperor planned to call him in to his assistance.

Cuernavaca, May 16, 1866.

My dear Marshal,—Now that you are generously placing at our disposal all the means in your power for organising the national army, I am about to ask you to add a fresh service to those for which we are already indebted to you, by authorising M. Friant to lend us the powerful aid of his remarkable administrative talents, in founding the management of the Mexican army on a solid basis.

The system elaborated by the above officer for the auxiliary division is distinguished by so much simplicity, united with such perfect security of due control, that I anticipate the most happy results from M. Friant's co-operation.

MAXIMILIAN.

Maximilian obtained without difficulty the concession that this high functionary should be placed at his disposal, although the latter was really necessary in the administration of our expeditionary corps.

One of the most striking features in Maximilian's reign is the confidence which he seemed to feel in his work. His energy seemed only to increase under the pressure of adversity. When he had once recovered from the shock which, after the mission of Baron Saillard, the news of the approaching evacuation had given him, he coolly confronted the position in which he was placed; and, though expecting some modification of the instructions given by his ally Napoleon III. in consequence of the efforts of M. Almonte, he looked to find in his adopted country all the necessary resources for bringing his undertaking to a favourable issue. He hoped much that time would shed a softening influence on conflicting passions, and felt persuaded that in the course of time the malcontents would be induced to return under his flag. Thus, as the following letter proves, he already accepted more readily the idea of the gradual departure of our troops, and was working actively to organise his national forces. The only thing was that he often nursed himself in fond illusions, and cherished ideas which, as he himself said, *'breathed the spirit of the middle ages.'* Whilst drawing up his army on paper, he fancied he was dealing with German soldiers, and forgot that the chief need in Mexico was an iron hand, which could hold firmly all the threads of this complicated web, leaving nothing to chance or to the dangers resulting from want of discipline; he forgot, too, that for about fifty years the country had been trodden under foot by partisan bands. A scheme like his might have been practicable for the energetic Yankees, who often operated in this way during the war of secession; but in Mexico it would only have the effect of increasing the number of what the emperor himself called 'hordes,' which were nothing more than a destructive scourge.

Cuernavaca, May 17, 1866.

My dear Marshal,—The Emperor Napoleon, having been compelled to settle formally and publicly as to the gradual recall of his troops, has informed me in his last letter that he has given the most definite orders that the co-operation, which is indispensable to the achievement of the work he has so gloriously begun, should be afforded to my government; and that every assistance should be rendered me for organising a substantial national army, for forming mixed troops, and for setting to rights the voluntary corps. To attain this end, I look upon it as an obligation on me and even as a conscientious duty to place myself in the closest and most continuous relations with you, my dear marshal, in order to definitively settle on the plans for organisation, to ensure their execution, and to determine the expenses that are to be incurred, and the men that are to be chosen. The most effective means of not wasting the little and so valuable time which is now left us appears to me to be, in the first place, to solicit you, my dear marshal, to let me have in writing your views and wishes on the subject of the fresh organisation, and of the detailed plan which must be followed to rapidly and entirely tranquillise the country, basing it upon the remarkable *data* which have been lately furnished us from all points of the empire; and, in the second place, by you and I meeting once, or, if necessary, oftener, every week, the minister of war, and the Commissary Friant, whose co-operation will be valuable in administrative questions.

I also intend to call upon the Commandant Loysel to take a part in these meetings, in which all the principal points will be discussed both of the organisation generally and also of the expenditure and the persons to be employed; he will also draw up confidentially an official record of our proceedings, without which we shall not attain either the order or promptitude which are desirable. If the marshal should be of opinion that it would likewise be useful to summon General Uraga to be present at these meetings, as a representative of the active portion of the Mexican army, he will be kind enough to let me know.

At the present moment, it appears to me that the military question is to be looked at in three essential points of view.

The immediate organisation of 20,000 national troops, the firm consolidation of the mixed corps who are styled by you the *cazadores* of Mexico, who are in my opinion the principal basis for the future army and for the systematic pacification of the country.

As regards the first point, it appears to me that we must avail ourselves of the few honourable corps now existing, such as those of Mejia, Mendez, Garcia, &c., so as to form a national nucleus, and that we must immediately dismiss all those men that constitute nothing but a valueless body of soldiery. This measure, however, can only be considered as the beginning of the matter.

In order to be in a position to form quickly some good battalions of infantry and a few good regiments of cavalry, I only see one way of proceeding, which will doubtless appear to you singular enough, and perhaps *breathes the spirit of the middle ages*; it is to choose reliable men, men possessing both your confidence and mine, one half of whom should be European officers of long experience, and to nominate them as chiefs of battalions and regiments; and then, after having summoned them to Mexico, and given them their instructions distinctly and clearly, to say to them:—' The responsibility lies upon you, choose your own officers, act, and you will be supported. But as a result you must give us the rapid and effective formation of your corps.' Your direct action, and that of the minister of war, who is completely at your disposal, would contribute much, as I think, to the execution of this plan.

The second point is completely in your hands, and your wisdom and your thorough knowledge of the country cannot fail to ensure a right solution.

As regards the third point, it appears to me that it would be very useful if we were to acquaint ourselves with all the reports and communications which have been lately furnished by the imperial commissioners and the generals commanding the territorial divisions, copies of which are to be found in my secretary's office. By this means, it would be easy to form a clear idea of the number of troops which would have to be set in movement, and the expenditure to which we should have to look forward.

If the execution of this is possible, *we should have the advantage of implicating all the high functionaries* who have furnished the reports, by showing them that we have complied with their desires, and that the responsibility of the ulterior state of things would therefore fall upon them.

If we set courageously to work, I think that in a few months we may reckon on a brilliant result which *will crown the efforts of valour and of wisdom which you have displayed for the service of this country.* MAXIMILIAN.

As may be easily seen, the army was always in a state of transformation. These commissions absorbed precious hours, and too often in vain. Nevertheless, time pressed, and such serious alterations could not be made in a day. Besides, it kept up a state of uncertainty among the Mexican regiments, already too prone through their fickle nature and the traditions of former *pronunciamientos* to go over easily from one chief to another. Maximilian was much deceived when he thought that 'implicating his high functionaries' would give pledges of their future fidelity. This stratagem was hardly worthy of a sovereign, and, besides, he ought to have known that Mexicans would never consider themselves bound because they were *implicated* in any particular course of action. For the latter were accustomed, at each new revolutionary movement, to disappear so as to let the storm pass over, and then to rally round the victorious side until the propitious moment came for a fresh revolt. This contempt for all political faith formed Juarez's power; he was always certain of being well received by his countrymen, even when they had just taken an oath of allegiance to the empire. Thus, as will be recollected, our troops had rushed to the very extremity of the empire, to the city of Chihuahua, to expel from it the president of the republic. After some months' occupation, which had certainly restored calm to these distant districts, the French forces were compelled to deliver up this state capital to its own garrison, and left it in order to seek fresh dangers. Chihuahua immediately opened its gates to Juarez, who had returned from Paso del Norte at a time when Maximilian thought that his enemy had crossed the American frontier without intention of returning. The president's presence on Mexican territory deeply affected Maximilian, who imagined that the resistance of the malcontents was due to this cause only. In spite of the want of troops which was felt in the central states, the court of Mexico itself resolved on a second expedition against Chihuahua, and it signified its desire to the commander-in-chief in terms which clearly prove that the emperor reigned and governed in complete independence.

Chapultepec, May 28, 1866.

My dear Marshal,—Both the home and foreign news that I receive prove to me the imperious necessity of expelling Juarez from Chihuahua, and of occupying this town definitively so as to deprive the United States of their only plausible pretext for accrediting an ambassador to him, and also of the occasion of putting forward every day new requirements.

It is evident that it is as much to the interest of your glorious sovereign and *my august ally, the Emperor Napoleon, as it is to mine that we should put an end to the pretensions of the Washington cabinet* by expelling Juarez from the above capital. It is a matter, indeed, on which our honour depends.

I repeat that the foreign news which I have just received strongly shows the urgency of this measure, and, as chief of my army, you will have the goodness to immediately see to its execution.

I again urge the prompt formation of Franco-Mexican battalions, and the necessity of instantly appointing their French *cadres*, for time presses.

I am writing on all these points to the Emperor Napoleon, whom I shall apprise of my resolutions.—Your very affectionate MAXIMILIAN.

Thus the Mexican court ignored the whole conduct of the French cabinet, and still clung to the hope of putting an end to the claims of the Washington cabinet, flattering itself that it would be able to allure its ally into the same course. Two powerful reasons forbade our return to Chihuahua. First, the expenses which this long journey must involve would press heavily on the Mexican treasury, which was already sadly exhausted; and, besides, our head-quarters had orders from their government to avoid at all hazard the chance of an engagement on the northern frontier, especially on those parts where the Americans exercised any direct action. Moreover, an expedition like this was a mistake, for it was easy to foresee that an occupation at such a distance could not be a permanent one. It would uselessly fatigue our operating columns, which could be better employed elsewhere.

The imperial order was, however, carried out. Commandant Billot marched rapidly on Chihuahua, whence

Juarez fled again towards Paso del Norte, followed by a few travelling companions only. The soldiers and the liberal officials were already scattered to the winds. For six weeks the French troops had worked at constructing a fort in the town, so that it might be defended from any further attack; and after the completion of this work, they gave up the place to the care of about twelve hundred imperialists, who were not long before they were attacked. Their generals, instead of keeping them in the fort, and thence defending the environs, undertook a sortie with their forces to a spot half a mile from the town. That night their overthrow was complete, and Chihuahua definitively welcomed the republic.

This military episode was reproduced on many points of the territory; and Maximilian, whom the French and foreign press has so often represented as constantly disagreeing with our head-quarters, desired nothing better than its concurrence in the means of defence for the empire. The prince could not make the marshal responsible for the acts of his government, and, in spite of all, was pleased with his exertions. Does the following letter testify to any hostile feeling on the part of the crown, or any dissatisfaction with the management of military operations, when, on the contrary, its aim is to concentrate absolute authority in the hands of the general-in-chief?

Mexico, June 3, 1866.

My dear Marshal,—Unity of action is the first requisite for finishing promptly the organisation of the army.

The ideas which you have put forward in council on this subject are most just and full of practical good sense. You are already commander-in-chief of the army, and sole director of all military movements, and, therefore, the very best judge there can be of what ought to be done, and you are also in the position to carry it out.

I now desire to invest you with absolute authority for the organisation of the Franco-Mexican battalions, and the re-organisation of the national army.

. . . All orders given by you, and sent to the minister for war, should express, 'by order of the emperor.'

Such is the plan that I have definitively adopted, since you have favoured me with your advice; it is conceived solely with a view of concentrating in your hands an organisation which you alone and your valuable officers can carry out properly.

MAXIMILIAN.

To any impartial mind, which has entered thoroughly into the cordial feelings which had hitherto prevailed between the Mexican court and the marshal—to any-one who, without prejudice, has appreciated the efforts made at our head-quarters for the consolidation of the imperial throne, by aid of the limited means and powers the French government had provided them with—in short, after the perusal of the conciliatory correspondence of which we have given several extracts, it would seem strange that the Emperor and Empress of Mexico could secretly complain to the Emperor Napoleon of the general-in-chief, and demand his recall. This is, however, what had been taking place for several months past unknown to the marshal, who only learnt the truth some time afterwards from Paris, at the time of the Empress Charlotte's journey to Europe. Everything should have dictated candour: it would have become a sovereign to state his grievances openly and straightforwardly, if he thought them well founded. It was all the more a duty for the crown, because at another time it had manifested to the general-in-chief, on his promotion to be a marshal, sentiments which no little contributed to keeping him on Mexican soil, where he believed himself doing good service to the monarchy; sentiments, too, which he knew that he had deserved.

Pengamillo, October 7, 1864.

My dear Marshal and Friend,—It is with the greatest pleasure that I have just heard of your promotion to the rank of marshal.

By distinguishing you with so high a mark of favour, the emperor fulfils the desire of all good Mexicans, to whom, in his name, you have brought liberty and peace, for which they will always be grateful to you. *One thing alone could lessen the joy which this happy event causes us, it is in case it should result in your leaving our country. I trust that the Emperor Napoleon will not deprive Mexico of services which are so necessary to her well-being.*

Repeating my cordial congratulations . . . Your very affectionate

MAXIMILIAN.

Was there not in these words something more than mere courtly language? The note of the Empress Charlotte, who was eager to be the first to apprise the commander-in-chief of the happy event, by sending him the Belgian newspapers, was redolent of the same goodwill. But at the commencement of 1866, a real misunderstanding interrupted for a short time the good understanding which existed between the throne and head-quarters. A French officer had, by order of the Emperor Napoleon, returned to Mexico after leave of absence. Maximilian, who at that time did not appreciate the services of this officer, addressed the following note to the general-in-chief:—

My dear Marshal,—The telegraph has just acquainted me with the sudden return of M—, who has just landed at Vera Cruz. I have every reason to feel surprised at the return of this officer, and beg you will inform me why the instructions which followed a special meeting which we held in Mexico on the subject have been departed from.

MAXIMILIAN.

As we here see, Maximilian spoke with an air of authority; but, as it may be imagined, the marshal could not countenance any such control over the acts of his sovereign, who alone had the right of choosing officers to serve in Mexico. That same evening, in the saloons of the palace, in the presence of the *corps diplomatique*, and after the departure of the commander-in-chief, Maximilian thought it his duty to denounce this act in rather strong terms. The procedure of the marshal, when acquainted with this painful incident, was determined on by him; but the Emperor of Mexico, who had a noble heart, did not delay in being the first to efface every trace of this disagreement. Neither this sovereign nor the empress ever made the commander-in-chief acquainted, either directly or indirectly, with the grievances which they revealed to the court of the Tuileries; and, but for the indiscretion of the Empress Charlotte during her stay at the Grand Hotel in Paris, the marshal might have remained much longer in complete ignorance of them.

But the marshal was gravely wrong, in a way, too, which increased every day in the eyes of Maximilian and his august spouse. This offence was his desire, above all things, of remaining true to his own country. The instructions of the French cabinet, dated January 6, 1866, and incessantly repeated since that time, prohibited the head-quarters *from exercising any influence, except with great reserve.* ' Notwithstanding the complaints of Maximilian,' they wrote, ' we will not grant another soldier.' At the end of the same month, they wrote to the marshal from Paris:—' You have acted wisely in concentrating your troops between San Luis, Aguas Calientes, and Matehuala. Let our share in military operations gradually die out.' At the latter end of the month of May 1866, the French government ' was even then hoping for some definite resolutions on the part of Maximilian,' weighed down as he was by the poverty of the treasury, and appealing to the devotion of the commander-in-chief that he would not yet return to Europe, as he was preparing to do with the first troops going home, but that he would undertake the charge of the evacuation until its completion. Maximilian had himself testified to the commander of the expeditionary corps his entire satisfaction with such a measure. But in spite of all this, the Mexican court allowed itself to be persuaded into begging that a much larger French force should be sent, and that large credits should be opened; and on account of the resistance from head-quarters to these projects, it was convinced that the marshal was the only obstacle to fresh sacrifices being made by our country, which would, in its opinion, ensure triumph to the cause. This court had unfortunately entertained the idea that France was still quite inclined to come to their help. But the marshal, who since the end of 1865 had been thoroughly enlightened, both as to the intentions of the cabinet of the Tuileries, and also as to the course public opinion was taking in France and in the United States, would in no way ask for an augmentation of forces, which would have been certainly refused. His personal opinion was that we had wasted enough, both of men and money; and, as he never failed to represent to Maximilian himself, he had been too much struck by the weakness of the Mexican element to consent to plunge his country into fresh dangers. The Mexican sovereign was right in seeking for further resources for his country, and the marshal would have been proud of commanding a more imposing army; but would not France have cried out if one of her generals had led away some thousands of men more? What a fatal story would there have been to tell to-day! Some believed, and will continue to believe, that an increase of the effective force at its disposal would have been sufficient to decide the triumph of the monarchy; but these persons have never witnessed the intrigues and disloyalties of a court, and have never scanned the distressing picture of financial difficulties springing up again and again. They could hardly have been aware of the French instructions directing that the towns should be evacuated in the beginning of 1866; and they had not had to deal with the premeditated sluggishness of the very highest officials, acting as a dead weight on nearly all the imperial territory. Maximilian was to be pitied; but it is not the commander-in-chief who must be blamed.

To be better convinced of this, one need only glance at the despatch which, at this very time, Mr. Bigelow, the American minister at Paris, addressed to his government, which had enjoined him to demand explanations from the cabinet of the Tuileries as to the asserted movements of troops intended for Mexico.

To Mr. Seward, Under Secretary of State at Washington.

Paris, June 4, 1866.

Sir,—I called on his excellency the minister of foreign affairs, last Sunday, to confer with him on the subject indicated in your instructions marked 'confidential.' As he had already been informed of the contents of this despatch by the French minister resident at Washington, I had not to explain it to him afresh.

. . . I then told him that the object of your instructions, as I understood them, is simply to obtain an explanation which would certainly be required of you in reference to the embarkation in France of large bodies of troops for Mexico, after the intention of withdrawing the whole army had been officially announced.

To this his excellency replied that, since he had seen me, he had received from his colleagues, the ministers of war and marine, the information that no troops belonging to the expeditionary corps had been sent to Mexico this year, excepting the number of soldiers that were necessary to replace those that were missing, but in no case would there be any augmentation of the effective force. The embarkation of troops mentioned in the newspapers, and in your despatch, is very probably that which took place on board the transport ship 'Le Rhône,' in the beginning of the year. This vessel touched at Martinique, and not at St. Thomas, as was stated. It had on board 916 soldiers, and not 1,200; and they belonged to the foreign legion, and not to the expeditionary corps.

These soldiers had been waiting for some time in France and in Algeria for means of transport to rejoin their regiments. No enlistments have taken place for the foreign legion since the emperor announced his intention of withdrawing his flag from Mexico, and there is no idea, as far as he knows, of making fresh enlistments.

Regarding the embarkation of troops recruited in Austria, his excellency told me that this is a matter entirely between the Austrian government and the Mexicans, and that France had nothing to do with it. Since I pointed out the fact to him, he has confirmed his own convictions on the subject, by a correspondence with the ministers of war and marine, and he has satisfied himself that there has been no kind of engagement entered into, either for the enlistment or for the transport of Austrian troops into Mexico.

He then stated that the intention of his government is to withdraw the whole of their army from Mexico at latest within the time specified in the despatch which he sent you, and even sooner, if the climate and other considerations permit it; also, that it is not their intention to replace this army by other troops from any source whatsoever.

In concluding this long conversation, with *the important result of which I have acquainted you*, I expressed to the minister the satisfaction which his explanations gave me, and the pleasure I should have in communicating them to my government.

This despatch has been submitted to M. Drouyn de Lhuys, who has approved the summary of our conversation contained in it. JOHN BIGELOW.

After reading this despatch, could any hopes be

entertained of reinforcements of troops for Maximilian? Thus, then, the United States followed step by step the actions of French policy, counting, nearly to a man, the detachments which were necessary to keeping up the number of our effective force. Even the recruiting of Austrians was forbidden. The government of France had not for a long time been subject to dictation so tyrannical as this! The only source of military recruitment left to Maximilian consisted for the future in re-enlisting those discharged soldiers of the French force who, instead of re-embarking for Europe, consented to enter his service amongst the *cazadores*.

CHAPTER XI.

Bad System of Enlistment followed—Energy of the Empress Charlotte—Destruction of Mejia's Division—The Emperor Napoleon's harsh Reply to M. Almonte's Mission—Its Effect on the Mexican Court—Maximilian's Project of Abdication stopped by the Empress—Her Expedition to Europe—Painful Incident—Fresh Imperial Disasters—Maximilian's Idea of Declaring a State of Siege—It is opposed by Marshal Bazaine.

AS we have seen, Maximilian set great value on the increase of the nine battalions of *cazadores*. He had a right to reckon on the good disposition of the French who had consented to join them, for the two sovereigns excited the ardent sympathies of our noble army. But the efforts of our head-quarters and the devotion of the French officers who had accepted the difficult task of commanding and forming these nine battalions would all be fruitless if the country itself, the imperial commissioners, and the great landed proprietors did not unreservedly help them by some substantial system of recruitment. The *leva*, a kind of military impressment, had been abolished in former days by the regency, obeying the noble suggestion of Marshal Forey. The empire had renewed the formal prohibition of resorting to this brutal and inhuman system of swelling the ranks of the Mexican army. But, nevertheless, the *leva* was still practised. Indians taken by force by the *hacenderos*, the dregs of the Mexican community discharged from the public prisons, —such were the miserable elements that the political prefects of the provinces persisted in placing at the disposal of the French commandants; and it may be easily understood what our volunteers, conscious of their own dignity, must have felt when they elbowed in their ranks comrades who had just exchanged the convict's chain for the musket. Yet our officers were not disheartened.

Depending upon the imperial orders which had directed the recruitment in the states of Mexico, Queretaro, and San Luis, they endeavoured to arouse the apathy of the political prefects, and, in some cases, to baffle their hostility. They personally visited all the *haciendas*; they appealed to the patriotism as well as to the self-interest of the great landed proprietors, whose safety could only be ensured by the legal enlistment of the labourers living on their property, or by the arrival of volunteers to serve under the flag. The whole population, if the imperial commissioners did not betray the crown, ought to furnish its contingent to the recruitment. And never had sacrifices of this sort been more called forth by pressing emergencies. General Mejia found in his front Escobedo and Cortina threatening to annihilate his division, the best disciplined amongst the Mexican troops, and composed of veteran bands well seasoned to the hardships of the sierras. Yet Maximilian did not lose heart. It should also be told that he felt his powers doubled by the energy of his devoted wife, who directed affairs at Mexico whilst he was traversing the country. From Cuernavaca, where he then was, and where the news of a great disaster had just come upon him without prostrating him, he demanded without delay from our head-quarters the means of retrieving the misfortune.

Cuernavaca, June 24, 1866.

My dear Marshal,—I have learnt with much pleasure from your last letter that the organisation of the nine battalions of *cazadores* and of the national army is going on without interruption, and I have to thank you cordially for it. The news of the almost complete destruction of Mejia's division has much surprised me, and has grievously affected me. On these brave troops I founded a great part of my hopes for the future.

To turn in another direction, the re-opening of the communications between Matamoros and Monterey is very necessary to relieve our finances; but I confide in the measures which your great experience will suggest, and I beg of you to send me a plan of campaign which should be followed to retrieve the misfortune which has just fallen upon us, and to restore order in the insubordinate departments. MAXIMILIAN.

A second and still more painful blow fell on the court of Mexico at the end of June. This was the Emperor Napoleon's reply to the embassy of M. Almonte, on which both Maximilian and the Empress Charlotte had built such fond hopes. Napoleon III. notified to his ally certain conditions which were harsher than any of those which had been hitherto drawn up. Although the form of the imperial message, which contained a statement of certain well-founded grievances, might be wounding to Maximilian's self-esteem, the resolutions it contained passed the sentence of death on the Mexican monarchy. Mr. Seward had triumphed!

Paris, May 31, 1866.

General Almonte has handed to the emperor the letters of his majesty the Emperor Maximilian, and has made the communications with which he was charged for the French government. His majesty regrets to be compelled to express the surprise which these communications have caused him. For more than a year the instructions sent to the French agents in Mexico, and inspired by the feeling of the reciprocal duties and obligations which we have contracted, have aimed to bring before the Mexican government certain recommendations dictated by the interest of the two countries no less than by the sincere friendship which his majesty feels for the Emperor Maximilian.

These recommendations do not appear to have been understood. The propositions laid before us by General Almonte sufficiently show this, and, at the same time, reveal a complete misconception of a situation the full explanation of which to the court of Mexico can no longer be delayed.

There is no need to go back to the origin of the French expedition; its justification is founded on our grievances. Compelled, as we were, to do ourselves justice, the experience of the past taught us for the future to seek for guarantees against the return of actions which had so often drawn down on this country (at the cost of burdensome expeditions) severe but always ineffective repressions. These guarantees were to result from the foundation of a regular government, strong enough to put an end to the traditions of disorder bequeathed by a succession of ephemeral powers. However desirable might be the establishment of such a government, we, least of all, could think of imposing it on others, and we have always loudly disavowed any such design. We have not, however, liked to believe that the elements of an indispensable political regeneration were altogether wanting in the Mexican community, and we resolved to further all the efforts which should be made by the country to rid itself of the anarchy which was destroying it. This enterprise was a grand one, and it allured the Emperor Maximilian. Being appealed to by the Mexican nation, without allowing himself to be deterred by the difficulties and dangers of the task, he courageously devoted himself to it. He, like the Emperor Napoleon, thought the great questions of conciliation and counteraction were connected with the independence of Mexico, and with the integrity of its territory when guaranteed by a stable and regenerative government; *and he knew that he would not want for our help in aiding him to realise a work profitable to the whole world.*

The duties of the Emperor towards France required him, however, to proportion the extent of the assistance that he could offer to Mexico to ensure the success of this enterprise to the importance of the French interests engaged. The treaty of Miramar was concluded to this effect.

. . . Now, in the contract which established our rights and our obligations, France has fully discharged the duties which she accepted, and she has but very incompletely received the equivalent compensations which were promised her. This is a fact which we are bound to assert, since it no longer rests with us to keep silence as to its consequences. We are far from not comprehending the obstacles and difficulties of every kind against which his majesty the Emperor Maximilian has had to strive. Although we have often deplored that his loyal intentions were not better appreciated, we have always applauded his active solicitude and his generous purposes.

.... The results did not answer our hopes in spite of the skilful and energetic management of the marshal and the devotion of an army which nothing wearies. ... The French government facilitated the negotiation of loans which relieved the embarrassments of the Mexican treasury, and yet our claims were compensated only by fallacious settlements. Friendly advice has been given, but the councillors of his majesty manifested a systematic resistance in everything which concerned the interests of France. Must we recall what exertions it cost the French Legation to obtain only an insufficient reparation for the injuries suffered by our countrymen, when the English claims were settled without question; when resources were found to discharge without delay and with ready money doubtful and perhaps illegal debts? We found the very principle of the French demands contested,—those demands which had been recognised by the treaty of Miramar as the determinative cause of our expedition; which, too, in default of any stipulation, *should have constituted an undoubted and indisputable debt of honour.*

After having, in all circumstances, pointed out to the Mexican government the necessity of itself individually providing for its own conservation, and after having many a time stated that the assistance which we were affording it could only be maintained in proportion as the corresponding obligations due to us should be strictly fulfilled, we have acquainted it with the stringent considerations which forbid us any longer to demand fresh sacrifices from France, which also decided us to recall our troops.

Nevertheless, whist adopting this resolution, we have directed that, in its execution, those delays and precautions should be employed which are necessary for avoiding the dangers of too sudden a change. We have been compelled, at the same time, to substitute for the now valueless stipulations of the treaty of Miramar other arrangements intended to ensure the security of our claims. The emperor's minister at Mexico has consequently received instructions to conclude a new convention for this purpose.

These instructions, like all the acts of the Emperor Napoleon, are inspired by the natural sentiments which attach him to the Emperor of Mexico, and by a sincere desire to reconcile interests that he does not wish to see separated. He has duly appreciated the reasons *which have led his representatives not to press for the immediate conclusion of the arrangements which had been prescribed*; but he has regretted to see that the Mexican cabinet has profited by their compliance to remove to Paris the scene of a negotiation which can only be usefully carried on at Mexico.

The Emperor Napoleon has especially regretted to find included in the draft of a treaty submitted to his government by General Almonte certain propositions which have already been laid before them, and have been necessarily declined for the most powerful reasons every time that they have been brought forward. The stay of the troops (it is said) must be prolonged beyond the assigned periods; fresh advances are demanded of us, in the anticipation of a deficiency in the resources of the Mexican treasury, and the repayment of these advances is put off to undetermined dates; no pledge is offered, no guarantee is given for the security of our claims. After the frank, loyal, and full explanations of the French government, *it is difficult to account for the persistency of illusion which must have guided the conception of this scheme.*

It is impossible to accept the propositions brought by General Almonte, or even to authorise their discussion. It will be necessary to consent to a new convention.

If the combinations which will be proposed to him are accepted by his majesty the Emperor Maximilian, the times fixed for the gradual departure of the French troops will be maintained; and Marshal Bazaine, in conjunction with his majesty, will settle the measures necessary, in order that the evacuation of the Mexican territory may be carried out in the mode most favourable to the maintenance of order and the consolidation of the imperial power.

If, on the contrary, our propositions are not accepted, we must not conceal that we shall henceforth consider ourselves free from every engagement, and, firmly resolved to prolong no further the occupation of Mexico, *we shall direct Marshal Bazaine to proceed with all possible expedition to send home the French army, taking into consideration those military expediencies and technical matters of which he will be sole judge.* He will also have to direct his attention to procuring for French interests those securities to which they have a right.

The Emperor Napoleon is conscious that he has hitherto aided in a joint work. Henceforth it will fall upon Mexico itself to assume its position. Prolonged foreign protection is a bad school, and a source of perils; in domestic matters, it habituates a people not to reckon on themselves, and paralyses the national activity; abroad, it excites animosity and awakens jealousies. The moment is now come for Mexico to satisfy every doubt and to elevate its patriotism to the pitch required by the difficult circumstances through which she has to pass. At home as well as abroad, the attacks directed against the particular form of government she has adopted will doubtless gradually weaken *when it will be she alone who defends it*, and they will be powerless against an union of the sovereign and the people firmly cemented by trials courageously accepted and endured together. It will be an honour to his majesty the Emperor Maximilian and to the Mexican nation to have thus accomplished that work of civilisation which we shall always feel proud of having encouraged and protected at the outset.

The court of Mexico was stupified, and even showed openly all its grief at the conduct of the Tuileries, feeling it all the more strongly as the Mexican treasury had been emptied to meet its engagements to France. At the time when this message arrived from Napoleon III., it is an undoubted fact that Maximilian, with the exception of 400,000 francs, owed nothing; for some time he had been devoting all his care and all his efforts to satisfy the conditions of the treaty of Miramar, which was henceforth to be trodden under foot; and now a fresh convention was to be exacted from him, which would take away his last available resources—the customs' duties at Tampico and Vera Cruz, the half of which he was to consent to assign to France. If this convention was not accepted by him, the marshal had orders to fall back at once and abandon Maximilian to his own resources. The imperial family gave vent to their feelings in bitter complaints, some of which transpired beyond the precincts of the palace. The revelations of the future will justify the following words which, we assert, were pronounced by Maximilian in the hearing of those around him: 'I am tricked: there was a formal convention entered into between the Emperor Napoleon and myself, which guaranteed me absolutely the assistance of the French troops until the end of the year 1868; without this I never would have accepted the throne.' As a matter of fact, which was not unknown in London, this secret treaty existed.

Maximilian felt that he had but one step to take, —that of abdication. On July 7, he took pen in hand to sign the fall of the monarchy; the Empress of Mexico stayed his hand. Then it was that the Empress Charlotte, moved by a generous but ill-considered feeling, crossed the seas, braving all the fatigues of the voyage and the fevers of the *Terres Chaudes.* She hoped that at Paris and Rome she should be able to gain her cause; that is, that she would be able to settle favourably the three questions which must decide the fate of the monarchy—the maintenance and increase of the corps of occupation, some financial assistance, and the acquisition of an ecclesiastical *concordat.* If her undertaking was not crowned with success, the emperor, after having placed his authority at the disposal of the nation, was to rejoin his courageous and admirable helpmate in Europe. The court of Mexico still blinded itself as to the real state of things; but certain intimate confidants, who could not make up their minds to abandon their high positions, urged the empress to embark. As to General Count De Thün, he had already returned to Austria. On July 8, the official journal of Mexico announced that the empress was leaving for Europe, where she was about to enter into negotiations as to the affairs of Mexico, and to settle various international matters. Allusion was made to the approaching visit to Rome, to reassure both the clergy and the holders of ecclesiastical property. To provide for the expenses of the august traveller it was necessary, as the treasury was exhausted, to have recourse to the funds of the 'inundation tax'* to provide a sum of 30,000 piastres.

An incident, painful in every respect, marked the visit of her majesty to the port of Vera Cruz. The department of the Mexican marine, for which the marshal had spontaneously opened a credit of 500,000 francs to form a coast-guard service to cope with the smugglers who interfered with the customs' receipts, did not possess a barge, and had not thought of preparing one for the use of their empress. The Empress Charlotte, on arriving at the quay, found nothing but a French boat at her command. She declined distinctly to embark under the shadow of our flag to go on board the vessel which was lying in the roadstead. The unequivocal signs of dissatisfaction which her majesty manifested whilst waiting on the quay, showed clearly enough that she quitted the Mexican soil with a heart thoroughly embittered against the French government.

* A fund which was raised by taxes levied for the works intended to preserve Mexico from inundations.

Her departure, which was considered as the last effort of the monarchical *régime*, was the signal of important Juarist demonstrations. Symptoms of dissolution openly showed themselves in the imperial army; and the Belgian legion, already weakened by desertions, began to mutiny just at the time that the northern frontier was lighted up with all the fires of revolt. General Douay announced that the whole country was cut up by the republican cavalry. General Olvera allowed a convoy to be taken from him, defended by 250 Austrians and 1,500 Mexicans, and a portion of the latter went over to the victorious Escobedo. General Mejia had given way, losing definitively the port of Matamoros, and was compelled to return to Vera Cruz by sea almost alone. In the south, Parras' troops had deserted and gone over to the enemy. Colonel Medina had betrayed the empire by raising into rebellion the central town of Tula, and the empty coffers of the state having failed to furnish pay for the troops of Lopez and Quiroga, they had disbanded. Moreover, the French treasury had received orders not to give another piastre to the battalions of *cazadores,* which the commander-in-chief had hitherto taken the responsibility of paying. On hearing of all these disasters, the marshal thought it prudent to proceed personally to the northern frontier, where the storm was principally gathering. He immediately formed a light column which, in conjunction with the French *contra-guerillas,* were commissioned to operate across the zones of the revolt. Before quitting Mexico, the commander-in-chief had presented himself at the palace in the hope of taking his orders from the emperor, *but he was not received.*

With what kind of feelings was it possible for Maximilian to look at the representative of France?

Besides, the emperor had not yet made up his mind as to the fresh convention, and he preferred to keep his own counsel. On July 20, on arriving at San Luis, the marshal sent a summary of the state of the country to the palace of Mexico, and announced 'that the Belgian legion could no longer be left alone in the town of Monterey, for it was not to be depended upon. The want of discipline had assumed such proportions that General Douay had not ventured to execute the orders which he had received to disband his forces, fearing to provoke an armed revolt.' In concluding this letter, the marshal, obeying the formal instructions of the Emperor Napoleon, said to Maximilian, 'I cannot undertake anything before I know the decision of his majesty as to the note he has just received from France, the latter portion of which directs the immediate concentration of the French troops, in case the emperor should not acquiesce in the substitution of a fresh convention instead of that of Miramar.'

Fifteen days after a courier arrived from Maximilian at Peotillos, where our head-quarters were fixed, and handed to the marshal a letter more fatal even than the unhappy decree of October 3, which must have been extorted from the weakness of the sovereign by a minister infatuated by fear at the report of the insurrection which was now reaching the very heart of the empire. It must, besides, be stated, that if urgent persuasion had not been used, the emperor would not even have consulted the commander-in-chief, and would have immediately placed the whole empire in a state of siege.

Mexico, August 7, 1866.

My dear Marshal,—By two decrees dated August 1, I have declared a state of siege in the departments which appeared to me the most disturbed at this moment. These are, on one side, the departments of Michoacan and Tancitaro; and, on the other, the departments of Tuxpan, of Tulancingo, and the district of Zacatlan (department of Tlaxcala).

On this subject, I must inform you *that several members of my ministry solicit me to declare a state of siege over the whole empire.* They assert that the only means of tranquillising the country, and also of obtaining some degree of order in the administration and finances, is to place the power in the hands of the chief military commanders, who should be chosen, wherever it is possible, among the French officers. This measure can only be legal through the departments being declared in a state of siege.

The question is a highly important one; it affects the most serious interests, and I did not wish to decide upon it before knowing your opinion. You have just traversed a large portion of the empire; you have observed closely the state of things in various departments, and you better than anyone are in a position to enlighten me with the information you have obtained, and the observations you have made.

I shall therefore be glad to know if you consider it necessary to declare a state of siege throughout the whole empire; or, if it would be best to declare it in certain departments, and what those departments should be; and, finally, if you are disposed to specify any French officers who might be named chief commandants in the departments placed in a state of siege. *Under these circumstances, I doubt not that you will again consent to come to the aid of my government.*—Your very affectionate, MAXIMILIAN.

The marshal, to whom some have so complacently attributed certain dreams of personal ambition, which would certainly have accepted the offer of a military dictatorship like this at a time so critical for the crown, replied to the emperor from his bivouac as follows:—

Peotillos, August 10, 1866.

Sire,—I have the honour of acknowledging the receipt of your majesty's letter of August 7, in which you ask my advice as to the expediency of placing in a state of siege the whole or a part of the territory of the Mexican empire, and request me to specify any French officers who might be nominated chief commandants in the departments or districts placed in the above-named state of siege.

As your majesty remarks, the question is a very important one, and affects the most serious interests.

A state of siege is in fact a transitory state in which all the powers are combined in the hands of the military authority; a state which extraordinarily modifies the administrative and judicial machinery, and places the citizens in an abnormal and unnatural position.

It is likewise only in the public interests and at some great unforeseen crisis, that the sovereign authority should resort to these extreme means to point out that force is the only argument which is left for it to employ.

Is it necessary at the present time to apply this measure to the Mexican empire? I do not think so; and I ask the emperor's permission to prove to him that this measure is a useless one.

The normal state, so to speak, of this country for the last fifty years, has been a state of war, which will not be altered for a long time yet. Does not this afford all the facilities which could be wished for obtaining by force that which neither persuasion nor the efforts of a regular administration have been able to effect?

The substitution of one sole authority, and of one sole power instead of all those which before ruled the community, could only give more unity to the proceedings of government, so far as the authorities temporarily suspended (for, as I repeat, the state of siege can only be transitory), may be simultaneously and everywhere replaced by others on whose valour and good faith dependence may be placed.

Does it not seem more natural to act than to issue edicts? and, in the unquestionable state of war in which the country now is, is not the gradual transition to a state of siege both simple and easy? There are generals and chief commandants close to all the points where their actions would be indispensable.

Courts-martial are now at work over the whole extent of the empire. Would a state of siege give more force, more activity, more prestige to the military authority? No, sire; it would simply have the effect of putting a stop to any direct action on the part of the civil authorities.

The same end may be arrived at without frightening anybody: by remaining in a state of war without deviating from strict legality, and by remodelling the administrative, judicial, and financial staff.

As a corollary to the feeling which urges me to oppose a state of siege, except in urgent cases and exceptional localities, allow me now to add to the general considerations which I have had the honour of submitting to your majesty, some other considerations founded on the peculiar position of the French army in Mexico, now that it has for the last two years restored to the Mexican authorities all the powers which it exercised before the arrival of the sovereign.

Whatever might be my desire of placing at your majesty's disposal all the officers whom you might require, there are limits which I cannot pass.

At a time when a portion of the French army is preparing to quit Mexican soil, I could not, in fact, disorganise its ranks and deprive it of its *superior* officers, the only ones who possess a sufficient authority for exercising the functions of chief-commandants in the departments in a state of siege.

Still less can I think of removing the superior officers belonging to the corps destined to remain in Mexico.

And, finally, would it be prudent, when two officials of the French army already fill two of the most important positions in the Mexican government—would it be prudent, may I venture to say to your majesty, to augment the share of responsibility which already falls upon us, by allowing us to absorb all the powers in the country, and by thus annihilating all the national elements on which your majesty has hitherto relied, which also may still be made useful?

In a word, the state of siege would become the source of active discontent: it would afford a pretext for general disaffection, which would extend from the sovereign of Mexico (who appeared to despair of his people) to the allied power, whose action would only then be felt by severities imposed by French officers alone; and it would impute to your allies the whole odium of these exceptional measures. The state of siege, under these conditions, would increase the enemies of the empire, and would give credibility to the calumny which is employed by the malcontents to stir up the national spirit, namely, that France came to Mexico with the aim of conquest.

The means which, as I think, ought to be first tried, are as follows:—You must oblige the prefects and the sub-prefects to send to the generals and chief-commandants (whatever may be their nationality) political reports as to the state of the country and its requirements. You must deprive them of the right to dispose of any troops without the assent of the military authority, to whom they must address a requisition in writing. And, finally, you must actively push forward the organisation of a good *gendarmerie*, and must endeavour to bring about a *solidarité* between the military and civil powers, instead of setting them in opposition one to the other.

Your majesty will pardon this long statement, which is dictated by the sincere desire that I have to be of service to you in every way, and by the dread I feel of seeing you involved in a course of proceeding which would be more hurtful than useful.—With profound respect, Sire, &c.

BAZAINE.

If it had not been for this language, so worthy of the French people, the severities incumbent on a state of siege would have desolated the whole of Mexico; and the Americans, now ready to cross for a second time* the frontier of the Rio Bravo, would have hurled defiance at the tri-coloured flag, which our army, less patient than our policy, would certainly never have allowed to be humbled.

* The American negroes had already some months before taken possession of Bagdad, then occupied by the Imperialists, and had evacuated it after having plundered it. Bagdad was immediately re-occupied by the French.

CHAPTER XII.

Arrival of the Empress Charlotte at Saint Nazaire—Her Journey to Paris—Conversation with M. Drouyn de Lhuys—Her exciting Interview with Napoleon III.—American Despatches as to her Arrival—Maximilian's *Coup d'état*—The Abbé Fischer—The Emperor's Reactionary Policy—Concentration of French Troops—American Assistance to the Liberal Party.

AT the very time (August 10, 1866) when Marshal Bazaine, operating in the north of Mexico to uphold the imperial cause, was replying to the Emperor Maximilian that he could not approve of a state of siege being declared over the whole territory, the Transatlantic Company's boat flying the imperial flag suddenly landed the Empress of Mexico at the port of Saint Nazaire. The surprise of the local authorities, who hastened to make this event known in Paris, was even less intense than that of the court of the Tuileries. Our government was very far from expecting this visit, the announcement of which, as will be recollected, caused a great sensation in our capital; for public opinion had already a presentiment of some mysterious incidents in this Mexican drama, the circumstances of which were becoming more and more involved. On the very evening before she landed, the *Mémorial Diplomatique* and certain other journals, which were known to derive their inspirations from official sources, had protested against the report, saying, 'that they were authorised to denounce as an arrant calumny the mere supposition that the Empress Charlotte was on her way to Europe.' As soon as the princess landed she announced her intention of travelling incognito, and that she would not demand hospitality of the court of the Tuileries.

Whilst waiting for the time for leaving, the august traveller visited the quay. She was accompanied by M. Martin Castillo, her minister for foreign affairs, by her high chamberlains, the Count de Bombelles, and other officers who had followed her. Her face bore the impress of painful cares, increased by her extreme fatigue; her eyes already shone with all the brilliancy of fever. The voyage had sorely tried the young empress. At her own desire, in order to be more retired, she had been placed at the stern of the ship, and had been unable to enjoy quiet sleep on account of the continual motion of the screw. The next day the empress arrived in Paris, and proceeded to the Grand Hôtel. As the end of her journey drew near, her excitement seemed to increase. The imperial family being then staying at the palace of Saint-Cloud, the empress, having asked that one of the court-carriages should be placed at her disposal, demanded an immediate interview with Napoleon III. In the meantime she received a visit from M. Drouyn de Lhuys, and spent a portion of the day in conversation with this minister. Although the emperor had replied that he felt indisposed, and that he regretted that he was unable to give her an audience, the Empress Charlotte, allowing no postponement, proceeded to the palace.

Her entreaties were so passionate that Napoleon at last consented to receive her. She then set forth Maximilian's demands, who still required from France fresh assistance, both financial and military. The conversation was long and vehement, replete on both sides with recriminations, which ended in altering the friendly tone of the explanations exchanged. The empress, seeing the gradual destruction of the structure of hope which her ardent imagination had been flattering itself in building up, from her leaving Chapultepec to the very threshold of Saint-Cloud, and feeling that her sceptre was crumbling in her hands, gave way to all her impetuosity. After having enumerated her wrongs, the daughter of King Leopold thought that she recognised, but too late, that, when she accepted a throne from the munificence of the emperor of the French, she had been wrong in forgetting that she was a daughter of the race of Orleans.* From the scene at the palace of Saint-Cloud must in reality be dated the insanity of this interesting princess, whose courage only failed together with her reason. Her sinking energies were scarcely sufficient to enable her to drag herself to the feet of the Holy Father, from whom she came to implore both assistance and consolation.

The United States had never lost sight, for a single instant, either of the journey of the Empress Charlotte, or of the actions of French policy. To the latter Mr. Seward, the American secretary of state, never ceased to give an impetus calculated both to satisfy the republican tendencies of the Congress, and to disarm the enemies of President Johnson, who was taxed with a want of vigour in his dealings with France. Mr. John Hay, the *ad interim* chargé d'affaires at Paris, wrote to Mr. Seward:—

Paris, August 10, 1866.

Sir,—Articles have lately appeared in the Paris newspapers announcing the approaching departure from Mexico of the wife of the Archduke Maximilian. This intelligence has naturally given rise to ideas which are generally unfavourable to the imperial cause in Mexico. To put an end to these

* After the interview at Saint-Cloud, the Empress Charlotte herself dictated the account of her conversation with the Emperor Napoleon.

prejudicial remarks, the *Mémorial* and the *Pays* have published contradictions of these reports.

. . . Yesterday, to the great confusion of these friends of the cause, who were so positive in their assertions and so full of indignation, *the lady in question* arrived in Paris, and proceeded to the Grand Hôtel.

. . . The most painful conclusions are drawn from this visit, especially by those who have the misfortune to be large holders of the Mexican loan. It is generally looked upon as a supreme and final effort to obtain, by means of personal influence, the assistance that is indispensable to the Mexican empire, which has been refused to its accredited diplomatic representative.
JOHN HAY

The style of this diplomatic missive is certainly rather deficient in courtesy. On August 17, Mr. Hay thus reported to his government the visit of the Empress Charlotte to the palace of Saint-Cloud:—

Paris, August 17, 1866.

Sir,—Under the advice of Mr. Bigelow, who is staying for a few days with his family at Ems, I yesterday waited on the minister of foreign affairs. I spoke to his excellency as to the news which was published generally in the Paris newspapers, on the subject of the visit of the Princess Charlotte to France. These articles stated that Maximilian's stay in Mexico depended on some modification of the resolutions adopted by the French government, and announced in the recent communications made by his excellency to the Marquis de Montholon and to Mr. Bigelow. Some journals even go so far as to state that the princess had succeeded in obtaining a change in the programme. I asked the minister if any modification had been made, or was intended to be made, in the policy of the imperial government as regarded Mexico. M. Drouyn de Lhuys replied, that 'there had been no modification of our policy in this respect, and that there would be none. All that we have stated to be our intention to do, that we shall do.' He also added: 'Of course we received the empress

with courtesy and cordiality, but the plan previously settled by the emperor's government will be carried out as it has been stated.
JOHN HAY.

At the time when the whole of Europe, feeling for the blow which was about to fall on the unfortunate Maximilian, was grieving over the despair and insanity of the Empress Charlotte, events in Mexico were hurrying on apace. The emperor, struck, as it were, with blindness, let loose the revolution with his own hands, by effecting an actual *coup d'état*. He turned out his ministers, and instead of trying to recruit the councillors of the crown among all parties, so as to be able to depend on the country and public opinion generally at the approach of the French evacuation, he threw himself, body and soul, into the arms of the ultramontane faction which had circumvented him with its intrigues and its promises. The 'reactionaries,' Lares, Marin, Campos, and Tavera, formed a part of the new council. The Abbé Fischer became chief of the imperial cabinet, and MM. Osmont and Friant,—the one chief of the staff, and the other chief commissary of stores in the expeditionary corps—whose temporary assistance had been afforded to Maximilian by the marshal during a critical movement, now definitely held the portfolios of war and finance. The news of this *coup d'état*, which was effected at Mexico on July 26, was late in reaching the French head-quarters authorities, whose astonishment only equalled their regret. For the choice which the emperor had made of this most extreme party was equivalent to a declaration of war against the great majority of the nation; moreover, the formal introduction of two French officers into public matters in Mexico was in positive contradiction to the orders of our government, which prohibited any interference in the political management of the country. It was, on the other hand, hardly to the interests of our army, that these two high functionaries should hold this plurality of offices. It was also much to be regretted that a decision on such a point as this was arrived at and even carried out without the consent of the commander-in-chief.

The confidence which Maximilian placed in the Abbé Fischer (who subsequently fulfilled a melancholy office) was to be deplored in every respect, and most certainly the religious scruples of the sovereign would not have been beguiled if he had known the real history of this Lutheran apostate, now become a Catholic. Augustin Fischer was of German origin, and about 1845 joined a body of colonists proceeding to Texas. After being a clerk to a notary without much success, he went off to California to seek for gold. He soon renounced the Protestant faith, received holy orders in the Roman Catholic church in Mexico, and obtained a post as secretary to the Bishop of Durango. Being soon after banished from the episcopal palace by reason of his profligate morals, he was received at Parras at the house of M. Sanchez Navarro, who, deceived by appearances, presented him to Maximilian. Father Fischer, who is endowed with rare intelligence, soon found himself intrusted with a diplomatic mission to the Holy Father; however he returned to Mexico having totally failed at Rome. Notwithstanding this, he increased in repute, and just at this time, the ambition of the imperial secretary, which knew no limits, was looking for the bishopric of Queretaro, the richest clerical benefice in Mexico. The direct favour of the sovereign was a sure means of success, but the selection of this priest was not calculated to soothe and rally round him the disaffected.

Did Maximilian hope that he should thus pledge himself to the Holy See and conciliate its good graces by this appeal to a reactionary ministry; and was facilitating the proceedings of the Empress Charlotte his only aim? This is credible, especially if we recall the aspirations of his life as delineated in the 'Tableaux de sa Vie,' which has just been published at Leipsic. The archduke's turn of mind was profoundly Catholic, as much by instinct as by education. The tendencies of his devotion as a prince of the royal Austrian race inclined him towards mysticism, just as the pride of his descent from the great Charles V. made him boast there was nothing superior to the 'right divine.' Before this right alone the young prince had bowed his head until he accepted from a pretended popular suffrage the crown which he had so often caught a glimpse of in his dreams. For Maximilian believed that he was predestinated to it; and this is the secret of his Mexican adventure, which, in his thoughts, as we shall subsequently see, was not the limit of his hope. Looking at the religious aspirations which his visit to Rome would necessarily excite, it would not have been surprising, although impolitic, in our opinion, if Maximilian, on his first taking possession of the throne, had thoroughly embraced the clerical cause, and had striven boldly from the first onset against the liberal movement. This, however, would have been followed by a war *à outrance* as disastrous to the dignity of the throne as it would have been irreconcilable with the presence of our flag; for, although the French clergy take the lead in setting a high example in both the old and new world, the Mexican priesthood, with very few exceptions, is corrupted by the desire and misuse of pleasures; and the late long revolutionary periods and the total absence of discipline had caused an increase of these abuses. It was not from the bosom of the Mexican church that the new sovereign could hope to derive any living power; from this quarter there was neither sincerity nor disinterestedness to be hoped for. We cannot forget that the first words pronounced by Mgr. La Bastida, the Archbishop of Mexico, when he returned to the capital of his country, which he had not seen for years, were an enquiry 'if the olive trees on his episcopal domain at Tacubaya had been respected by the ravages of war.' The subject of the church and her faithful ones was as nothing before the question of his revenue. Maximilian, therefore, now committed a second grave error. From the very first he made the serious mistake of placing his dependence upon individuals hostile to the French name, when he might have placed a much better class of persons round him. At the present time, he was allowing himself to be carried away on the overflowing torrent of a reaction against which all true conservatives, and the greater part of a generation brought up in republican principles were bound to contend. These principles, at variance with the new programme of the throne, could not fail to regain the ascendency in all the populous centres which the French army in its evacuating movement had given over to the military defence of the imperial troops.

Nevertheless, all the early part of 1866 had been devoted by our soldiers to improving and completing the fortifications and armaments of the towns of the interior, such as Monterey, San Luis, Durango, Zacatecas, Guadalajara, and Matehuala. Our artillerymen had succeeded in placing in position on the works of these towns more than six hundred cannon in good order and plentifully provided with ammunition. But these defensive works being confided in succession to the Mexican troops, would now remain powerless against the revolt of the country, irritated as it was at the selection of the new ministers, which destroyed all hope of any liberal revival. After this *coup d'état* the Mexican government, in despair, gave its adhesion to the new convention extorted by France. By this contract, which was to come into execution on December 1, 1866, and was substituted for the treaty of Miramar, half the proceeds from the custom-houses of Vera Cruz and Tampico was assigned for the payment of the French debt. In signing this, Maximilian entered into a fatal engagement, which he knew well he could not keep without soon lapsing into a national bankruptcy. It would have been more dignified in the emperor if he had at once laid down his crown and retired from the scene, leaving to the French government all the enormous responsibility of the situation. But this sovereign did not know how to resist the seductions of royalty. Perhaps he still hoped for the success of the mission of the empress to Paris and Rome. This is his only excuse.

During this time, the French army, in conformity with the plan of evacuation to be carried out as settled at the successive periods, was concentrating its forces. To facilitate its retrograde movement, the marshal remained on horseback on the northern roads, ready to give his assistance to either of his two *corps d'armée* which might be menaced. On the left Castagny's division leaving gradually the immense tracts of La Sonora, and the plains of Zacatecas and of Durango, was falling back upon the town of Leon, its new headquarters. On the right, General Douay was quitting all the positions of the north close to the American frontier, and his troops, having been concentrated on Saltillo, were pitching their tents under the walls of

San Luis, fronting the contingents of Zébéda, Pedro Martinez, and Aureliano Rivera. The French *contre guerillas*, who were operating on the confines of Matehuala, were preparing to go down into the *Terres Chaudes* of the State of Vera Cruz. This vast retrograde movement exposed the whole breadth of the states farthest from the centre, such as Tamaulipas, Nuevo-Léon, Cohahuila, Sinaloa, and La Sonora. This concentration would have been a wise step from the very outset, even if it had not been compelled by the orders of Napoleon the Third. Maximilian had dreamt of an impossibility when he desired to keep all these immense solitudes under his sceptre, and our head-quarters authorities would, in my opinion, have acted wisely in resisting still more strongly than they did the impulse of the crown; for our troops traversing Mexico resembled a ship gliding through the water and leaving behind it no traces of its track. This centralising movement was all the more prudent, as information sent to Maximilian himself by the prefect of Zacatecas established the fact that the liberals were on the point of obtaining the guarantee of a loan of fifty millions of piastres from the United States. In order to negotiate this loan, the Juarists offered to sell them Lower California. By means of this American assistance, Gonzalez Ortega, with ten thousand filibusters, a hundred thousand muskets, forty pieces of artillery, and a large quantity of stores, was to enter the territory by Piedras-Negras, so as to attack Zacatecas. Cortina was preparing to assail Monterey and Saltillo. Negrete had undertaken to land in Tamaulipas, and to penetrate into La Huasteca, whilst Corona moved down on Culiacan. To assist this well concerted plan, our consul at San Francisco advised us that General Miller, the collector of customs in this city, had authorised the transit and embarkation of the arms and stores which were sent to the Mexican rebels by the official agents of Juarez; whilst General Vega was clandestinely engaging on a large scale certain disbanded American soldiers, to send them on by small detachments to La Sonora. Moreover, the provinces of the interior needed to be firmly kept to their duty. Nearly all the Mexican regiments were worked upon by the liberals; even the generals themselves received secret propositions from the enemy, and some listened to them. General Quiroga, it must be stated to his honour, denounced these intrigues to the French authorities. Desertion, however, was the order of the day. Thus, General Lopez, who commanded at Matehuala, mustered a force of five hundred men; their pay had been wanting for several days; the French *contre guerillas*, moved at the destitution of soldiers deprived of food and clothing, consented to grant them an advance from their own coffers. As soon as they were clothed and paid, three hundred of these Mexicans deserted in eight days.

CHAPTER XIII.

Reactionary Influence of the new Ministry—Maximilian's injudicious Innovations—Fall of Tampico—Correspondence thereon—Marshal Bazaine's Explanations—Mutiny of the Belgian Contingent—Singular Loss of Belgian Despatches—Bad State of the National Army—Complaints made by the French Commandants of the *Cazadores*—Well-founded Appeal of General Guttierez—Clerical Interference with the Course of Justice.

IT was to be expected that the influence of the new ministry would soon begin to show itself; anxious as they were to take revenge for the liberal measures which were inaugurated before Maximilian's arrival at Mexico, when the commander-in-chief declared that the sales of mortmain property were valid, except in cases of fraudulent acquisition. Our head-quarters authorities felt displeased at having to be associated with a policy of so decidedly reactionary a character. It was not long before hostilities broke out between the crown, now alas! subjected to untoward influences, and the military representative of the French government. The marshal might now congratulate himself that he had been the means of sparing Mexico all the severities of a state of siege, which would indeed have been terrible in the hands of religious fanaticism.

The capture by the rebels of the port of Tampico, —so important for its customs' receipts—formed a pretext for an attack by the ministers, who had for a moment flattered themselves that our flag, being compromised by a sudden conflict with the United States, would become so committed to the war, that France, so far from being able to withdraw, would find herself compelled to send for fresh reinforcements. Maximilian, it must be confessed, had found out that the policy of the Tuileries spoke two languages; that the ministers contradicted the assurances of his ally, who had never ceased to promise his material assistance and moral support; and that at last the Emperor Napoleon had placed him in a cruel dilemma, by forcing him to sign the convention of July 30.

The Emperor of Mexico also had profited by these lessons of a political conduct now much in request in Europe. Thus he no longer hesitated in sowing the seeds of discord in the French camp, appealing to certain feelings of devotion in some, who, in consequence of their complete ignorance of the instructions sent by the cabinet of the Tuileries, deplored the severity of the measure of evacuation, although the latter had been modified by our head-quarters authorities. Forgetting that discipline is the first law of an army, Maximilian sought to create for himself partizans in our ranks, in the hope that their counteraction might find an echo in France which would be powerful enough to retard the movement of evacuation.

The constant innovations which were experienced by Maximilian's military household had often revealed a real want of experience on the part of the sovereign as well as a complete forgetfulness of the etiquette of government. Thus, the following letter from the imperial cabinet, was intended to compel a marshal of France, as well as all the ministers of the crown, to correspond with the emperor through the medium of a captain of the expeditionary corps.

Military Cabinet of the Emperor,
Mexico, March 7, 1866.

Monsieur le Maréchal,—I have the honour of informing

your excellency that the cabinet of the emperor is abolished, and is replaced by a *secrétariat*.

His majesty places Captain X—— at the head of the military section of this office.

For the future, the emperor desires to correspond with your excellency, the chief of the staff, and the various ministers, through the medium of this officer.

I cannot at present acquaint you with the name of the head of the civil section.

Maximilian now felt himself, and rightly so, relieved of all gratitude to the French government, and had only one aim with regard to them; namely, to derive all the advantage he could from our help, and to make use of our soldiers as long as he could, in order to save his crown. And he had a right to do this. Thus, he constantly expressed his wishes that the French should guard specially the northern frontier line, and the neighbouring ports of the United States. In this sphere of action there was a chance of their coming in collision with the Americans; but our authorities kept on their guard and obeyed the instructions which came from Paris, although at the same time they afforded complete co-operation to the crown of Mexico which they were still charged to defend, the convention of July 30 being now signed. Impressed by these hopes now deceived by our total abandonment of the northern frontier, Maximilian thus wrote to the Commander-in-Chief:—

Alcazar de Chapultepec, August 4, 1866.

My dear Marshal,—The capture of the city of Tampico by the rebels and the evacuation of Monterey apprise me that the result of the campaign in the north will be attended with the most serious consequences to my country.

I desire, therefore, to be informed of the plan which you propose to follow in your operations, so that I may try to save, if possible, those adherents to the empire and unfortunate officials who have sacrificed themselves in our cause.

MAXIMILIAN.

This letter manifests considerable irritation, which was hardly uncalled for, on the part of the Prince, who was still feeling the blow inflicted by the imperial note of May 31, and saw that all his hopes were betrayed. If the commander-in-chief had been received at the palace, when he presented himself there before his departure for his northern tour of inspection, these questions might have received a more conciliatory solution. As this painful history goes on, we shall see that the sovereign's correspondence with the marshal, as far as regards all personal relations with him, never ceases to manifest feelings of cordial good-will. But as soon as the great military interests of the Mexican crown, now put in jeopardy by the anticipated withdrawal of our troops, again come into question, we shall find that Maximilian could only look upon the marshal as the representative of a government against which he had the most bitter cause of complaint; and consequently the relations on both sides will be as stiff as the situation itself was awkward, since the headquarters authorities, having already received several rebukes from Paris, could not do otherwise than conform to their instructions.

The commander-in-chief replied from his camp:—

Peotillos, August 12, 1866.

Sire,—I have this instant received your majesty's letter of August 4.

In associating together the fact of the capture of Tampico by the rebels and that of the evacuation of Monterey effected by my orders, your majesty seems to wish to throw upon me the responsibility of both. By my two letters written from San Luis Potosi—No. 7, dated July 11, and No. 46, dated July 20—I believed I had so sufficiently explained the situation of Nuevo Leon and Cohahuila, that the necessity of the evacuation of Monterey (after the destruction of General Mejia's troops and the capitulation of Matamoros in the present moral condition of the Belgian legion) would have been fully recognised, not only in a political but also especially in a military point of view.

The capitulation of Matamoros, and the consequences which have resulted from it, are not my doing, and I have not yet been able to state my opinion on the subject. I had to meet the exigencies of a position which I found ready made to my hands, and I believe I have done my duty to the sovereign in placing before him all the documents annexed to my before-named letters, duplicates of which I have sent to my government.

With respect to the capture of the city of Tampico by the rebels, I must have the honour of respectfully reminding the emperor that, before undertaking what he is pleased to call *my campaign* in the north, at the time when the remains of General Mejia's troops were arriving at Vera Cruz, I asked that General Olvera, with the residue of his brigade, should be sent to Tampico. The urgency of General Mejia has, it appears, induced your majesty to modify your first decision, which was favourable to the contemplated movement. For Olvera's brigade has not gone to Tampico, and has indeed been sent on to Mexico contrary to the orders which I left, which were in harmony with a military combination, the foiling of which finds its material results in the state of Queretaro.

The want of a similar co-operation, which General de Thun refused to afford me, has not a little contributed to the disasters which have befallen Tamaulipas. General Mejia complained that his soldiers were exposed to the yellow fever at Tampico.

A small detachment of the *contre-guerilla*, which was all I had at my disposal to form a garrison at Tampico, was then embarked at Vera Cruz, without noticing the dangers of the climate, which cost us a whole battalion last year. I am not aware that this detachment has abandoned its post, or delivered up that which it was charged to defend.

Your majesty expresses a desire of being informed of the plan which I propose to follow in my operations.

If your majesty had deigned to receive me when, on the eve of leaving the city of Mexico, I solicited the honour of taking leave of you, I should have explained my intentions, which simply were—to see with my own eyes the effect produced in the north by the events at Matamoros; to assure myself of the correctness of the reports which had been sent me as to the little confidence that could be placed in the principal officials, and as to the generally hostile feeling of the population of those districts.

After having ascertained all these facts, and relying on the reports of Generals Douay and Jeanningros, I saw the impossibility (at least for a time) of preserving these advanced points, which could be nothing else but a source of danger and continual expense. I formed the resolution, and stated it to your majesty, of directing the evacuation of Monterey and Saltillo, so as to establish in their rear a strong line, easy to defend and separated from the former places by a complete desert, where neither allies nor enemies could reckon on any resources. My opinion was, and still is, that it is preferable for you to develope your influence in the interior, by concentrating your powers on a limited extent of territory, instead of exhausting your energies at the extremities of the empire which are subject to the evil influence of the American frontier.

Your majesty calls forth these explanations; and I give them to you in good faith.

The absolute state of isolation in which the former ministers of the crown left General Mejia at Matamoros was the real cause of the capitulation of that place; the painful position in which General Montenegro has been placed at Acapulco—and this in spite of my numberless demands, and in spite of promises made but never kept—will lead, I doubt not, either to the early defection of this body of troops, which has really given proofs of self-denial and devotion, or to the capitulation of the place.

In the face of all this sluggishness, and flagrant unwillingness of action (which I have no fear in again denouncing to your majesty), whilst I will devotedly and conscientiously fulfil towards the emperor of Mexico the mission which has been confided to me by my sovereign, my first business must be the cares which are imposed upon me by my duty as commander-in-chief of the French army.

My letter of July 11 has set before your majesty the duties which fall upon me in connection with the approaching withdrawal of a considerable portion of the army under my command.

As a natural consequence of the apprehensions which I am justified in conceiving as to the part which the Mexican element plays in this country, I have the honour of acquainting your majesty that it will be impossible for me to leave any of my troops at Guaymas and at Mazatlan.

For a long time the Mexican government has been able, and ought, to have taken in hand the maintenance of the imperial power in these two places. I find myself compelled to leave La Sonora and Sinaloa to those resources alone which the government of your majesty has at its disposal, and I shall not delay in recalling the French troops who are occupying these far-off districts.

With regard to the officials who have given their support to your majesty's government, I take them to be too clever either to have compromised themselves fruitlessly, or to expose themselves to danger from events which they must have foreseen.

They have all of them understood hitherto, and I think will still understand, how to keep themselves clear from all danger.

Upon the whole, sire, I do not think that the evacuation of Monterey and Saltillo can produce the serious results for your country which you appear to dread.

In war, it is necessary to know how to make allowances for emergencies, and to be able to sacrifice a portion of territory in order to preserve the main part; and then, when the enemy is weakened by exhaustion or desertion, the offensive must again be resumed and victory established.

In order to arrive at this end, your majesty has and will continue to have at your disposal means (the Foreign Legion and the Austrian brigade) which will not leave you in embarrassment.

With the deepest respect, sire, &c.,

BAZAINE.

This letter—which, by the way, clearly shows the

stiffness which had crept into official relations in consequence of the attitude of the French cabinet—proves that our army was still holding the most dangerous positions, which were avoided by the Mexican troops. Our French ports, which witnessed the return of the marine-infantry, can testify how their sons had been swept away by their stay in the *Terres Chaudes,* and especially at Tampico. The French *contre-guerillas* were, in their turn, sadly tried there, both by pestilence and by the fire of the enemy.

Yet Tampico fell into the power of the Liberals only through the treason of the Mexican soldiers, who caused a portion of our men to be slaughtered in the fort of Iturbide. The valorous defence by Captain Langlais can never be forgotten, who, in defiance of famine and *la vomito,* held out for weeks with only two hundred men of the *contre-guerilla* against two thousand Liberals under Pavon; when he surrendered the fort of Casa-Mata, he marched his troops out freely in front of the enemy, with their arms loaded and their flag proudly flying.

With respect to Monterey, which was left to the safe keeping of the Belgian Legion, Maximilian's letter, which we quote here, shows sufficiently what kind of support was to be expected from the cabinet of Brussels and the Belgian corps, which had recently mutinied. The unhappy prince did not derive any more benefit from the help of the foreigners whom he had been so unwise as to call in for the defence of his throne.

Chapultepec, August 30, 1866.

My dear Marshal,—The state of excitement which exists in the Belgian regiment is proved by the last telegraphic despatch from the officers; it is produced by external causes—viz., the reorganisation which it is necessary it should undergo, and the fact that its officers must embark on September 13 at the latest, the Belgian government not having granted them an extension of leave. All this induces me to think that it would be desirable and prudent to bring the Belgian regiment for some time either to Mexico or any neighbouring town; and it would be well to give the necessary orders. You will please give me your opinion on this question, as important as it is disagreeable.

Accept, my dear marshal, the assurance of the sentiments of sincere friendship, with which I am your very affectionate,

MAXIMILIAN.

It must be stated here, that Maximilian only subsequently learned that the King of the Belgians had authorised his officers to prolong their stay in Mexico until the month of April 1867. But, unfortunately, the despatch from Brussels, dated July 30, 1866, and addressed to the Belgian *chargé d'affaires* at Mexico, was lost for six weeks, and did not reach this diplomatist, as he asserted, until October 21, at a time when all the Belgian officers but five had set sail for Europe.

Following the example of this foreign contingent, the national army was in a state of complete dissolution. In consequence of the poverty of the treasury, the imperial edifice was giving way on all sides. The *cazadores* themselves, this last resource for evil days, who had hitherto rendered important services, whose French commanders, too, did not hesitate to risk their lives, were threatened with extinction for want of money and recruits. Thanks to the course of action which the new ministry adopted, the public officials, the imperial prefects, and the great landed proprietors, who all took their watchword from Mexico, refused to provide soldiers. The clerical party, who wanted to have Maximilian delivered up to them bound hand and foot, employed all the means in their power to shake off the yoke of the French intervention, and to free themselves from French military administration. Disgust and weariness took possession of our officers, who asked to be recalled in all the provinces in which the *cazadores* were acting. At Queretaro, at Mazatlan,—in fact everywhere—the same complaints were raised, accompanied with tenders of resignation. The two documents which follow, which have been selected out of many others written in the same spirit, will relate the existing state of things more clearly than a mere recital:—

September 15, 1866.

Monsieur le Maréchal,—When you did me the honour of placing me in command of the . . battalion of *cazadores*, I thought I might be able to undertake this difficult, but not impossible, task. Certain advantages and guarantees were promised to the military men of these battalions, and it was likely that a large number of French soldiers would come forward on the faith of these promises. The system of voluntary enlistment was an element of strength; confidence was felt in the certainty that the *cazadores* would be treated like the foreign legion, with which they were connected; that they would be dependent on the commander and administration of the expeditionary corps, receiving their pay from French paymasters, their food from the French commissariat, and their stores from the state magazines and from the camp; finally, that they would be cared for in the hospitals of the expeditionary corps. This confidence was increased by the certainty *of remaining for at least eighteen months along with the French army*, the aid of which was to facilitate and further the organisation, the instruction, and the solidity of these battalions.

At the present time, the advantages and the guarantees are daily disappearing. The system of enlistment is completely changing; the paymasters have already received orders to pay no longer the battalions of *cazadores*. The French administration now does little for us;* nothing is left us but a pro-

* It must be recollected that the marshal, who had taken the initiative in paying these troops through the French treasury, had found his action disapproved of at Paris,

spect of every kind of poverty and privation, just as it is with the Mexican corps, for the public treasury can pay no longer. The officers, generally the last to be paid, will find themselves reduced to a deplorable state, from which they will be unable to extricate themselves without leaving behind them their dignity and their honour. In spite of the emperor's instructions, enlistment by means of *la leva* is now being adopted. Thus, the imperial commissary Iribarren claims to send me, to be looked after and maintained, six hundred Juarists, every one of them prepared (everyone here is aware of it) to turn against us at the first opportunity; this, too, is done at a time when we ought certainly to avoid arming a number of certain enemies *within* our lines, for those *without* are *numerous* and *strong*, and are becoming more so every day. However, I cannot accept the command over the recruits of the *leva*; nothing but prisoners who must be looked after night and day, in action as well as in quarters. With a recruitment of this kind, the task of organising and instructing is an impossible one, and corps will be formed in which the French element will only meet with future mortification of every kind.

I therefore profess myself incapable of commanding a corps which is subject to this sort of recruitment, and it is my duty, monsieur le maréchal, to state this to you, and to beg you to withdraw me from the command of the . . battalion of *cazadores*. THE COMMANDANT . .

September 23, 1866.

Monsieur le Maréchal,— . . . All the Mexican coffers are empty. The imperial commissary has just laid upon us a most iniquitous ordinance, the decree of which I send you. Many a person will be reduced to poverty, and everyone is complaining. The various consuls have protested, but nothing has come of it. The most painful part of it is, that it is imagined here that this notorious decree has been issued under the protection of the French bayonets, as we are compelled to repress all the disorders which this unhappy decision has called forth.

A *leva* has been made to form the guard, and every inhabitant ought to take a part in it. But in consideration of the payment of a few piastres, many have been able to get off.

We get nothing but vagrants, or men who are well known as enemies, whom we are obliged to keep in confinement. These are the elements on which the imperial commissary depends for preserving this city for the Emperor Maximilian. Everyone asks whether it is madness, or some project which will not bear disclosure. If no reinforcements arrive here, it will be a crime to leave a handful of Frenchmen in the place, who will fall as victims to their devotion. There is no mistake as to this, the liberals are fully expected here, and fêtes are getting ready to receive them. THE COMMANDANT . .

The following deposition of the Mexican general commanding at Guadalajara, the second city of the empire, is not less curious. This high functionary, placed at the head of the fourth military division, which was one of the most important, wrote to the emperor to complain of a want of co-operation on the part of the civil authorities:—

Head-Quarters, Guadalajara.

The revolutionary movements, which are to be observed in various parts of this military division, the indefatigable activity of the agents of disorder, and the apathy and indolence which the greater part of the political authorities in these departments manifest in the execution of their duties, render my task more and more difficult every day.

I shall always insist on the obligation incumbent on the civil authorities to assist our military operations in every possible way. My work is condemned beforehand to failure, if I am to continue as now to contend with the unwillingness of certain prefects.

I think that it is indispensable to dismiss all the authorities except those of Zacatecas and Colima, and they should be replaced by men who are loyal and possessed of bright ideas— partisans both of the intervention and the empire.

GENERAL J. GUTTIEREZ.

Such were the fruits of the new policy! When the establishment of French courts-martial was asked for, the marshal replied officially, that he could not concur in the appointment of such tribunals, because it was altogether contrary both to his instructions and his intentions.

The administration, too, sought to get off any culprits in whom the clergy were interested. No other proofs of this are needed than the following telegraphic despatch from a general of the expeditionary corps. 'A telegram from the imperial secretary directs that the sentence on Rosada should be reprieved. The bishop is interested in him. It is wished that he should make his escape. In spite of all I have written, in spite of a refusal by the emperor, Rosada will escape well-deserved punishment. I am distressed to see numbers of poor wretches shot, and the greatest culprits get off. This sort of thing produces a very bad effect for the imperial cause.' Thus it was that the emperor found himself disobeyed in the provinces in which Father Fischer was beginning to make his influence directly felt.

CHAPTER XIV.

French Officers in the Mexican Administration—Correspondence on this Subject—Marshal Bazaine's Acquiescence—Disavowed at Paris—Neglect of the Mexican Naval Department—Convention of July 30—Sudden Alteration in the Views of the French Cabinet—The Mission of General Castelnau—Matters getting Worse in Mexico—Maximilian's Plans to ensure his safe Retreat—Marshal Bazaine receives fresh Orders from Paris—Mr. Seward's Despatch—Complaints of the Mexican Ministry rebutted by Marshal Bazaine—Mysterious Aim of General Castelnau's Mission—The Four-fold Drama—Maximilian's Protest.

THE commander-in-chief thought it right, for fear of thwarting Maximilian's projects whilst at a distance from him, to wait for his own return to Mexico before he came to any decision as to the selection of MM. Osmont and Friant as ministers. When he arrived, the new cabinet was not completely constituted; but as soon as its organisation was finished, the marshal gave the above high functionaries to understand that the presence of French officers in the Mexican council might give rise to incidents which would be annoying in a political point of view; but that it would be preferable, if they wished to connect themselves with the imperial fortunes, to resign their military positions, their prolonged absence from which might endanger the interests of the expeditionary corps. Notwithstanding their natural sympathies for the court of Mexico, the French officers could not consent, without the leave of their government, to forthwith quit their flag. This important question caused the following correspondence between the Palace of Mexico and our head-quarters:—

Palace of Mexico, September 15, 1866.

My dear Marshal,—I think that advantage has been taken of your good faith in putting this ministerial modification before you as the commencement of an era of reaction which would be incompatible with the presence of two French generals amid their new colleagues.

My past actions, and my well known political tolerance are, I have a right to think, a sure pledge that the change will be one which events call for, and worthy both of my glorious allies and of myself.

Receive, my dear marshal, the assurance of my feelings of the sincere friendship with which I am your very affectionate

MAXIMILIAN.

Mexico, September 16, 1866.

Sire,—In reply to the letter which your majesty sent me yesterday evening, I have the honour of acquainting you that I have called upon MM. Osmont and Friant to make their election between the duties which they are fulfilling in your majesty's service and those which have been assigned to them in the expeditionary corps; experience daily shows that their double functions are incompatible, and that annoyances are thereby caused such as the various services of the army have been too long suffering from.

It is not my province to express an opinion on the shade of political opinion which is represented by your majesty's new cabinet, and this is not the motive which has induced me to come to the above determination.

Immediately on my return to Mexico, I allowed MM. Osmont and Friant to remain in your majesty's service because the number of ministers was deficient; now that the cabinet is fully constituted, I thought that they might withdraw without inconvenience.

Nevertheless, I have the honour of repeating to your majesty, that I am quite disposed to afford to your government the co-operation of these officers, if they are willing to resign the functions they have to fill in the expeditionary corps.

I have written to my government to this effect by the last

courier, and this is the only way in which this affair can be looked at.

With the most profound respect, sire, &c.   BAZAINE.

Mexico, September 16, 1866.

My dear Marshal,—I regret that you place MM. Osmont and Friant in a position which will leave them no alternative but to resign their portfolios. Both of these officers fulfilled their duties to my entire satisfaction. The former has managed to secure the good feeling of the Mexican army; the latter has just prepared a series of decrees calculated to increase our resources, but which he alone is able to carry into execution. *If, therefore, it is true that the alliance between my own and the French government is to be considered as a reality, as I flatter myself that it is*, it is my desire that these two officers should continue in their ministerial functions, for, I am pretty sure, it will not be impossible to replace them, at least temporarily, in the offices which they occupy in the expeditionary corps.

Your reply will at all events inform me as to which class of ideas I must now make up my mind to.—Your very affectionate
MAXIMILIAN.

Mexico, September 17, 1866.

. . . Taking into serious consideration the desire which your majesty expressed in your letter of September 16, I have the honour of informing you that, until the arrival of fresh instructions from my government, the present positions of MM. Osmont and Friant will not be altered.

These two gentlemen will remain at your majesty's disposal, and the duties which belong to them in the expeditionary corps will, until further orders, be fulfilled by their respective assistants.

With the deepest respect, sire, &c.   BAZAINE.

Again, our head-quarters' authorities yielded to Maximilian's wishes. The reply of the French cabinet, dated August 26, was not long before it arrived. It was as the marshal had foreseen; 'it was of serious consequence to us,' they wrote, 'to keep aloof from the administration of the country. The Emperor

Napoleon felt bound to send instructions directly. It was inadmissible in any case that a chief of the staff and a commissary of stores should simultaneously be ministers of the Mexican empire.' In the meantime, in the beginning of the month of September, a despatch arrived in Paris from the Marquis de Montholon, laying before the Cabinet of the Tuileries the following note from Mr. Seward:—

Mr. Seward to the Marquis de Montholon.

Washington, August 16, 1866.

Sir,—I have the honour of calling your attention to two orders or decrees which it is said were issued on the 26th of last July by the Prince Maximilian, *who lays claim to being Emperor of Mexico.* In these orders he states that he has made over the direction of the war department to General Osmont, chief of the staff in the French expeditionary corps, and that of the treasury department to M. Friant, chief commissary of stores to the same force.

The president considers it necessary to acquaint the Emperor of the French that the nomination by the prince Maximilian of the said French officers to administrative functions *is calculated to be prejudicial to the friendly relations existing between the United States and France*; because the congress and the people of the United States might consider this fact as an indication which would be incompatible with the engagement entered into for the recall of the French corps from Mexico.

WILLIAM H. SEWARD.

After this almost menacing communication, the *Moniteur* of September 13 announced, without delay, that MM. Osmont and Friant were not authorised by the French government to accept their respective portfolios. The commander-in-chief was also informed in writing, alluding to the unexpected nomination of these officials, that he ought to have opposed it even after it had been carried out; and a formal disavowal was also sent him from the Tuileries of this interference in the public affairs of Mexico. Although the duty of our military commander became more and more difficult, what was Maximilian to think, who had just asked, '*If it was true that the alliance between his own and the French government was to be considered as a reality, as he flattered himself that it was?*'

The attitude of the United States, full of a logic which was never inconsistent with its purpose, was at all events an attitude of open hostility. Just at this time President Johnson issued a proclamation, declaring null and void a decree of Maximilian, which ordered the blockade of certain ports in Mexico.

One cannot help wondering at the illusions of a prince who thought proper to order a blockade at the very doors, as it were, of the United States, and yet did not possess a single Mexican ship ready to enforce with its guns the will of the sovereign. Nevertheless, Mexico lies between two seas, and possesses an extensive line of coast. What had her naval department been doing for the last three years? Although it might not, perhaps, have been able to launch large ships, or to measure their strength with the American *Monitors*, surely they ought to have constructed gunboats and light vessels fitted to go up the rivers, and to protect the shores against *duerilleros* and smugglers.* Certainly, France, as an ally of Maximilian, might, with her fleet, have maintained an effective blockade of Matamoros, and especially of Tampico, where, by the convention of July 30, she had powerful interests at stake. She preferred to abstain from doing this, and again gave way before the Americans.

It will be recollected that when the convention of July 30, so ruinous to the Mexican monarchy, was so dictatorially exacted, the Emperor Napoleon promised

---

* It had not even made use of the credit opened by the marshal for this very purpose.

Maximilian that, if he accepted the new conditions laid before him, the French army should not all return at once, but in three portions, at fixed dates, up to November 1867. But the interview at St. Cloud had called forth certain resolutions as extreme as the conversation of the two sovereigns had been violent: the irritation had been equal on both sides. The court of the Tuileries, yielding to passion which should always be banished from politics, conceived the sudden resolution of recalling its troops, at a short notice, in one mass, thus treading under foot the promise it had first made. Nevertheless, it was well understood in Paris that a cancelling of plighted faith, although recommended by an excessive impatience to have done with this fatal expedition, was a matter of deep moment; but that its importance might be lessened, if Maximilian, either with or against his will, could be snatched from fresh hazards, and could be induced to abdicate. By this plan, whilst they restored to Europe an archduke somewhat disgraced, it is true, but still safe and sound, they would run the chance of constituting a new Mexican Republic, with which they would have to deal.

Such was to be the result of five years of grievous sacrifices! Time had been when Admiral Jurien de la Gravière could have negotiated successfully without firing a shot! In 1861, the rise of Maximilian was plotted; in 1866, they were plotting his fall, and were prepared, in case the unfortunate sovereign declined to lay down his crown, to hasten on the end, by entering into mysterious negotiations, through our diplomacy and through the medium of the United States, with the liberal chiefs in Mexico. In the first place, an attempt was to be made to procure Maximilian's abdication by means of persuasion. For this second and delicate mission, which was of rather a complex character, the French cabinet cast their eyes on General Castelnau, aide-de-camp to the emperor, who was then in attendance on his sovereign. His majesty's envoy was invested with full powers for every eventuality. This mission conferred on a mere general certain prerogatives superior to the authority of the commander-in-chief himself, and gave him a right of control over the acts of the latter, which right (although not avowed) was prejudicial to the dignity of a marshal of France. The French cabinet would certainly have been stopped in a course so contrary to military etiquette, if it had not taken advantage of Marshal Randon's temporary absence from Paris; but we cannot help thinking that the tried loyalty of the minister of war, who thoroughly understood the Mexican question—both the promises which had been made, and also the immense difficulties which our military commander had had to grapple with—would not have lent his aid to the almost forcible subversion of Maximilian.

General Castelnau set sail on September 17.

At this time the Mexican horizon was getting darker and darker. The rebels were forcing their way to the very heart of the empire. The French alone made any head against the progress of the insurrection. The battalions of *cazadores* were rapidly melting away, and the Austrians themselves gave unequivocal signs of a feeling of discouragement which can easily be accounted for, when we consider that Maximilian was compelled against his will to neglect his countrymen. This apparent unconcern on the part of the sovereign had a bad effect on the Austrian legion; the wounded men of this corps had not yet received any alleviation of their lot from the Mexican government. At the end of September, 1866, the officers of this force found themselves compelled to give up generously a portion of their pay to assist their mutilated comrades. It must, however, be stated, in justification of the court of Mexico, that the civil list itself, which at first took away every morning 27,500 francs in gold from the daily receipts of the capital, was now much diminished owing to the financial crisis, which was afflicting the whole empire, so that the court was often powerless to render assistance, although actuated by the most generous intentions. As to the regular and auxiliary Mexican army, of which the ministry had the sole management, it was dwindling away to nothing. Maximilian now learnt, through the medium of the United States, the failure of the interview at St. Cloud: he kept this news secret until he heard the result of the empress's negotiation with the Holy See, whose moral support might, he thought, counterbalance the gradual withdrawal of our troops. But from this moment he quietly began to make his preparations for departure; and to make sure beforehand of an escort, he sent the following letter to the commander-in-chief, who had just arrived at Puebla, having marched to the assistance of an Austrian column which was in serious danger:—

Palais de Mexico, September 26, 1866.

My dear Marshal,—I send you annexed some documents as to the invasion of Llanos de Apam by the rebels; and you will have the kindness to adopt the necessary measures with all the haste that the state of things requires, so as to prevent the rebels from taking complete possession of these points so rich and so important.

You will also have the goodness to give orders that the three squadrons of Austrian hussars should be summoned to Mexico *in order to get remounts and to recover from the fatigues of the long and rough campaign which they have just made.*

Receive, my dear marshal, the assurance of the good will and friendship of your very affectionate

MAXIMILIAN.

After having executed these orders, the marshal hurried on his march along the road to Jalapa. In spite of his advice and the objections he made, the minister of war, who was operating without the marshal's privity, had undertaken the pacification of the *sierra* of Tulancingo, and the Austrian troops had been put in motion. This difficult and troublesome mountain warfare, now also especially inopportune, looking at the general disturbed state of the country, must have been fatal to these foreign soldiers, who were put to rout and closely blockaded in the town of Perote. Scarcely had the commander-in-chief got within reach, with the intention of extricating them, when an officer of the French cavalry came at full speed from Mexico to his bivouac; he was the bearer of the following imperial message:—

Chapultepec, October 11, 1866.

My dear Marshal,—The arrival of the empress is likely to take place between the 20th and the end of the present month. As I wish to receive her in person at the port of disembarkation, I propose to quit the capital in the early part of next week. Consequently, as I am desirous to leave the tranquillity of Mexico well assured, and as I also wish *to discuss with you certain important points*, it is indispensable that we should meet, and I should be glad to have an interview with you next Sunday.

I hope that you will be kind enough to come, *whatever obstacles may be in the way, on account of the superior importance* of the conference I wish for. I regret that *I did not know of this necessity* before you left Mexico; for I should have saved you all the trouble of the journey you will have to suffer; but I reckon on your well known kindness that you will not think much of it.—Your very affectionate

MAXIMILIAN.

In spite of fatigue and the long distance, the commander-in-chief proceeded as quickly as possible to Mexico, leaving to General Aymard (who acquitted himself with success) the task of extricating the foreign troops. The hurried departure of our head-quarters was immediately commented on, and the American papers vied with one another in repeating that the Austrians had been left to be massacred. Whilst the commander-in-chief was gallopping along on the road to Mexico, a second enclosure was handed him from Maximilian:—

Alcazar de Chapultepec, October 19, 1866.

My dear Marshal,—At the end of the present month I shall be expecting the empress on her return from her journey to Europe. Be kind enough, my dear marshal, to tell me if you have taken any measures for her escort, and in case this should not yet have been done, you will be good enough to look to the safety of the empress, *not losing sight of the state of insurrection in which the departments adjacent to the road now are.* I leave the safety of the empress in your hands with the greatest confidence, and thanking you for it beforehand, I am glad, my dear marshal, to assure you of my good will and sincere friendship.—Your very affectionate,

MAXIMILIAN.

The emperor was well aware that the Empress Charlotte could not yet be *en route,* even supposing that she had achieved a rapid success at the Vatican; for the accession of King Leopold had made it necessary for the Empress of Mexico to stay some time at Brussels. But the expressions in this letter had a double aim; first, not to reveal his projects to the rebels in case the letter should have fallen into their hands; and next, to get a cordon of troops placed along the line of road from Vera Cruz to Mexico, so as to ensure Maximilian's safety in his descent from the high plateaus. All the military arrangements pointed out were made as far as the *Terres Chaudes.* On the Sunday, the commander-in-chief went to the palace to meet the emperor. The grand chamberlain, who received the marshal, begged him from Maximilian to defer the intended interview until the next day, and to wait for fresh notice from his majesty. The sovereign's fickleness of mind was such that he did not yet dare to take any decisive course, and the important interests which he had declared to be so urgent seemed no longer in question.

On his return to Mexico, the marshal heard of the landing of General Castelnau; he also received the following urgent instructions, dated at Paris, September 12 :—' As matters get worse and worse every day, and as the capture of Tampico has disappointed us of the customs' receipts, Napoleon III. has decided to recall the troops *en masse,* and to push forward their complete evacuation in the approaching spring.' It was, however, thought necessary to retain the regiments which were just upon the point of sailing, and it was added :—' *Protect our flag against every insult, and assert, if necessary, the power and the preponderance of our arms.*'

An order worded in this way and communicated to our head-quarters could only have in view the possibility of insults on the part of the Juarists, or of the United States. Now, how can we understand this, when at this very time the French government, as the two following despatches prove, had already asked leave of the American cabinet to delay the evacuation of our army, and had been sounding through our diplomatists, both in Washington and Paris, *as to the restoration of a Mexican republic?*

Despatch from Mr. Seward to Mr. Bigelow on the subject of the French troops leaving Mexico, dated October 8, 1866.

Sir,—The question which you submit to me in your last despatch—namely, 'What our government would think of the recall of the whole body of the French troops in the course of next year, instead of their retiring in three detachments during the space of eighteen months?' has never been directly laid before me.

What I have to say on the subject is this: The arrangement proposed by the emperor for the recall of his troops in three divisions, the first of which would leave in November, was likely to be forgotten (in the midst of the political agitation which has accompanied every Mexican question), even before the execution of the above arrangement had commenced.

The frequent and varied incidents mentioned by the press both in France and Mexico, and represented as manifesting a disposition on the part of the emperor not to fulfil this engagement, have had the inevitable effect of *creating and spreading doubts even as to the sincerity of the emperor in entering into the engagement, and on his fidelity in carrying it out.*

Through this very fact, this department has continually found itself under the evident necessity of protesting against acts which were calculated to weaken the confidence of the people in hopes which were as just as they were well defined.

The government, however, most confidently hopes that the emperor's engagement will be fulfilled at least to the letter; and it has even expected that, going beyond the mere letter, this promise would be kept with a sincerity of intention which would have hastened, instead of retarding, the departure of the French forces from Mexico. But, at the present time, we have not yet seen even the beginning of the evacuation. *When this operation is completed, the government will willingly listen to any suggestions wherever they may come from, which tend to ensure the re-establishment of tranquillity, peace and a native constitutional government in Mexico.*

But, until we are permitted to verify the commencement of this evacuation, any attempt at negotiation would only have the result of misleading public opinion in the United States, and of rendering the position of things in Mexico still more complicated.

I scarcely need inform you that the surmises which have been made by a portion of the press on the subject of certain relations existing between this department and General Santa Anna, have no foundation in fact. W. H. SEWARD.

Despatch of Mr. Bigelow to Mr. Seward reporting his first interview with the Marquis de Moustier, the new Minister of Foreign Affairs, dated Paris, October 12, 1866.

Sir,—The Marquis de Moustier received the *corps diplomatique* for the first time yesterday.

He asked me if it was true, as the newspapers reported, that our official relations were soon to cease. He expressed his regret to learn that this was the case, and the desire which he should have felt to co-operate with me in cultivating very friendly relations between our two respective countries.

In reply to a question I put to him, he stated that the policy of his government towards the United States and Mexico would undergo no alteration through his accession to the ministry.

His excellency added that he was devoting all his leisure time to studying the different American questions with which he had not yet had an opportunity of becoming familiar, and that as soon as he was prepared, he should be glad to converse at greater length either with me or my successor. Nevertheless, he wished to inform me, and begged me to apprise you of the fact, that he had seen the emperor at Biarritz; that his majesty had expressed his desire and intention of withdrawing his troops from Mexico as soon as it could be done, and *without taking cognizance of the convention entered into with Maximilian.* His excellency added that, according to the last reports, the malcontents were gaining territory, but *that it was not the emperor's intention to undertake any fresh or distinct expeditions for the purpose of subduing them*; that there had been an idea of recapturing Tampico, but that nothing had transpired at Paris on the subject.

He said that the position of France was a delicate one, and that the emperor desired nothing so much as *to disembarrass himself of all his engagements with Mexico* as soon as he could do it with dignity and honour; and that, with our aid on which he reckoned, the time might be considerably hastened.

To this I merely replied in general terms, that I had no reason to doubt that the future relations between the United States and France would be marked by the same friendly considerations which had hitherto characterised them.

I did not ask what kind of aid from the United States he meant, presuming that he reckoned *on forbearance rather than on any active co-operation.*

I may also mention on this subject that I returned yesterday from Biarritz, where I was informed by M. Pereire, the proprietor of the Franco-Mexican line of packet-boats, that his agent had finally signed the contract with the minister of war for bringing home the whole French army during next March.*

He had received the day before, as I understood, the letter advising him of this fact. Some detachments of troops, he said, would be brought home this autumn, and all the rest before the end of March. I have reason to think that he had been requested to give me this information.

JOHN BIGELOW.

From these two documents it is easy to see, what was thought of French policy on the other side of the ocean. And it was nothing but justice. Whatever might be the cause, our head-quarters still remained in complete ignorance of these diplomatic manœuvres. As to General Castelnau's mission, its almost threatening character was not long in transpiring. The public feeling spread as far as Mexico, and M. Larès, the president of the council, undertook to express the general impression to our head-quarters authorities. The reply only reaffirmed the principle, which its powers and personal conviction fully confirmed, that

---

* The alteration in the first contract with this line of packets, which was made with an idea of withdrawing the troops in three divisions, was a great loss to the French treasury.

the expeditionary corps had but one duty, that of protecting the empire. At the same time, the marshal honestly pointed out to the Mexican cabinet the mistakes which had been made, and met the pretended complaints which were brought forward against the expeditionary corps.

Mexico, October 16, 1866.

Monsieur le Ministre de la Justice,—In reply to your excellency's letter of October 9, I have the honour to inform you that, in consequence of the arrival of General Castelnau, aide-de-camp to his majesty the Emperor Napoleon, who certainly is the bearer of instructions from my august sovereign which I have not yet seen, I am not in a position to inform you of the future disposition of the French troops. In the meantime they remain in their positions, continuing to render assistance wherever necessity arises, both to the authorities and to the people of the empire.

With regard to the national and auxiliary troops, your excellency, having been away from the government, is doubtless not aware that, since the arrangement of military divisions, these troops have been completely at the disposal of the Mexican generals commanding these divisions, and consequently under the orders of the government which directs their movements, either through the medium of the minister of war, or of the imperial commissioners.

Since this took place, my duty has been confined to giving advice which has scarcely ever been followed, or to lending the assistance of my troops in recovering the warlike stores, or repairing the fortifications in the most important places; in short, in helping as far as I possibly could in the reorganisation of the national army. This army comprises, at the present time, twenty-two battalions of infantry, including the Mexican *cazadores*, ten regiments of cavalry, four companies of *gendarmerie*, with artillery and engineers to correspond, the whole forming an effective force of 17,254 men.

By adding to this the 6,811 men of the Austro-Belgian legion, and the auxiliary or permanent guards who still exist, it amounts to a total of about 28,000 men. *On the 28th of last*

January, *this effective force reached* 43,520 *men.* The artillery and engineer services have been made over since last year to Mexican officers nominated by the minister of war, and the inventory which was then made out was placed in their possession.

Owing to the trouble taken by the Austrian staff, there exists at Puebla a powder-mill and a percussion-cap manufactory, as well as workshops for iron, wood, and leather, which would provide for all the wants of the national army; all these appliances are at the sole disposal of the minister of war.

The imperial government has, therefore, all these elements under its control, with regard to which, however, I have never exercised any direct action. It also has the artillery, which exists in the fortified places, and 46,000 muskets and other arms, which have been distributed during the last three years to the Mexican army and to the population generally. A commander-in-chief's duty, as it is usually understood, is not to interfere with the discipline, advancement, and administration of the troops, but only to put them in operation, so that there may be unity of action.

I am sorry to have to say that this has not been the case, notwithstanding my reiterated observations; the generals commanding have more frequently acted according to their own caprice, or in consequence of orders proceeding directly from the minister of war.

Nothing prevents this course being continued, and the question as to the national troops being placed at the disposition of the government, is already solved as you wish it.

But it is necessary that generals nominated to divisional commands should proceed to their posts, as, for example, Generals Chacon and Severo Castillo, the one to the 8th, and the other to the 9th, military division.

Your excellency labours under another error, due doubtless to your absence from state business, which, however, I hasten to rectify. It is that you attribute the evacuation of the towns to the French troops. *The latter did not evacuate them, but gave them over to the Mexican troops, who, for some cause or other, have not defended them; this is the truth*, and it is right for your excellency to know it.

No other causes than the real ones need be sought for to account for the late events; these causes are well known to his majesty, as our reports have thoroughly described them to him.

Your excellency, too, ought to know them, but I will abstain from again enumerating them. In short, the imperial government can dispose, as it has before done, of all the elements of the national army; but it is only honest in me to say that, if the recruiting and the administration are not better managed than in times past, and if, on the other hand, there is not more energy, fidelity, and devotion shown on the part of the said troops, *the imperial government will act wisely in not relying with any certainty upon its help.*

THE MARSHAL OF FRANCE, BAZAINE.

The liberal camp of Porfirio Diaz was better informed than our head-quarters authorities as to the proceedings of our government. Just at the time when the envoy of Napoleon was ascending the high plateaus, the republican newspaper thus expressed itself: —' The packet from St. Nazaire has just brought over General Castelnau and the Marquis of Galliffet, both of them aides-de-camp of Napoleon III. . . .'
'. . . Castelnau makes no mystery of his important mission; he says that he has brought the order to make Maximilian abdicate. It is asserted that, after the fall of the Austrian prince, a convention will make its appearance, which has been concluded beforehand between the cabinets of Washington and the Tuileries as to the French debt. It will be understood that Maximilian's abdication is inevitable, either voluntary or forced; the proceedings of France are well comprehended; and the sun of the new year will see the triumphant arms of the republic glittering all over the Mexican territory.'

Our troops continued to concentrate on the centre of the country. After the last orders were received from Paris their retrograde movement was about to be hastened, and our head-quarters authorities brought these military arrangements to the knowledge of Maximilian, leaving to Napoleon's envoy the task of dealing with the political side of the mission, with which he alone was charged, and of which he alone knew the full import. What a complicated drama was this, the exciting scenes of which were now being acted at Paris, Rome, Washington, and Mexico! The whole weight of it fell upon two persons,—Maximilian and the Marshal. The Emperor of Mexico began to feel his energies giving way, but ere he gave up the contest he issued this final protest against the actions of our policy.

Mexico, October 18, 1866.

My dear Marshal,—I have learnt with the deepest regret from your esteemed letter of yesterday's date, that we are threatened with the immediate abandonment of Matehuala, which is a strategetical point of great importance as regards the rebels.

I have at once given orders that the necessary funds should be provided to pay the troops in full. I am firmly persuaded that one vigorous attack would be sufficient to put to flight the undisciplined forces of the rebels; whilst, if the Franco-Mexican forces retire, not only will the number of the enemy be increased, but the communications between Tamaulipas and San Luis will be cut off, and we shall be deprived of the resources of this territory. It will also be the means of giving to the rebellion a fictitious importance, to which, up to the present time, it has never attained.

You well know, my dear marshal, that the *government cannot in so short a time combine a sufficient force, which by itself would be able to face the enemy*, and consequently the proposition of relying on our local resources is only an illusion. I hope, my dear marshal, that in accordance with article 4 of the treaty of Miramar, in virtue of which you dispose of the whole forces of the empire, you will have the kindness to take the measures necessary to prevent a military and political disaster more considerable than all we have before experienced.—Your very affectionate, MAXIMILIAN.

Maximilian still dreamt of appealing to the treaty of Miramar, which had been revoked three months before, when, too, the Emperor Napoleon had declared to Mr. Bigelow, that he would undertake no further expeditions to subdue the rebels.

CHAPTER XV.

Maximilian prepares for Departure—Last Moments at Chapultepec—Arrival of sad News—The Health of the Empress Charlotte—Maximilian resolves to leave—Cowardly Conduct of the Ministers—Marshal Bazaine's Firmness—Maximilian leaves the Capital—His Three last Wishes—His Journey—Peculiarities in Maximilian's Character.

NOTICE was given that the new French Embassy was two days' march from the capital. The emperor, resolved to avoid it, hastened his preparations to go down to meet the Empress Charlotte as he had announced to his ministers. But the report had already spread, that the baggage of his household and his retinue had been sent forward to the port of Vera Cruz; and it was well known that the three squadrons of Austrian hussars, which had been recalled to Mexico on the pretext of resting after their fatigues, had already received the order to be ready to mount.

The news of the probable departure of the sovereign produced a great sensation among the inhabitants of Mexico.

History shuts out romance; yet the historian cannot without emotion recount the scene of sorrow which was presented by the last moments which were spent by the emperor in the palace of Chapultepec.

The hour for departure approached; the sovereign, worn out by fever and vanquished by events, thought over all his broken hopes, and longed for his fatherland. Full many a time had he regretted it when his heart had thrilled to the distant war-echoes of Sadowa and Lissa! A telegraphic despatch, forwarded from the United States, was handed to him; it announced that the reason of the Empress Charlotte had received a shock. There are intensities of anguish, there are struggles of despair and rebellions against fate felt by a broken heart, which the pen is unable to describe.

The whole town, in which the empress was adored, was disconsolate. Maximilian gave the order to depart that night, and, on the morning of October 20, announced to the marshal that he was leaving Mexico:—

> Alcazar de Chapultepec, October 20, 1866.
>
> My dear Marshal,—I have been deeply touched by the expressions of consolation and sorrow that you have just sent me in your own name and that of your wife. I wish to express to you my deepest gratitude. The terrible blow caused by the late news, which has so grievously wounded my heart, and the bad state of my health caused by the intermittent fever which I have suffered from so long, now of course much increased, have necessitated (under the express order of my physician) a temporary sojourn in a softer climate.
>
> In order to meet the express courier who is coming to me from Miramar, whose intelligence I am expecting with an anxiety easy to be understood, I intend to leave for Orizaba.
>
> To your good judgment I confide, with the greatest confidence, the maintenance of tranquillity in the capital and in the most important places which are at the present time occupied by the troops under your command.
>
> In these painful and difficult circumstances I rely more than ever on the *loyalty and friendship* that you have always shown me.
>
> I shall travel according to the annexed itinerary, and I shall take with me the three squadrons of hussars of the Austrian volunteers, and all the disposable men of the *gendarmerie*.
>
> This letter will be handed you by M. Herzfeld, a councillor of state, and my former fellow traveller at sea, whom I place at your disposal to give you every elucidation.
>
> I repeat to you as well as to Madame Bazaine my warm

gratitude for the kind expressions of feeling which have done so much good to my poor heart.

Receive, my dear marshal, the assurance of my sincere friendship. MAXIMILIAN.

At this critical moment, when devotion might become dangerous, M. Larès presented himself at the palace, and declared, in the name of his colleagues, that all the ministers would retire if the emperor quitted Mexico. M. Herzfeld immediately informed the commander-in-chief of this.

Mexico, October 20, 1866.

Excellency,—M. Larès has just tendered the resignation of all the ministry, and has stated that, as soon as the emperor leaves the capital, *there will no longer be any government.* As his majesty is in a state of extreme weakness, and insists upon leaving, it is necessary that some measures should be taken. I beg that your excellency will be pleased to consult with the emperor again this evening.—I am, &c., HERZFELD.

On being informed of this significant incident, Marshal Bazaine wrote immediately to the president of the council, that the ministers must be wanting both in loyalty and generosity if they abandoned the emperor in an hour like this, after having sought for all his confidence; and that he (Marshal Bazaine) should feel compelled to adopt certain measures towards the ministers if they persevered in their resolution.

If it had not been for this energetic and necessary firmness, the whole government of the country would have suddenly fallen on the French commander at a time when the exact information received at our headquarters proved that all parties were on the point of rising *en masse* against the foreigners, and to massacre the small bodies of French which were still scattered over the territory, as if in another night of 'Sicilian Vespers.' In the evening, M. Herzfeld, by Maxi-

milian's wish, came to Buena-Vista to ask advice from the marshal. In the meantime the now frightened ministers replied, that they were only too happy to continue to discharge their accustomed duties. The marshal, to whom Maximilian's envoy had confidentially broached the definite intention of his sovereign, who had now decided on abdication, replied that his majesty might leave and travel in perfect safety, and that he would take everything upon himself. The commander-in-chief thought, in fact, that the chances for the monarchy could now only get less and less, and he had not the heart to detain Maximilian, whom he left free to follow the suggestion of his own ideas. Delay, however, was especially necessary to allow the small French detachments, many of which were at this time six hundred leagues from Mexico, to get together and close in upon the main body. A sudden abdication would let loose the insurrection over the whole country: to obviate this, it was needful that Maximilian should feign a merely temporary absence, which would permit him to institute a regency which might lead the country on gently to another form of government. An abdication dated from Europe would be the only thing to prevent a great shock and to insure the safety of our army. This was the plan to which the marshal sought to incite Maximilian. At seven o'clock in the evening the prince was impatiently waiting in his palace the reply from head-quarters. At the moment it was handed to him, he was pacing up and down in a state of great agitation. After he had read it, he appeared somewhat relieved. The last words which he spoke before he left Chapultepec revealed all his thoughts:—
'I can no longer doubt it; my wife is mad. These people are killing me by inches. I am thoroughly worn out. I am going away. Thank the marshal for

this fresh proof of devotion to me. I am leaving to-night, and if he wishes to write to me, here is the itinerary of my journey.'

At two o'clock in the morning of October 21, three carriages, escorted by three squadrons of Austrian hussars, rolled along the road of La Piedad. Father Fischer, the minister Arroyo, Colonel de Kodolich, and Dr. Bash accompanied the emperor to Orizaba, where a public and definitive resolution (already anticipated in opinion) was to be adopted by the sovereign. That evening Maximilian, who had come to sleep at the *hacienda* of Zoquiapa, wrote a confidential letter, which an Austrian officer carried at night to the French head-quarters. This letter was only the corollary to the interview between the marshal and M. Herzfeld.

Hacienda de Zoquiapa, October 21, 1866 (evening).

My dear Marshal,—To-morrow I propose to place in your hands the documents necessary to put an end to the onerous and perplexing position in which my person as well as the whole of Mexico is now placed. *These documents must be kept in reserve until the day which I shall intimate to you by telegraph.*

Three points weigh upon my mind, and I desire at once to throw off the responsibility incumbent on me in respect to them.

The first: That the courts-martial cease to interfere in political delinquencies.

The second: That the law of October 3 be revoked *de facto*.

The third: That there should be no political persecutions on any ground whatever, and that all kinds of hostilities should cease.

I wish you to summon the ministers, Larès, Marin, and Tavera, in order to agree on measures to secure these three points, *without allowing the intentions which I have expressed in the first paragraph to transpire ever so little.*

I doubt not *that you will add this fresh proof of your true friendship to all those which you have before given me*, and I express beforehand my feelings of gratitude, at the same time renewing the assurance of respect and friendship with which I am your very affectionate, MAXIMILIAN.

Maximilian, as we see, urgently requested that his project of abdication should not transpire, even to his own council; in the second place, he begged the marshal to assemble the ministers to communicate his orders to them—orders all the more important as the law of October 3 was therein revoked. When he was just on the point of leaving the country, he did not wish that blood should be uselessly shed. The very next day, on the morning of October 22, the commander-in-chief (although the French government had charged him not to interfere in political matters), impelled by his devotion to the Emperor Maximilian, hastened to summon and assemble MM. Larès, Marin, minister of the interior, and Tavera, minister of war. He officially notified to them the will of their sovereign, and gave the order to put it into execution. It must be added that the ministers Larès and Marin professed themselves to be disinclined to accede to the generous ideas of Maximilian. The marshal replied to the emperor, informing him of the execution of his orders, but stating that hostilities could not be put a stop to at points where the rebels and parties who had not recognised the empire were attacking the French troops. In fact, the commander-in-chief had not the power of signing an armistice with the liberals. He had no right to modify, by his private authority, the military programme of the expeditionary corps, whose only duty was to save the empire. The general evacuation, however, still followed its course, and the number of places occupied by our troops lessened every day.

Maximilian appears to have changed his mind on this occasion too; for he never sent to the marshal either the important documents or the telegraphic despatch alluded to in his confidential letter of October 21. An incident, which should be related, marked the commencement of the young sovereign's journey. The halting-stages of the imperial *cortège* had been purposely arranged, so that General Castelnau should be unable to fall in with Maximilian. Nevertheless, the two travellers met for an instant in the village of Ayotla at breakfast-time; and although the envoy of Napoleon III. sought admittance to the young emperor, he had to leave without having obtained an audience.

The emperor's journey proceeded rapidly without his being annoyed by the guerillas, who, if they had not been held in check by the display of our troops, had intended to seize his person. An important movement of Juarist contingents had taken place on the coast of Oajaca, which Porfirio Diaz was menacing. During the whole journey, Maximilian only stayed at the houses of the Mexican clergy. On October 24, he slept at the priest's house at Acacingo. The road between this large village and La Canada is furrowed out by the rains of winter, and in the dry weather is smothered with dust. The country is rough, and covered with woods, in which redoubled watchfulness against attack was requisite. On one occasion the attendants of the sovereign were put in dread.

On the road ahead of them, a whirlwind of dust was stirred up under the tread of a party of red-clad horsemen. It turned out to be a squadron of the French *contre-guerilla*, who had come to flank his majesty's road. Maximilian made a few enquiries as to the positions which the *contre-guerillas* occupied in the *Terres Chaudes*, and then relapsed into the obstinate silence which he had maintained since his departure from Chapultepec. On alighting at La Canada, he demanded hospitality at the half-ruined priest's house in the little town. The night passed away sadly enough, spent in a cold room, and the next morning, about seven o'clock, the *cortège* moved in the direction of Orizaba. A thick fog spread over the narrow defiles of the Cumbres, and at a little distance obscured the valley below. During the whole journey Maximilian was distressed by fever; he left his carriage to descend on foot the zig-zag road leading down from the great mountain range which hangs over the *Terres Chaudes*. Wrapped in a long grey garment, and with a light-coloured, narrow-brimmed *sombrero* on his head, the emperor walked rapidly with his head bent down, followed by his faithful companion the German, Dr. Bash. Sometimes at a turn of the road he would stop to wait for his escort, and to cast a last look at a prospect which he thought he should never see again. About eleven o'clock the *curé* of Aculcingo, a miserable hamlet situated at the foot of the Cumbres, offered a slender repast to Maximilian. When they wished to start again, they found out that the eight white mules which drew the royal carriage were stolen; and they had to wait two long hours before they could find animals to replace them. The sun was already disappearing below the horizon ere they arrived at the lovely village of Ingenio, almost hidden in foliage. There, on the road, a numerous crowd of horsemen, pedestrians, and *curés* on horseback, followed by Indians and the inhabitants of Orizaba, were waiting to welcome the emperor with their acclamations, and to escort him to the city, which was still a mile and a quarter distant. When they came in sight of the towers of Orizaba, Colonel de Kodolich ordered the French cavalry to slacken their march, as his majesty desired to pass unattended through the streets in which he knew the inhabitants were waiting for him.

One of Maximilian's most decided tendencies, which distinctly manifested itself during his whole reign, was his desire to show himself to his people as seldom as possible when he was surrounded by the French, for whom he in general felt a deep antipathy. M. Dubois, a talented critic, who published in the *Temps* a conscientious review of the ' *Souvenirs de Voyages,*' a work written by the archduke in his early youth, certifies to the constant expression of feelings unfavourable to France. He, indeed, concludes by avowing that his study of the prince's character has tended to lessen in his eyes this descendant of Charles the Fifth. ' It must be admitted,' adds this writer, ' that when Maximilian accepted the Mexican crown, others drew the sword for him; and he does not seem to have been very fond of his allies. His writings show, in fact, that he was full of prejudice against France and the French. The Emperor Napoleon is almost the sole exception to this dislike, which is so forcibly contrasted with the prince's infatuation for the Spaniards. In 1852, some months after " December 2," before the proclamation of the empire, the future emperor of Mexico recognised in the future emperor of the French " the powerful mind of the statesman who rules his age." There is no doubt that this impression existed; and that, at the decisive moment, it justified the prince's confidence in himself and his star, to which he was always quite disposed. But we must again repeat that, in general, the prince refuses us his sympathies; we are neither sufficiently catholic, nor sufficiently romantic for him. Perhaps, too, the prejudices which he manifests proceed from that deep and secret resentment against France, over which political necessities may sometimes cast a veil, which however, for both good and bad reasons, is bound to be hereditary in the house of Hapsburg. However this may be, the prince does not even like our language, and he congratulated the Emperor Francis Joseph on having, as much as possible, banished it from his court; he does not like our fashions, and he congratulated the Spanish on not having adopted them; but the features in us which he most of all detests, are our ideas and our character.'

Many of the questions which arose between Maximilian and Marshal Bazaine might have been discussed in a more conciliatory way by friendly conversation than by correspondence; but Maximilian often requested the marshal to come but seldom to the palace at Mexico, as the visits of the French commander-in-chief to the sovereign might (so the emperor fancied) be unfavourably interpreted by the Mexicans. When he was residing at the more secluded palace of Chapultepec, he expressed the contrary wish. This very same rule of conduct is met with in the last letters from Maximilian to his minister of war, dated from the town of Queretaro: he expresses in them all his impatience of the French yoke, and his joy at the cessation of the intervention, to which, nevertheless, he owed his throne. This peculiarity, adopted at the very outset of his reign, was certainly wanting in logic.

CHAPTER XVI.

Maximilian's Entry into Orizaba—His enthusiastic Reception—Retires into Seclusion—Intrigues of Father Fischer and the Clerical Party—Disaster to the Austrian Contingent—Fall of Oajaca, and increasing Liberal Successes—Maximilian still undecided—His kind Thought for the Austro-Belgian Contingent — M. Eloïn's Letter—Decides Maximilian to renew the Contest.

MAXIMILIAN now made his entry into the city of Orizaba, which received him with enthusiasm: he passed through lines of French infantry and National Guards drawn up in the streets, accompanied by the sound of fireworks and ringing of bells. He soon retired into the house belonging to the rich family of Bringas. The reception rooms of Bringas—the most notorious smuggler in Mexico—were the well known *rendezvous* of all the enemies of the intervention: quite recently, several secret cabals had been held there under the presidency of General Uruga, who was then in the town on his way to embark at the port of Vera Cruz. During his short stay (of a week) in Orizaba, the young emperor only showed himself in public when he visited the bath-rooms. As soon as the courier from Europe brought him the heart-rending details of the empress's state of health, he retired to the *Hacienda la Jalapilla*, adjacent to the town, and almost lost amongst the sugar-cane and groves of coffee trees. He still hesitated to abdicate. Father Fischer, taking advantage of his influence over the young emperor, decoyed him into this secluded spot, under the pretext that both his body and mind had need of complete repose. The intrigues of the reactionary party, who felt sure enough that the ruin of the clergy and its decisive spoliation would immediately follow the fall of the monarchy, kept back from the sovereign both the importance and the rapidity of the liberal successes. The visits of the agents of the clerical party, whose only aim was to detain Maximilian on Mexican soil to fight for their party alone, needed both concealment and mystery; and in this *hacienda* they could follow each other without interruption.

Nevertheless, a portion of the imperial luggage had been already embarked on board the Austrian frigate 'Dandolo' anchored in the port of Vera Cruz; and the German attendants of the prince, though they saw with bitter regret the fall of the throne to which they had attached their fortunes, could not but acknowledge that the game was lost. In fact, the news of a serious disaster which had befallen the Austrian troops on October 18, had just reached Orizaba. A column, about fifteen hundred strong, which was on its way to help the Mexican general Oronoz and the *cazadores* blockaded by Porfirio Diaz in the city of Oajaca, had been attacked by the Juarist bands on the heights of Carbonera, and were completely routed with great losses both in men and munitions of war. Domestic matters also seemed to get worse as the time arrived for bringing in force the convention of July 30, and of handing over to the French commissioners the moiety of the daily receipts in the Port of Vera Cruz. All resources seemed to be vanishing at once. Nevertheless the marshal was obliged to put his finger on this sore place.

Mexico, October 25, 1866.

Sire,—The time draws near for putting the convention in force which has been entered into between your majesty's government and that of France. M. Dano, not having received any reply to the notification which he gave on this subject, has informed me of his intention to refer it to me in order that it may be carried out.

I have the honour of bringing the above statement under your majesty's notice, and to beg you to be pleased to give your orders for the fulfilment of the said convention.

Your majesty is certainly aware of the disaster which has befallen the column which was going to assist Oajaca. I shall have the honour of acquainting you with the details as soon as I am in possession of the official documents.

General Douay is at this moment on the other side of Matehuala, pursuing a pretty considerable body of cavalry.

With the most profound respect, Sire, &c.,

BAZAINE.

Some days after, the city of Oajaca, the garrison of which were compelled to lay down their arms, capitulated and opened its gates to the victorious Porfirio Diaz, notwithstanding the heroic defence of the chief of the *cazadores*, the brave commandant Tétard, who was killed during the siege. This double feat of arms accomplished by the liberal troops made a great noise in Mexico. In the *Terres Chaudes*, the guerilla chiefs getting bolder commenced to threaten the environs of Médellin, Tehuacan, and Pérote. At this crisis, Maximilian, surrounded by the clerical party, could not yet make up his mind to take any decided course, so great was the vacillation of his character and the extent of his reluctance. It cost him much to resign this crown, which he had been dreaming about since his infancy. One is struck with the precocious ambition which is breathed in his *Souvenirs de Voyage*, written after he had contemplated in the church at Grenada the royal insignia of Ferdinand the Catholic. 'I handled,' said Maximilian, 'the golden circlet and the sword once so powerful, with mingled feelings of pride, longing, and melancholy. What a glorious, brilliant dream would it be for the nephew of Hapsburg of Austria, to draw the sword of Ferdinand to reconquer his crown!'

These few words help to explain the painful uncertainty, and the deep anguish to which Maximilian's ambition was a prey, during his stay at the *Hacienda la Jalapilla*.

The following letter was written when he was under the impression produced by the disaster suffered by the Austrians, whose valour had been so unfortunate: in it, too, he generously forgets his causes of complaint against the Belgians. It sufficiently testifies that even now, when he had determined in his mind on abdication, he was still desirous of making a last attempt before he finally let drop the sceptre which was costing his heart and his pride so much pain.

Orizaba, October 31, 1866.

My dear Marshal,—In the difficult circumstances in which I am placed, which also, *if the negotiations I have just entered upon do not produce a happy result*, will force me to resign the powers with which the nation has entrusted me, the matter I first lay to heart is to settle the destiny of the Austrian and Belgian volunteers, and to guarantee the full accomplishment of the conditions entered into with these corps.

For this purpose, I send to you my aide-de-camp, Colonel de Kodolich, to whom I have given the command of the Austrian volunteers, and have provided with full powers for settling this question, which interests me more than any other.

This officer enjoys my entire confidence, and when I place in your hands—that is, in the hands of France, so susceptible to a feeling of devotion—the lot of these brave and faithful men, I feel that I may expect with entire security the satisfactory issue of this matter.

Receive, my dear marshal, the assurance of my feelings of sincere friendship, with which I am your very affectionate,

MAXIMILIAN.

At the time when Maximilian sent Colonel de Kodolich to our head-quarters at Mexico, he was thoroughly acquainted with the aim of General Castelnau's embassy. Napoleon's envoy had come to see with his own eyes, by investigating facts and ascertaining the state of public opinion, if the monarchy was able to stand its ground alone. Under the contrary alternative, which the cabinet of the Tuileries knew beforehand was the right one, he was to instigate the immediate abdication of the emperor; and in case of the refusal of the young sovereign to return to Europe, he was ordered to announce the recall of the whole expeditionary force *en bloc* and at once. These instructions given by his ally Napoleon III.—the *full* purport of which Maximilian was still ignorant of—were not of a nature to encourage him to throw himself again into the *mêlée*; and, besides, he no longer retained any illusion as to the elastic powers of the Mexican element in the country. His mind was fluctuating between, on the one hand, a humiliating return to Austria after a public rebuff which might compromise his political future, and, on the other, a well-founded dread of attempting an impossible task joined to a justifiable wish of rejoining his wife, the victim of her devotion to his evil fortunes.

Now intervenes a painful event with which but few are acquainted, which greatly influenced the destinies of the unfortunate prince, and was, in fact, the means of bringing him to the fatal ditch at Queretaro. Maximilian had been foiled in his negotiations with the liberal chiefs and with the United States, which he had for a second time blindly attempted. The state of health of the Princess Charlotte, which was almost despaired of, seemed to draw him more than ever to the château of Miramar. He was now preparing to set sail for Europe without intention of return, when a letter from M. Eloïn, the Belgian councillor, was handed to him. It was dated from Brussels, but had been submitted, in its passage through the United States, to the dark closet at Washington.

Brussels, September 17, 1866.

Sire,—The article in the *Moniteur*, disavowing the appointments of the French generals, Osmont and Friant, to the ministries of war and finance in the Mexican government, proves that, for the future, the mask is unreservedly thrown off. The mission of General Castelnau, aide-de-camp and confidant of the emperor, secret as it is, can have no other aim, in my opinion, but to bring on a conclusion as soon as possible. With a view of explaining away its conduct (which history will judge of), the French government would prefer that an abdication should precede the withdrawal of its army, and that thus the possibility should be offered them of *alone* reorganising a new state of things calculated to ensure its own interests and those of its countrymen. I am fully persuaded that your majesty will not be induced to afford this satisfaction to a policy which will, sooner or later, have to answer for its actions, and the consequences which have resulted therefrom.

The language of Mr. Seward, his 'toast' to Romero, the attitude of the president (the result of —— of the French cabinet), are grave facts which are calculated to increase difficulties and to discourage the bravest. I am persuaded, however, that the abandonment of your party before the return of the French army would be interpreted as an act of weakness; and, as your majesty holds your right of authority under a popular vote, a fresh appeal should be made to the Mexican people, *when relieved from the pressure of a foreign intervention*; and it is to them that a demand should be made for the material and financial assistance requisite for the maintenance and growth of the empire.

If this appeal is not listened to, your majesty, having then completely brought to a close your noble mission, will return to Europe with the same *prestige* which accompanied your departure; and, *in the midst of the events which are sure to spring up, you will be able to play the part which so eminently belongs to you.*

Having left Miramar on the 4th of this month with the resolution of embarking at Saint Nazaire, I was induced, after receiving the orders of her majesty the empress, to again put off my departure. It needed this august influence to change a determination which my devotion as well as my duty dictated to me.

I have been bitterly disappointed at learning that my numerous despatches of June and July did not reach your majesty in good time. They were placed under cover to our devoted friend Bombelle, and accompanied by long letters addressed to him, and intended to be communicated to your majesty; but I had not anticipated your departure from Mexico. They have now lost all the interest which they derived from the unforeseen events which were then so rapidly occurring. I especially regret this annoying incident, if it can have for a moment awakened doubts in your majesty's mind as to my unfailing desire to faithfully perform my duty.

When I was travelling through Austria, I was enabled to ascertain the general discontent which is prevailing there. Nothing is yet done. The emperor is *disheartened*; the people are becoming impatient, and publicly demand his abdication. A sympathy for your majesty is visibly spreading over all the territory of the empire. In Venetia, there is a party ready to welcome their former governor; but when a government arranges elections under the *régime* of universal suffrage it is easy to foresee the result.

According to your majesty's last orders, I forward by this courier a telegram in cipher to Roccas, to advise your majesty of the arrival of General Castelnau and of the disavowal of the appointments of MM. Osmont and Friant. ELOÏN.

Can it be believed that a royal councillor would have ventured to use language like this, if he had not been authorised by the secret wishes and confidence of his sovereign? Maximilian, then, was still dreaming of fresh adventures, and his ambitious glance was turned away from the crown of Mexico only to be thrown back again upon those of Austria and Venetia, the latter now become an Italian province: perhaps, in imitation of his ancestor Charles V., whom he used to call the 'Poet Emperor,' and whom he thought to imitate, he had seen in his visions of the future the two sceptres merged in his own hand. At every step that we take through the mazes of this lamentable story (the result, as it is, of a double-faced policy), intrigues and conspiracies are continually obstructing our path.

Looking at all these underhand plots, to which Sadowa had given fresh life, we cannot be astonished that the Austrian court had taken offence, and forwarded to the Baron de Lago, its ambassador at Mexico, a despatch, which forbade the archduke to set foot on Austrian soil if he returned to Europe bearing the title of emperor.

After he had thought over M. Eloïn's letter, Maximilian, forgetting all the perils before him, and obeying only the voice of a mad ambition, again seized the reins of power; and having resolved to surrender himself into the hands of the clerical party, who promised him both men and money, he prepared to make an appeal to the Mexican people.

CHAPTER XVII.

General Castelnau proceeds to the Capital—Marshal Bazaine's ambiguous Position—His Difficulties and Error—Dark Views of the French Cabinet—Agitated State of the Country and City of Mexico—Mexican Ingratitude—French Intrigues with Ortega—Attitude of the United States—Campbell and Sherman's Mission to Mexico—Mr. Seward's Instructions to the Envoys—They arrive at Tampico.

AFTER General Castelnau had fallen in with the Emperor Maximilian in the village of Ayotla, and had failed in obtaining an interview with the sovereign, he went on to Mexico, where he arrived October 21, 1866.

Dating from this epoch, so important to the destinies of Mexico, Marshal Bazaine's moral responsibility totally ceased. Public opinion was purposely misled when it has been attempted to throw upon the commander-in-chief the onus of any one resolution which was taken, or of any one act which was committed in this distant country after the arrival of Napoleon III.'s aide-de-camp. And, in fact, the instructions from the Tuileries, dated September 12, 1866, enjoined our head-quarters authorities neither to determine on nor execute any measure, either political or military, amidst the important events which were presenting themselves, without previously submitting everything to the assent of General Castelnau, assisted by M. Dano, the French minister, whose authority, hitherto almost effaced, now acquired fresh force.

The marshal consequently was now nothing more than a military commander, entirely subordinated to the full discretionary powers of Napoleon's envoy; placed, in fact, under the control of a mere general of brigade, invested by his sovereign with an unlimited confidence, which looked forward to every eventuality. Certainly, the commander-in-chief continued to speak and act in his own name; but the liberty of action which he appeared to preserve was only deceptive, for his power of taking the initiative disappeared at the moment of action. Only when a thing was once accomplished he was compulsorily saddled with the responsibility, since General Castelnau was only the secret prime-mover, whilst he was the visible agent. Well! we do not hesitate to say that, from the day when the policy of the French government showed itself to be ambiguous, when the official instructions came into collision with the semi-official, when policy became only a system of mental reservations; when, in short, the full confidence of the Emperor of the French was transferred from the commander-in-chief to the imperial aide-de-camp, Marshal Bazaine was led into a great and continuous error for which he pays the penalty; for he made himself responsible, before the tribunal of France and Europe, for acts which he did not originate, but to which, by his military obedience, he made himself a party. In our opinion, as regards the commander-in-chief, who was naturally loath to overturn the throne which for four years he had been helping to raise, the day had now come for him to sheathe his sword.

A protest like this would have been a great lesson: we can, however, well understand, that at this crisis a feeling of duty got the upper hand in the commander-in-chief's mind. The French army was still scattered far and wide. A retreat to be carried out over eighteen hundred leagues of territory, every stage of which he had himself worked out, needed all the experience of a man thoroughly acquainted with the country, its resources, and its hostility, if success was to be attained. Our government besides had appealed to the self-devotion of the marshal, to preserve the French flag from any insult before it left the Mexican soil. Now, if the monarchy was suddenly hurled down, it was to be expected that the two great parties in the nation would both rise against us. In the absence of the two generals of division, Douay and de Castagny, who were both away from Mexico, and necessarily engaged in the concentration of their troops, to whom could the chief command be safely entrusted? General Castelnau, being only just landed, and ignorant both of the people and country, being also inferior in rank to the above generals, was unable, in spite of his high authority as an imperial envoy, to take to the command of the expeditionary corps. The marshal, impelled by his cares for the future, and his attachment to the army, resolved, in spite of his thus being thrown into the shade, to follow out the work he had undertaken. Thus only can we explain the motives for the marshal's conduct.

One of the reasons which had decided Maximilian not to receive Napoleon's aide-de-camp at Ayotla (the aim of whose mission had already transpired), was the fact that General Castelnau was not accredited to the young sovereign, but only to our head-quarters, to whom he was sent to give the impulse desired and foreseen at the Tuileries, according to the various turns which events might take.

According to the first instructions given by the French cabinet, the programme was a very plain one, —Maximilian's abdication. The precautions taken by our government in withdrawing all assistance to the

Imperial cause, had already prepared for this project, and made them hope for its success. If it had succeeded it is certain that it would have prevented that long agony, the consummation of which stained Queretaro with blood. 'If Maximilian abdicates,' the order ran from Paris, 'a congress is to be assembled. The ambition of the various disaffected chiefs, who are holding the country, is to be excited, and the presidency of the republic is to be conferred on that one amongst them (Juarez alone excepted), who will consent to grant the most weighty advantages to the intervention.' General Castelnau therefore, in spite of the bad reception which the young emperor had given him, must have rejoiced at the turn which things had already taken by Maximilian's own will, and by his spontaneously leaving the territory. For the difficulties of his mission were thus singularly diminished. The approaching downfall of the throne gave liberty to any combination of government and to the prompt withdrawal of the expeditionary corps, which nothing need detain when the interests of our countrymen were once guaranteed. Now it had been thought in Paris, that the best means of obtaining this guarantee—means which seemed recommended by the long contest and successes of the Liberals—was to aid in the restoration of the presidential chair, in attempting to overthrow which we had uselessly expended so much money and so many lives.

The French authorities were, therefore, waiting with keen impatience for the decisive news of Maximilian's embarkation. This event seemed the more desirable, as the country was a prey to a deep-seated agitation which might break out at any moment. The Mexican government, although the ministers still remained passively at their posts, existed only in name, and there was great danger in allowing a crisis to be prolonged which might develope into an insurrection of all the factions combined together against the foreigners. These symptoms, which were manifest even in the ministers themselves at the time when Maximilian, still undecided, had left Orizaba to retire to the *Hacienda la Jalapilla*, had assumed so menacing a character in the capital, that our head-quarters authorities were compelled to adopt measures of precaution: this is proved by the marshal's letter to the French general in command in the city.

Mexico, November 2, 1866.

My dear General,—I am informed of disturbances having taken place yesterday evening at the foreign theatre established on the *Place d'Armes*. I have written to his excellency the president of the council to request him to have this establishment closed to-day.

If the Mexican government should not think right to close the said theatre, as his majesty the Emperor Napoleon has been publicly insulted in it, and as his name has been received there with hootings and cries of hatred and contempt, you will be pleased to give orders to Captain Oudinot and to the gendarmerie that, in virtue of the state of war now existing, this theatre should be closed this evening.

You will adopt the necessary measures that the public peace should not be disturbed, and that anyone making a tumult should be immediately arrested.

BAZAINE,
Marshal commanding-in-chief.

Already were they thus insulting the sovereign of France: the Italians, after the battle of Villafranca, recompensed us with similar gratitude.

The cabinet of the Tuileries felt so certain of the approaching downfall of the Mexican throne, that, without loss of time, they had secretly called upon their diplomatists to enter into correspondence with Ortega, the former defender of Puebla, who had escaped from our hands in 1863 (thereby breaking his parole), and had since waged an implacable war against us,—a war dictated by personal ambition alone. This general had seemed to be the most formidable competitor that we could oppose to Juarez, both from the influence he wielded, and from the legal right he had to succeed to the former president, whose powers, according to the republican constitution, would have already expired had there been a state of peace.

This was not the way the United States looked at the matter. Until the country was tranquillised, they had neither recognised, nor intended to recognise, any one but the old Indian as the real chief of the nation. As soon as the Washington cabinet was advised of the mission of General Castelnau, it planned the mission of Mr. Campbell and General Sherman. This embassy was originated by President Johnson, who fancied that he should strengthen his somewhat compromised position by certain acts of foreign policy calculated to flatter the American pride: it was intended to rally round Juarez the principal republican chiefs, and to put a stop to the efforts of Ortega. The really important man in this mission was General Sherman—a high-minded and conciliatory man. Campbell only played a secondary part. A secretary of legation was associated with them, who had lived a long time in Mexico: he was a man of ardent temperament and rather disposed to strong measures. By quoting the instructions given by the White House to these two principal personages, we shall understand the attitude which the American government were then taking both towards Mexico and towards France.

Instructions from Mr. Seward to Mr. Campbell.

Washington, October 22, 1866.

Sir,—You are aware that a friendly and explicit arrangement exists between our government and the Emperor of the

French, by which the latter has engaged to withdraw his military forces from Mexico in three detachments: the first of these will leave Mexico next November, the second in the March following, and the third in November, 1867: that when the evacuation is accomplished, the French government will immediately adopt towards Mexico a policy of non-intervention similar to that which is practised by the United States. Doubts have been conceived and expressed in certain circles as to the good faith in which the French government will carry out this measure. Doubts of this kind have not been entertained by the president, who has received reiterated and even recent assurances that the complete evacuation of Mexico by the French will be concluded at the dates agreed on, or even sooner, as military and other arrangements may permit. There are grounds for supposing that two incidental questions have already engaged the attention of the French government, namely, in the first place, whether the departure of the prince Maximilian for Austria ought not to take place before the French expedition leaves; secondly, whether it would not be preferable, on account of questions relating to the climate and to military and other matters, to withdraw all the expeditionary forces at one time, instead of withdrawing them in three detachments at different periods.

Nevertheless, the Emperor Napoleon has not made any formal communication on this subject to the government of the United States. When the question was incidentally brought forward, the state department replied, by order of the president, that the United States were awaiting the execution of the agreement for the evacuation at the times fixed by the French government, and that they would rejoice to see this evacuation carried out even more promptly than had been agreed upon. Under these circumstances the president expects that, *in the course of the next month (November), a part at least of the expeditionary French force will leave Mexico*; and he thinks that it is not improbable that the main body of the expeditionary force may retire at the same time, or almost the same time.

An event like this cannot fail to produce a crisis of great political interest. It is of importance that you should be present, either on the republican territory or in the immediate vicinity, in order to be able to exercise your functions as minister plenipotentiary of the United States to the Mexican republic. We cannot positively know the course which Prince Maximilian will decide on taking in case of a partial or complete evacuation of Mexico; nor can we determine beforehand the course which M. Juarez, the president of the Mexican republic, will adopt under like circumstances.

We are informed that various political parties exist in Mexico besides those of which President Juarez and Prince Maximilian are the respective heads: these various parties entertain conflicting opinions touching the most prompt and suitable means for restoring the peace, order, and civil government of the republic.

We do not know what these different parties will do after the evacuation; in short, it is impossible to foresee the conduct of the Mexican people when this event becomes known.

For the above reasons it is impossible to give you precise instructions as to the line of conduct which you should pursue in carrying out the high mission which the government of the United States has confided to you. Much must be left to your personal judgment, and you must take as your basis the political movements which the future may produce. There are, however, certain principles which, in our opinion, must guide the political conduct which the government of the United States looks for from you. The first of these principles is that, as representative of the United States, you are accredited to the Republican government of Mexico of which M. Juarez is president.

Your communications as American representative must be addressed to him in whatever place he may be, and, at all events, you will be unable to recognise officially either the Prince Maximilian, who claims to be emperor of Mexico, or any other person, chief, or commission, carrying on the executive power in Mexico, without having previously referred to my department, and without receiving the instructions of the President of the United States.

Secondly, in case the commanders of the French army and fleet carry out in good faith the agreement for the evacuation of Mexico before the time fixed, the engagement that you must make under this supposition is, that neither the United

States, nor their representative, would interpose any hindrance or any obstacle to the departure of the French.

Thirdly, that which the government of the United States desire for the future of Mexico is, not the conquest of this country nor of any part of it, nor the aggrandisement of the United States by the purchase of lands or provinces; but, on the contrary, it desires to see the Mexicans delivered from all foreign military intervention, so that they may be able to regulate the conduct of their own affairs by means of the existing republican government, or any other form of rule which, when they enjoy perfect liberty, they shall adopt of their own accord uninfluenced by foreign countries, and also by the United States.

It follows from these principles, that you must not make any stipulations with the French commanders, or with the Prince Maximilian, nor with any party which may show a tendency to thwart or oppose the administration of the President Juarez, or to delay and put off the restoration of the republican authority. On the other hand, it may happen that the president of the Mexican republic may claim the good offices of the United States, or some effective action on our part to further and hasten the pacification of a country so long rent by civil and foreign war, and thus to accelerate the re-establishment of the national authority on principles in accordance with a republican and domestic system of government.

It is possible that some movement may be made by the land and sea forces of the United States, without intervening within the limits of Mexican jurisdiction, or violating the laws of neutrality, but in order to further the restoration of law, order, and republican government in that country.

You are authorised to confer on this subject with the republican government of Mexico and its agents, and even to confer, for the sake of inquiry, with any other parties or agents, in case an exceptional conference should become absolutely necessary; but in this case only.

You will thus be able to obtain information which will be important for our government to know, and you will transmit it to my department with your own suggestions and opinion as to any other measures which might be adopted on our part in conformity with the principles developed above. You will confine yourself to thus referring to my department, for the information of the president, any important proposition which may be started on the subject of the reorganisation and restoration of the republican government of Mexico.

The lieutenant-general of the United States is already in possession of a discretionary authority as to the disposition of the United States forces in the vicinity of Mexico. His military experience qualifies him to advise you on questions of the kind which may arise during the transitory period which will bring Mexico from a state of siege maintained by a foreign enemy, to the political condition of self-government.

At the same time, being near the scene of action, he will have the power of issuing any orders which may appear to him expedient or necessary to fulfil the obligations of the United States in respect to what is going on on the frontiers of Mexico. For these reasons, he has been requested and has received the president's order to accompany you to your destination, and to fulfil towards you the duties of an official councillor, who is recognised by the department of state in all that touches the matters pointed out.

After having come to an understanding with him, you will be able to proceed to the city of Chihuahua, or any other place in Mexico in which President Juarez may be; or, at your choice, you may go to any place in Mexico which, at the time of your arrival, is not occupied by the enemies of the Mexican republic. You might also stay at some point in the United States close to the frontier or coast of Mexico, to wait for the time when you might enter that portion of the country which may be subsequently occupied by the republican government. WILLIAM H. SEWARD.

Note from President Johnson to Mr. E. Stanton, Minister of War, directing the addition of General Grant to Mr. Campbell's Mission to Mexico, dated Washington, October 26, 1866.

Sir,—As recent advices announce the approaching evacuation of Mexico by the French expeditionary troops, the time is come for our minister in Mexico to enter into relations with that republic. To assist him in his mission, and to give a proof of the lively desire which the United States feel of settling all the pending questions, I think it important that our minister should be accompanied by General Grant. I therefore request that you will summon General Grant to proceed to some point of our Mexican frontier which may be convenient for communicating with our minister; or, if General Grant thinks it preferable, he may accompany him to his destination and assist him by his advice in carrying out the instructions of the secretary of state, a copy of which I send you for the general's use. General Grant will report to the secretary of war on any subject which, in his opinion, ought to be communicated to that department.

A. JOHNSON.

General Grant having declined this appointment, Lieutenant-General Sherman, who accepted it in his place, was ordered to leave for his destination without delay. As may be seen, both by their language and by their military demonstrations, the United States, rejecting at once any other candidate for the presidency, asserted more decidedly than ever the authority of Juarez; but they did *not* require that the Emperor Napoleon should modify his well known decision of evacuating Mexico at three separate periods. On this occasion, therefore, the court of the Tuileries had resolved entirely of its own will to accelerate the downfall of the Mexican monarchy, by hastening on the fixed date for the withdrawal of our troops, and by altering its plans of a gradual withdrawal, which would have given Maximilian time to see his real position, and to have retired honourably, which he would doubtless have done with the last detachment of our rear-guard.

On November 11, the American envoys left New York, on board the war-frigate 'Susquehannah,' and put to sea, first steering to the port of Matamoros, and afterwards to that of Tampico, both now in the power of the rebels. From the latter place they reckoned that they should be able to communicate with Juarez. Their real aim was to claim a vessel laden with arms for the Liberals, which had been captured by the Imperialists. But General Pavon, who occupied the place, had recently allied himself to the fortunes of Ortega. The Liberals, now in possession of the vessel, claimed the capture as their lawful prize. Nevertheless, the frigate remained several days anchored before the bar at Tampico.

CHAPTER XVIII.

Maximilian's new Resolutions—Generals Marquez and Miramon—Secret Imperial Envoys to Washington—M. Larès' Requests to Marshal Bazaine—Father Fischer's Diplomacy—Maximilian's final Requisitions—The French Representatives deceived—Marquis de Montholon's Letters to Marshal Bazaine—Accordant Views of France and the United States—Letter of Porfirio Diaz—Final Disappointment of the American Envoys.

WHILST the American mission was being organised in Mr. Seward's cabinet, events were hurrying on in the *Hacienda Jalapilla*. It will be recollected that Maximilian, impelled by M. Eloïn's letter, had resolved to assemble a national congress—a project which he had for a long time cherished. He flattered himself that the convocation of this congress, as soon as the French had left, would settle peaceably the contest which was in progress between the monarchy and the republic. If the principle of which he was the representative failed to get the advantage in a popular vote—an issue, however, which he had foreseen—he would be at liberty to return proudly to Europe as a prince who had gracefully given up his throne, and as one who would be worthy to play his part in the affairs of his country. But, in order to maintain his power up to the time of the French evacuation, it was necessary for him to depend upon the party which still held the insurrection in check, and would at least give him the means of treating upon equal terms with the various liberal chiefs, and insure the execution of his scheme —that is, the free assembly in Mexico of all the 'notables' belonging to the territory called upon to give an opinion. Now Father Fischer held in his hand all the threads of the plot constructing by the clerical party, and never ceased to hold out before Maximilian's eyes the pretended resources of the party of which he called himself the head. Just at this decisive moment the royal confessor received a powerful reinforcement. Generals Marquez and Miramon, whom the crown had dismissed to Europe about two years before, had just landed at Vera Cruz; some hours after, this mysterious visit was signalled at La Soledad. The day after they landed, forgetful of their disgrace, and feeling unable to turn a deaf ear to the appeal of their party, they presented themselves at Jalapilla, ready to throw their swords into the scale; and, if Maximilian consented to give himself up to the clerical party, prepared to open the campaign again under the imperial banners. Maximilian hesitated no longer; he passed his word to the clerical party, whom he engaged to reinstate in their property and honours. Miramon, fortified with the imperial promise, which was, however, to be kept secret for a few days, hurried to Mexico to communicate this important news to the ministers and council of state, to rekindle the zeal of all the partizans of the church, and to take the steps necessary to set on foot another army, and to get together twenty millions of francs in the imperial treasury.

From this time Maximilian, no longer feeling himself isolated, adopted a decided course with the French authorities. The report of the negotiations opened by our diplomatists with the liberal chiefs, and of Mr. Campbell's mission, sent by President Johnson to Juarez, had found its way to Jalapilla. The sovereign learned also from his tools at Washington that various agents had been sent from Paris to expedite his downfall.

A second secretary of legation had been dispatched by the Marquis de Moustier to the Marquis de Montholon; and, on his return from America, he obtained an advancement of rank.

Certain secret envoys, such as Colonel Estevan, who had had an audience of the emperor at Saint Cloud about this time, and a Frenchman of the name of Moreau, had been seen at Washington. At length M. Marcus Otterbourg, the American consul, preceding the 'Susquehannah' frigate, landed at Vera Cruz, and proceeded hastily to Mexico. Convinced that for the future General Castelnau was the mainspring of action, he resolved to unmask the intentions of the French policy at one stroke, and to compel it to decide openly one way or the other. Maximilian had by his side the Abbé Fischer, a well-practised diplomatist, inured to all the tricks of the trade, who directed the thoughts of the young sovereign, as well as his pen and his conscience. Under his ascendancy, the emperor now regretted that he had not received General Castelnau; for he thought that it would be interesting to have heard from his mouth the latest utterances of the Tuileries. M. Larès, the president of the council at Mexico, was charged to invite Napoleon's aide-de-camp to enter into some explanations. This attempt failed. General Castelnau, faithful to his part, replied to M. Larès that the presence of the marshal was necessary, the latter being qualified to deal with matters. MM. Larès and Arroyo were compelled to proceed to the French head-quarters, where they met the three French authorities. After this interview, the two Mexican ministers drew up a note, which was a faithful summary of the explanations exchanged, and sent it to the marshal: it was dated November 4, 1866.

In the first place, they declared formally that General

Castelnau had stated that his sole mission was to confirm the letter of January 15 and those that followed, by which the Emperor Napoleon notified to Maximilian that he could not continue to assist the empire, either with the French troops or with money. The question being thus stated, Maximilian was left at full liberty to make his decision. The ministers also demanded that the crown should be put in possession of all the arsenals, artillery, and munitions of war; and that it should have the entire disposition of the Mexican troops, in order to undertake any military operations that the national government should consider opportune. They also asked that the fortified places should be delivered up to their charge at a fitting time. The two last phrases of this document especially betrayed the feelings which dictated it: they were as follows:—
'We shall be glad to be able to acquaint our sovereign of the latest time to which the departure of the French army will be deferred, and what help it still intends to afford to his majesty's government in the pacification of the country. . . . Finally, in case the decision of the emperor should be not to continue to govern, *we must inform him* as to what the marshal and General Castelnau *have settled to do*, in order, *according to the Emperor Napoleon's instructions*, to avoid the anarchy and disturbances *which would take place in consequence of the absence of any government.*'

Only fourteen days before, MM. Larès and Arroyo showed much less anxiety about the future of their country, when they tendered their resignations at the palace of Chapultepec, and declared that, if Maximilian quitted Mexico, ' *there would no longer be a government.*'

On November 7 the three French authorities confirmed the resolutions of the Emperor Napoleon. All the Mexican forces and munitions of war were to be given up to the imperial generals, who were already in possession of all the military establishments. As before, all the towns would be placed under the Mexican authorities, who would have proper warning given them of the departure of our detachments. The French troops would continue to protect the officials and the inhabitants in the districts occupied by our soldiers, but no expedition would be undertaken.

'As to the last article,' it was replied, 'it was impossible *to state the measures which would be taken if the supposed case occurred*; but we can give the assurance that their especial aim will be to maintain order, to respect the wishes of the population, as well as to protect French interests.'

The above language, which was not devoid of artifice, was far from satisfying Father Fischer. Maximilian also drew up a letter which, although it was addressed to the marshal, called for a collective reply from the representatives of France. Under the pretext of settling certain questions, and, among others, the sending home of the Austro-Belgian Legion (whose interests had already been fully entrusted to the care of Colonel de Kodolich), he sought to provoke a more explicit declaration.

November 12, 1866.

My dear Marshal,—Before I decidedly resolve what I must do, and in case my determination should be to leave this country, I must ensure the settlement of certain points which are strictly just and deserve my especial attention. For this purpose I have no doubt that you will be kind enough to send me a document signed collectively by yourself, the minister of France, and General Castelnau; and in this document the following points should be stipulated:—

1. That the French government shall convey to their respective countries the individuals forming the Austro-Belgian Legion, by granting them a passage and the resources necessary to effect their return home. The individuals of the

Austro-Belgian Legion shall be the first to evacuate the Mexican territory.

2. The French authorities in Mexico shall make the necessary arrangements that, at the expense of Mexico, a sum should be assigned to afford a life-pension to each of the wounded and invalids of the above corps, in case a sufficient amount should not be produced for this purpose by the sale of the cannon of the Austrian legion, which are my personal property.

. The pensions of which this article speaks are to be paid by a commission nominated by you, to which Colonels Kodolich and Van der Smissen will belong, who will undertake on their part to distribute these sums amongst those legally interested.

3. The French authorities in Mexico shall make every arrangement that the Mexican treasury should pay ten thousand piastres, which shall be remitted to the Princess Iturbide on account of her pension.

At the same time, you will direct that ten thousand piastres should be sent to any town of France to the Prince D. Salvador de Iturbide, on account of that which is owing to him; and it must also be stipulated on the deed, that the young prince alone shall be able to dispose of the capital during his minority.

4. The same French authorities shall arrange that the sum of forty-five thousand piastres shall be handed, on account of the Mexican government, to Don Carlos Sanchez Navarro, in order to pay the debts of the civil list.

There shall also be remitted to the said Sanchez Navarro the sums necessary to settle the accounts of the office of the great seal, it being understood that these accounts, as well as those of the civil list, shall be paid from the sums which the state continues to owe the civil list.

5. The payments included in articles 2, 3, and 4, shall be fully made on the day when the last portion of the expeditionary corps shall leave the city of Mexico.

My personal property, my dear marshal, will remain confided to your safe keeping; and with regard to the produce of it I shall beg you, in conjunction with Sanchez Navarro, to comply with the tenor of my instructions.

Receive the assurance of my feelings of sincere friendship, with which I am your very affectionate, MAXIMILIAN.

When the sovereign gave this fresh proof of his confidence in the marshal, in whose safe-keeping he left his personal property, it seemed as if he plainly announced his abdication. The representatives of France received with joy this tardy manifesto, which would quickly put an end to the constantly increasing confusion in the kingdom and to the panic in the capital. They hastened to assent to all the emperor's wishes (who was certainly bound to fulfil all the engagements entered into by the crown), and the collective note, intended to do away with Maximilian's last scruples, was forwarded to Orizaba.

Mexico, November 1, 1866.

His majesty the Emperor Maximilian having expressed the desire to obtain a document signed jointly by the marshal of France commanding in chief the expeditionary corps, by the envoy extraordinary and minister plenipotentiary of France, and by the General Castelnau, aide-de-camp to the Emperor of the French, regarding the solution of several questions explained in an imperial letter dated Orizaba, November 12: The undersigned, who are glad of this opportunity to testify, as much as in them lies, of their good will to his majesty, have agreed to transmit to him the following declaration:—

The French government engages to convey home the whole of the men composing the Austro-Belgian Legion. This operation will be carried out as soon as circumstances permit, and at all events the Austro-Belgians shall have evacuated Mexico before the departure of the last French brigade.

The details relative to their being sent home shall be arranged by two persons, one of whom shall be designated by the Emperor Maximilian and one by Marshal Bazaine.

The undersigned engage to pay an allowance of half pay to the wounded and disabled of the Austro-Belgian Legion, and to grant the officers and soldiers of this legion an indemnity at the port where they land.

The settlement of the half pay allowances and indemnities specified above shall be confided to a commission to which the Colonels Kodolich and Van der Smissen shall belong.

The undersigned also engage to exert all their influence that an advance should be made to the princess Dona Josefa and to the young prince Don Salvador de Iturbide, on the pension which is due to them.

Finally, in accordance with the wish expressed by his majesty the Emperor Maximilian, M. Carlos Sanchez Navarro shall be charged with the payments of the debts of the civil list, and the settlement of the accounts of the office of the great seal. The sums resulting from the sale of the property belonging to the civil list shall be devoted to this purpose; and, in case of the insufficiency of the above sums, the undersigned will endeavour to obtain the concession that *the additional amount required shall be furnished by the new government of Mexico.*

In witness whereof the undersigned have signed this present declaration.

BAZAINE. DANO. CASTELNAU.

The representatives of France had fallen into the snare which Maximilian had set for them. The last statement of the collective note betrayed the approach of a new government, which was already prepared to succeed to the monarchy. The three joint-subscribers were deficient in perspicacity: they certainly would not have fallen into this error in diplomacy, if they had been wise enough to compare the language of the two imperial letters which spoke of the return home of the Belgian Legion, between which letters there was a space of only twelve days. The first, dated October 31, 1866, commenced thus:—

In the difficult circumstances in which I am placed, which also, if the negotiations I have just entered upon do not produce a happy result, will force me to resign the powers with which the nation have invested me. . . .

It was now known that these negotiations had failed, and, instead of resigning his power, Maximilian wrote in very doubtful terms indicating a complete change in his ideas.

Before I decidedly resolve what I must do, and in case my determination should be to leave this country. . . .

When he had read the French document, Maximilian could no longer feel any doubt: he then became certain that the French policy, having completely sacrificed him to its own interest without a shadow of regret, had decisively severed their two respective fortunes, and that all the measures which the French commander was taking were intended to substitute some new state of things in place of the empire. M. Eloïn's predictions were realised! Impatient to have done with France, being informed too by Miramon of the favourable change which had taken place in some of the state authorities, who were preparing to come down to La Jalapilla at their sovereign's appeal, Maximilian forwarded a despatch to Marshal Bazaine inviting him to a private interview. In a conversation of this kind he hoped that the commander-in-chief would let out the full import of the policy of the Tuileries.

To Marshal Bazaine.

[*Confidential and important.*]   Orizaba, November 18, 1866.

I must thank you, as well as General Castelnau and M. Dano, for having arranged those points which concern me so closely. But one important point still remains to be settled: a firm government to protect the interests which are compromised. This point cannot be discussed without a personal interview with you. The continuance of my fever will not allow me to come up to Mexico. I therefore request you to come here some day soon, and, in a few words, we shall be able to arrange everything in a satisfactory manner. I have summoned here for Saturday my council of state and my president of the council.   MAXIMILIAN.

These Mexican officials, who a short time back dreaded endangering themselves even in Mexico, would never have consented to traverse sixty leagues of country ripe for revolt, merely to register an abdication. They then knew the real aim of their assembling at La Jalapilla. When the above despatch arrived at our head-quarters, Miramon's arrival and his proceedings in the capital had already foretold the reaction which had taken place in Maximilian's resolutions; the attitude of the ministers, which had now become almost ungracious, was a sure sign of this. Nevertheless, the commander-in-chief, obeying to the letter the instructions of his government, directing him to respect the young emperor's liberty of action, thought it right to yield to his appeal. General Castelnau and M. Dano, who were joined with him in council, were opposed to it. Compelled to submit to this decision the marshal forwarded to La Jalapilla the following reply:—

To His Majesty the Emperor Maximilian.

Mexico, November 18, 1866.

I have received the telegraphic despatch from your majesty dated this day. Notwithstanding my great desire to visit you as you request, it appears to me very difficult to quit the capital which your majesty placed in my charge before the arrival of General Douay, and until I am set at ease as to the military movements which have been directed.

BAZAINE.

It was not till some days after he had written this reply that the marshal was, for the first time, enlightened as to the real intentions of the French cabinet, by receiving a letter from the Marquis de Montholon, the meaning of which appeared to him at first sight rather enigmatical, for he was in no way aware of the course of policy which was being followed at Washington:—

Washington, November 9, 1866.

My dear Marshal,—I can only announce the departure of Mr. Campbell and Mr. Sherman for Mexico in the frigate

'Susquehannah,' and beg you to read the despatch in cipher which I send by this courier to M. Dano. In a few days I shall be able to tell you more. The tendencies here are good; if there were any incidents to be feared, it would be only on questions of detail.

The news from Europe this morning announced no improvement in the health of the empress. What a fatality it seems! The news of the emperor's departure from Mexico has been received with pleasure, and his leaving is looked upon as the signal of an amicable and decisive solution of the difference with France on the subject of Mexico.

The Fenian question in Canada will henceforth form the principal feature of the foreign policy here. The result of the elections is entirely in favour of the opposition, and condemns the president's policy for the reconstruction of the union. The republican and radical party is however, as far as we are concerned, very plainly opposed to any foreign collision.

MONTHOLON.

Washington, November 8, 1866.

Frigate 'Susquehamah' conveys to Mexico Mr. Campbell and General Sherman to meet Juarez. Instructions to aid the establishment of a regular republican government, and to avoid all pretext for collision with the French authorities. No improvement in the state of the empress.

MONTHOLON.

To the Emperor's Minister at Mexico.

Washington, November 12, 1866.

Mission left yesterday. Instructions very vague. To come to an understanding with none but Juarez, except only in case of absolute necessity. No intervention. No acquisition of territory. Moral support to Juarez. Land and sea forces on the frontier at the orders of General Sherman. To avoid all collision with us. MONTHOLON.

General Ortega arrested at Brazos by the Americans.

Everything was explained to the marshal in a visit which he received in the meantime from M. Marcus Otterbourg, the American consul, who had arrived in haste from the United States, where it was believed that Maximilian had now embarked for Europe: he was commissioned to prepare the ground for two plenipotentiaries accredited to Juarez. In this interview M. Otterbourg announced to the commander-in-chief the approaching visit of his two countrymen, and the aim of their journey, and sought to sound him as to the mode in which he intended to deal with events. Subsequently, in an official conversation, he intimated that he was charged by his own government, acting in accordance with the court of the Tuileries, to restore, in conjunction with the commander-in-chief, the Mexican republic.

'The time has come,' said he, 'to look out for the Juarist general, to whom it will be best to give over the city of Mexico, so as to avoid the disturbances which may break out at any moment.' Porfirio Diaz appeared, in his opinion, to be worthy of being selected by the French. It would, therefore, be prudent, looking forward to contingencies, to invite him to approach the capital. He also apprised the commander-in-chief that he had already obtained from the bankers of the city funds sufficient to meet the pay of Porfirio Diaz's troops for a month.

The marshal manifested all the astonishment he felt at finding things so far advanced, and declared plainly to M. Otterbourg, that 'as long as Maximilian trod the Mexican soil and had not abdicated, he remained in his eyes the only lawful chief of the country who had any right to the French protection; that, until this moment arrived, no fresh measures could be taken, and every disaffected general necessarily preserved his character as a rebel, and must be dealt with as such.' Subsequently, when the archduke was once embarked, he could not see any objection to organising a government with the co-operation of Porfirio Diaz, for whom he professed to feel more esteem than for General Ortega (whose forfeiture of his parole he could not forget), although the latter was the candidate recommended at Paris. 'If this eventuality should occur,' continued the marshal, 'we should neither assist nor accept as a claimant to the presidential chair any republican chief who would not fully recognise the French debt by giving us solid guarantees for the same. If we come to terms, and in this I shall follow the instructions of my sovereign, we shall treat regularly as one government with another, and on this score we shall, of course, hand over to the new president the fortified places of the republic as well as the Mexican artillery and arms.'

In reply to a special observation as to the giving up of six thousand muskets, which had been ordered at Maximilian's request, it was stated that these would be included among the *matériel* which would be handed over to the future chief of the state when lawfully recognised. M. Otterbourg's own declaration would suffice to attest the authenticity of this conversation, in form as well as in import; as it was this declaration which gave rise to Porfirio Diaz's famous letter addressed to Romero, Juarez's minister, and lately published by the cabinet of Washington. The third party, to whom Porfirio alluded, is none other than this American consul, who was in no way authorised to make himself the mouth-piece, either official or semi-official, of the French head-quarters to this disaffected chief, as he himself can attest. The proposition which Porfirio alluded to as having been rejected as not very honourable, refers to the recognition of the debt and the French loans. As to the eventual giving up of the cannon and muskets, it is explained in the preceding statement. There still remains the design imputed to the marshal of having wished to deliver over secretly to Porfirio the arms, the fortified places of the empire, as well as the emperor and his generals; but this calumny will recoil upon the head of its author, whoever he may be.

The marshal never saw General Porfirio after the time when he took him prisoner at Oajaca with his whole army. It will be well to recollect that this chief was given up by the French to the Austrians by Maximilian's order, and escaped from the hands of the Austro-Belgian Legion. Our headquarters, as documents will soon show, subsequently negotiated an exchange of prisoners with this Mexican chief, whose honour was equal to his humanity; but this was all openly done at a distance from head-quarters through the French officers commanding at Tehuacan and Puebla. Porfirio, who must be honoured for the way in which he energetically claimed the rights of his country, must have yielded to perfidious advice or to a culpable feeling which he cannot fail to disclaim, when he wrote this letter of which Mr. Seward himself was the originator and sender in order to serve as a documentary support to his foreign policy. This document—inserted in the 'Yellow Book'—aimed to show that he had caused the American representative to act in favour of the 'Monroe doctrine,' and also to calm down the ill-humour of the Congress, which was irritated at the rebuff given to the mission of its two envoys. There is no mistake about it: the Mexican question has been for the last five years a means of gaining popularity for the cabinet of the United States, and an instrument it has been able to handle with as much boldness as skill in order to silence the cries either of the disaffected or of those who were hostile to Lincoln's successor.

The mission of the American plenipotentiaries had, in fact, completely failed. The United States consul at Vera Cruz had, on November 25, made the inquiry by telegraph at Mexico, 'if the frigate "Susquehannah," now at anchor before Tampico, might come to Vera Cruz, and if it would be well received there, as Mr. Campbell and General Sherman desired to have an interview with the French authorities.' Our headquarters replied, 'that the American frigate would be received the same as any other man-of-war belonging to a friendly nation, and that the persons in question would be well received at Mexico if they wished to come thither.' The consul hastened to forward this reply to Tampico by the English packet which was just starting. On November 29, in stormy weather, the 'Susquehannah,' proudly displaying her star-spangled banner, rounded the hills behind which the city of Vera Cruz is somewhat gloomily situated. Scarcely was she in sight of the roadstead, when a small boat was noticed leaving the port and rowing so as to follow in her wake: she soon stopped off the Fort St. Jean d'Ulloa to receive the person who had come to board the ship: he was the American consul from Vera Cruz. He was the bearer of important news, which much surprised MM. Campbell and Sherman. The city was in a state of rejoicing; they could already perceive the lines of lamps with which the principal buildings were illuminated, and the wind carried out into the roadstead the noise of the fireworks. All this commotion was occasioned by the news of Maximilian's fresh resolve, which had proclaimed to Mexico that its sovereign had renounced the idea of returning to Europe, and that, yieldimg to the entreaties of the high state authorities, he was going up to Mexico to add fresh vigour to his sovereignty by means of a popular vote. The American minister and the general, who had flattered themselves that they should see on their arrival the republican banner floating on the custom-house buildings of the port, ordered that the frigate should tack about and anchor at the 'Ile Vert,' some miles from Vera Cruz: there they waited events. The next morning an officer of the French fleet came, according to usual custom, to pay his respects to the commander of the American frigate. Lieutenant-general Sherman was advised by M. Ottenbourg from Mexico, *that the marshal would receive him with all the respect due to his rank and with the most sincere cordiality; indeed, that he would even give him the opportunity of witnessing a review of the French troops*; but Sherman replied that he would not proceed to Mexico except at the pressing invitation of the head-quarters authorities. It is very certain that the spectacle of a review of our troops was not the aim and end of the American mission.

CHAPTER XIX.

Conference of Mexican Ministers—Seductive Plans of the Clerical Party—Meditated Campaigns by Marquez and Miramon—Maximilian announces his fresh Resolve—His Manifesto—M. Larès' Letter to the French Representatives—Dissatisfaction in the French Camp—Destruction of the French Schemes—Harsh Measures of the Emperor Napoleon—Recall of the Foreign Legion—Mr. Bigelow's Despatch—Irritation at the Tuileries—The lost Despatch—Hostile Feeling between the French and Mexican Governments—Maximilian returns to the Capital.

WHAT, then, were the events which had taken place during the last few days at Jalapilla? The ministers and the council of state, having come down from Mexico to Orizaba under a French escort and with Miramon as their leader, had entered upon a conference, and had remained in consultation for three days (from Saturday until Monday) at the imperial residence. M. Larès, appointed to speak for all the members of the commission, had supplicated the emperor not to leave the territory, asserting, in the name of the clerical party (for whom Abbé Fischer vouched), that his majesty might reckon upon four millions of piastres and an army ready to commence operations. Marquez and Miramon both accepted commands. The former of these generals was to occupy the capital and protect the valley of Mexico and the plateaus of Inahuac against the attempts of Porfirio Diaz; the second was to make his way to the north and give battle to Escobedo's troops. Victory could not be doubtful, especially with the co-operation of the brave Mejia in the interior, whose military fame was no less potent in the Sierra than in the state of Queretaro, which had been aforetime witness of his triumphs. If necessary, immediately after the bands in the north were put to rout, the victorious forces of the monarchy might turn round against the rebels of Oajaca, whom they would soon bring to reason. As to the millions which were necessary, the president of the council confined himself to saying that they would be provided: *this was the secret of his party.*

This plan looked very seductive upon paper, and Maximilian fully adopted it. In order to put an end to the state of uncertainty in which the country had now been for more than a month, the emperor completely altered his course of action, and issued a telegraphic despatch, which contradicted all the events which had taken place. The visit to Orizaba of Mr. Scarlett, the English diplomatist, then on his way to Europe, did not a little contribute to hurry the adoption of this sudden measure by the young emperor, whom he advised not to abandon the throne.

Our head-quarters authorities received immediate communication from the imperial cabinet of the telegraphic despatch which left Orizaba, November 20, 1866.

None of the steps which I have taken authorise the belief that it is my intention to abdicate in favour of any party whatever. The appeal made to me by the council of state and the ministers was simply this, that, in conjunction with them, when the time to abdicate shall arrive, the *ad interim* power should be made over to those to whom it is due, and that, in the meantime, the vote of the nation shall settle the rest. The appeal made to Marshal Bazaine had no other aim than that these points should be arranged in conjunction with the commander-in-chief of the army.

The assertion that a provisional government will be recognised by the United States is more than doubtful. Why should it be so? Who guarantees this recognition? Who will go to solicit it? I think that it is right to remit the powers which I have received to the nation that conferred them on me, and to leave the other questions—as to the source and election of a new government—to the free choice of the nation. MAXIMILIAN.

This was the emperor's reply to the American mission, which he knew was now off Tampico; in it he relies for the future on the collective note of November 7. At the same time he counteracts the manœuvres of the cabinet of the Tuileries, which he knew were being carried on, both at Washington and in the liberal camp. After the publication of this fresh *coup d'état*, there was no further hope, for the present, of the abdication of the prince. This despatch was soon followed by a more official and explicit document. On December 1 appeared the imperial manifesto, dated from Orizaba, which announced to the country the assembling of a national congress.

Manifesto of the Emperor.

Mexicans,—Important circumstances affecting the welfare of our country, which vanish in the presence of our domestic misfortunes, have called forth the conviction in my mind, that I ought to give back to you the power which you formerly conferred upon me.

The ministerial and state councils which I have assembled are of opinion that the welfare of Mexico requires that I should remain in power. I have thought it my duty to yield to their urgency, and to announce to you at the same time, that it is my intention to summon a national congress, constituted on the largest and most liberal basis, and that in this congress all parties will participate. This congress will decide if the empire is to continue for the future, and, in the affirmative case, will concur in the formation of laws essential to the consolidation of the vital interests of the country. With this aim, my counsellors are at the present time devoting themselves to preparing all the necessary measures, and are also taking the requisite steps that all parties should combine in an arrangement on this basis.

Consequently, Mexicans, reckoning upon all of you, without excluding any shade of politics, I shall endeavour to follow out with courage and constancy the work of regeneration which you have confided to your fellow countryman,

MAXIMILIAN.

Two days after, the president of the council announced in the emperor's name, to the French authorities, that Maximilian had resolved for the future to depend only on his own forces. Nevertheless, it was settled that the expeditionary corps was to continue its protection to the monarchy during its stay in Mexico, now limited to the spring of 1867, and that it should defend all the points which it occupied, without undertaking any distant expeditions.

To His Excellency the Minister of France at Mexico, His Excellency Marshal Bazaine, and General Castelnau.

Orizaba, December 3, 1866.

The undersigned being appointed by the Emperor Maximilian to settle the measures which are rendered necessary by the mission of General Castelnau, a mission which the latter states he is fulfilling in conjunction with the Minister Plenipotentiary Dano and Marshal Bazaine, we now have the honour of acquainting you that, having communicated to his majesty the note of the 7th of last month, which was signed by Marshal Bazaine and General Castelnau, in reply to that which we had the honour of sending them on the 4th of the same month, his majesty, after long and serious consideration, by the advice of his ministers and of his council of state, has decided that, relying upon the authority conferred upon him by the nation, he will prolong and maintain his government with the resources of the country only; since the Emperor of the French has declared that it is no longer possible for him to support the empire either with his troops or his money, and perseveres in the resolution which he formed to withdraw the former in the beginning of 1867.

His majesty the emperor, in carrying out the execution of his designs, is employed in the measures necessary for the formation of the Mexican army, and in organising the forces which are to uphold the empire. He hopes that M. the Marshal Bazaine will be pleased to give orders, as far as it lies with him, to the French chief-commandants, that the Mexican troops, the military establishments and magazines, should now remain at the exclusive disposal of his majesty. His majesty also assumes that the French troops, so long as they stay in the country, will protect the authorities and inhabitants in the districts which they occupy, without undertaking any distant expeditions.

This co-operation, the points of which are specified in the note of November 7, above quoted, is gratefully accepted by his majesty.

His majesty the emperor desires us also to state, that any question relative to the matters spoken of in this note, or which may be called forth by the resolution he has adopted, may be discussed with the president of the council of state, who, in this capacity, has signed his name first.

TEODOSIO LARÈS,
President of the Council of Ministers.
LUIS DE ARROYO,
Minister of the Emperor's Household.

The rupture was now *de facto* consummated with the French government; and, from this day forward, Maximilian had no further direct communication with our head-quarters. The president of the council had the power of dealing with all questions, and of addressing himself to the three French representatives collectively. Maximilian well understood that the effects of the personal feeling of the commander-in-chief would disappear with his authority, and that the Mexican throne would henceforth have to treat with the aide-de-camp of Napoleon III. as if with the sovereign himself.

The sudden change in the political views of the

Emperor of Mexico excited deep dissatisfaction in the French camp. The scheme of the Tuileries was utterly destroyed. Nevertheless, the illusion of its success had strongly prevailed in Paris, to judge only from the despatches of our government, dated October 31, which had just arrived from Europe. 'The minister Larès,' they wrote, 'has no chance of a continuance of power; the mission of General Castelnau could not be more opportune; and the emperor's desire is to see Maximilian quit Mexico.' Two of the representatives of France thought that an energetic note, telling the undisguised truth as to the impossibility of the enterprise which he was undertaking, might perhaps open Maximilian's eyes, and cause him to relinquish his design.

The marshal, in his feeling as a soldier, persisted in believing that, with the sure help of the foreign legion and the Austrians, and with the numerous well-fortified places to constitute his base of operations, Maximilian still retained those elements of a continuance of power which would permit him to retire at some future day with more honour and in full security. He was, however, compelled to embrace the opinion of General Castelnau and M. Dano.

General Castelnau had already informed the Emperor Napoleon of Maximilian's irresolution; and, on December 7, he acquainted him of this new *coup d'état*, in which the monarchy, unfurling the banner of the clerical party, destroyed all hope of an amicable solution. It was, however, necessary to meet promptly a state of things so compromising to French interests. The same day a joint note was drawn up by the three French representatives, and the day after the reception of M. Larès' communication it was sent to the president of the council. It was intended to make a last effort against the reactionary party.

To His Excellency M. Téodosio Larès, President of the Council of Ministers.

Mexico, December 8, 1866.

The undersigned have received the note, dated the 3rd instant, which MM. Larès and Arroyo did them the honour of sending them.

The president of the council being charged with the duty of dealing with the matters which formed the subject of this note, the undersigned have to acquaint him with their opinion as to the determination adopted by his majesty the Emperor Maximilian to retain the authority which the Mexican nation has conferred upon him, and to uphold his government with the resources of the country only.

The sacrifices which the government of the undersigned has made, and their own personal efforts to establish a monarchy in Mexico, need not be recalled. The agents of France deeply regret the arrival of a crisis which they would have desired to render impossible. However, after having maturely considered the position of things, they have come to the conviction that it is impossible that the imperial government should be upheld by its own resources alone.

However painful it may be for them, and without pretending at all to influence the final decision, they consider that it is their duty to make the above declaration; and they must add that, in the actual state of things, the high and generous resolution which the Emperor Maximilian appeared a month back anxious to decide on could be the only one to allow a solution of matters calculated to hold harmless every interest.

As to everything which bears upon the military question and all connected with it, replies have already been sent by competent French agents. Fresh explanations will be furnished by them if they become necessary.

BAZAINE.   ALPH. DANO.   CASTELNAU.

The minister's reply was not long before it appeared. On December 10 he issued a long circular, summing up the efforts of the monarchy in the past, and its hopes for the future; disclosing, also, the disloyalty of the French government.

Circular.

. . . In the midst of this lamentable crisis, advantage is taken of the attitude of the United States, who have been always hostile to a monarchical form of government and to an European intervention. His majesty has been informed that the French government and that of the United States have entered into negotiations to insure a Franco-American intervention by means of which it is promised that an end shall be put to the civil war which is desolating this country. To carry out this intention it is considered indispensable that the government to be established under this mediation should assume a republican form, and should be suggested by the Liberal party. The hopes of our government for the consolidation of order, which were partly based on a loyal and firm alliance, are thus deceived.

The French government had not, however, yet reached the limit of its disloyalty. The American frigate, after several days of useless waiting in the gulf, had put to sea to proceed to the United States, carrying back on board the two plenipotentiaries, who had not even landed. The news from Mexico and Orizaba had ruined the hopes of the ministers at the Tuileries, who now had no fear of unmasking before Maximilian's eyes the whole of their hostile policy, by again violating their promise given and recorded by treaty.

The Emperor to Castelnau.

Compiègne, December 13, 1866.

Send home the Foreign Legion and all the French, soldiers or any one else who wish to return, as well as the Austrian and Belgian Legions if they demand it.

This despatch had the effect of depriving Maximilian of his last support, in defiance of Article 3 in the treaty of Miramar, which had been expressly reserved in the convention of July 30, and, as will be recollected, was to the following effect :—' The Foreign Legion in the service of France, composed of 8,000 men, shall remain six years in Mexico after all the other French forces have been recalled in conformity with Article 2. From this time the said legion is to pass into the service and pay of the Mexican government. The latter government reserves to itself the power of shortening the period of the employment in Mexico of this foreign corps.'

There was no doubt that the dissolution of this legion would entail the withdrawal of the Austro-Belgian legion, which by itself would be incapable of upholding the monarchy, even for a time. Besides this, the defection of the French volunteers engaged in the ranks of the Mexican army must also surely follow; for they reckoned, beyond everything, on having this almost French element always near them. This contempt for plighted faith on the part of our government affords the greater cause for surprise, because, in a conversation with Mr. Bigelow (November 7, 1866), *the Emperor Napoleon had stated to the American minister, that if Maximilian asserted that he could maintain his authority alone, France would not withdraw its troops sooner than M. Drouyn de Lhuys had stipulated for, if such should be the desire of the young sovereign.* This was saying clearly that the expeditionary corps should be brought home in three separate divisions, and consequently that the French protection should be secured to Mexico for another year. The day that Mr. Bigelow received this assurance at Saint Cloud from the imperial lips, General Castelnau, in Mexico, was doing the very contrary; for we have seen that the joint note of the three French representatives announced to Maximilian that the Emperor Napoleon had resolved to withdraw his troops *en bloc* in the early part of 1867. What change, therefore, had taken place in the state of things as admitted by our government?—absolutely nothing. But Maximilian, declaring that he was able to maintain his power with his own resources alone, intimidation was tried as a last resource, which, through his decisive refusal to abandon the throne, necessarily changed into reality, for General Castelnau could no longer retract. The Emperor Napoleon, who had fancied this stratagem would be infallible, and was convinced that the abdication of Maximilian would solve everything to his satisfaction, doubtless thought it preferable to make this last threat, which he hoped would soon be shrouded under the veil of oblivion. We shall see directly what menacing language this silence called forth on the part of Mr. Seward. It is nevertheless the case that General Castelnau withdrew from Maximilian the troops which the emperor said were to be left him. This will be seen if we refer to the language of the interview at St. Cloud, reported by the American minister himself, the principal passages of which it will be best to quote:—

Despatch from Mr. Bigelow to Mr. Seward as to the Withdrawal en bloc of the Expeditionary Troops from Mexico during the next Spring.

Paris, November 8, 1866.

Sir,—The minister of foreign affairs informed me last Thursday, in reply to a question which certain rumours in the newspapers had led me to put to him, that the emperor contemplated withdrawing his troops from Mexico in the spring, but that he would not recall any corps before that time.

I expressed my surprise and my regret at this determination, so clearly contrary to the assurances given by his excellency's predecessor, both to you through the medium of the Marquis de Montholon, and also to me personally.

The minister fell back upon considerations of a purely military character, not desiring to see, or not estimating at its value, as it seemed to me, the important effect which this change might perhaps have on the relations of France with the United States.

My first impulse was to send him a note the following day, asking for a formal statement of the emperor's motives for having paid no regard to the stipulations made by his minister for foreign affairs relative to the recall of a detachment of his army from Mexico in the course of the month of November.

I came, however, to the conclusion, that it would be more satisfactory to the president if I saw the emperor himself on this subject.

To-day, therefore, I waited on his majesty at St. Cloud. I repeated to him all that the Marquis de Moustier had told me, and expressed to him my desire to know if I could do anything to anticipate and prevent the dissatisfaction which I was persuaded the people of my country would feel if this news was received without any explanation.

I alluded to the approaching meeting of Congress, a time when any change in our relations, either with France or with Mexico, would probably be the subject of discussion. I also expressed my fear that his majesty's reasons for delaying the withdrawal of the first detachment of his troops would be imputed to motives that our people would be inclined to resent.

The emperor told me that it was true that he had resolved to delay any recall of troops till the spring, but that in acting thus he had been influenced by military interests exclusively.

. . . . This despatch, added his majesty, has not been sent in cipher, in order that no secret should be made of its tenour to the United States.

. . . His majesty continued by saying, that almost at the same time he had sent General Castelnau to Mexico, who was directed to inform Maximilian that France could give him neither another *sou* nor another man. *If he* (Maximilian) *thought that he could maintain his authority alone, France would not withdraw its troops sooner than M. Drouyn de Lhuys had stipulated for, if such should be his desire*; but if, on the other hand, he was disposed to abdicate, which was the conduct his majesty advised him to follow, General Castelnau was directed to find out a government with whom he could treat for the protection of French interests, and to send home the whole of the army in the spring.

I asked the emperor if the president of the United States had been informed of all this; and if anything had been done to prepare his mind for this alteration in his majesty's policy.

He replied that he knew nothing about it; that M. Moustier ought to have done it. . . . There is but one feeling here as to the determination of France to wash its hands of Mexico as soon as possible. I doubt not that the emperor is acting in good faith towards us; but I was not sure that the change in his plans which I have commented upon would receive an equally favourable interpretation in the United States.

In consequence of the late successes of the imperialists in Mexico, and the rather disturbed state of our domestic political affairs, I fear lest the conduct of the emperor should awaken suspicions in the United States which might be seriously prejudicial to the friendly relations of the two countries.

To prevent, if possible, a calamity of this kind, I thought it my duty to take the precautions of which I have just informed you. The emperor having admitted in this conversation that he had advised Maximilian to abdicate, I have been prepared every day to receive the news of this event; for advice to one in the dependent position of Maximilian is almost equivalent to an order.

The emperor said that he hoped to hear the final result of the mission of General Castelnau about the end of this month.

A telegram has appeared in the 'Star' and 'Post' newspapers of London, reproducing the report in circulation in New York on the 6th instant—that Maximilian had abdicated. As we have received despatches of the 7th which made no allusion to this news, I presume that it is at least premature.

JOHN BIGELOW.

General Castelnau, however, was less harsh towards Maximilian than the Court of the Tuileries itself; for the former did no more than notify the recall of the troops at once, but Napoleon III., doubly severe, gave the order to send home the Foreign Legion as well. This attitude on the part of the Tuileries can only be explained by the deep irritation which was felt there: first, on account of the non-abdication of Maximilian, which kept our policy, our flag, and above all our responsibility in regard to the young sovereign, still entangled in regard to Mexican affairs; secondly, on account of the check given to Sherman's mission which, if it had succeeded, would have smothered, by the restoration of the Mexican republic, the seeds of misunderstanding with the United States; and finally, on account of a despatch from Mr. Seward (recently communicated to the Emperor Napoleon, although disavowed by our government), which called forth from the *Moniteur* in its bulletin of December 24, the following remarks:—' The American press sends us very incomplete extracts of the diplomatic correspondence which has just been submitted to congress.'

' Amongst it we notice a despatch dated November 23, sent by Mr. Seward to Mr. Bigelow.

' *This document the French government have never had any knowledge of.*

' The United States newspapers confirm, however, the good understanding which exists between the Federal government and that of the emperor.'

Looking at the fresh document of a threatening character which now follows, our patriotism finds a difficulty in realising this ' good understanding,' the assertion of which indicates really too much complacency on the part of the official journal.

Despatch from Mr. Seward to Mr. Bigelow, as to the Return of the French Troops from Mexico, dated November 23, 1866.

Sir,—Your despatch of November 8 (No. 384) relative to Mexico has been received. Your conduct in your interview both with M. de Moustier and with the emperor is entirely approved of.

Tell M. de Moustier that our government is astonished and distressed at the announcement now made for the first time,—that the promised withdrawal of a detachment of French troops from Mexico, which ought to have taken place in November, has been put off by the emperor. The embarrassment resulting from this is considerably increased by the circumstance that this resolution was adopted by the emperor without having conferred with the United States about it, or even advising them on the point. Our government has in no way sent reinforcements to the Mexicans, as the emperor seems to presume; and it knew nothing at all about his counter-order to Marshal Bazaine of which the emperor speaks.

We consult the official communications only, when we want to know the aims and resolutions of France, just as we communicate our own intentions and resolutions in this way when France is in question. I am not in a position to say, and, for the present it would be unnecessary to enter on the question, whether the President would have been able or not to acquiesce in the delay intended by the emperor, supposing that he had been consulted at a fitting time, and that this proposition had been based as now on purely military considerations, and that it had been characterised by ordinary manifestations of deference to the interests and feelings of the United States.

But the decision arrived at by the emperor of modifying the present arrangement without any previous understanding with the United States, and of leaving, for the present, the whole of the French army in Mexico, instead of withdrawing a detachment in November as promised, appears at the present time to be in every respect to be regretted.

We cannot give our adhesion to it, firstly, because the time —' next spring '—which is fixed for the complete evacuation, is indefinite and vague; secondly, because there is nothing that authorises us to state to congress and the American people that we have even now any better guarantee for the recall of the entire expeditionary force in spring than we had before for the recall of a portion of it in November; thirdly, reckoning completely on the (at least) literal execution of the emperor's agreement, and therefore foreseeing the evacuation of the French troops, we have adopted measures for co-operating with the republican government of Mexico in the pacification of that country, as well as in the prompt and solid re-establishment of the real constitutional authority of the government.

As a part of these measures, Mr. Campbell, our newly-nominated minister, accompanied by Lieutenant-General Sherman, was sent to Mexico in order to confer with President Juarez, on questions which are of the highest interest to the United States, and of vital importance to Mexico. Our policy and measures, thus adopted in the firm conviction that the evacuation of Mexico was about to commence, have been brought to the knowledge of the French legation here, and you have doubtless fulfilled your instructions by communicating them to the emperor's government at Paris.

The emperor will see that we cannot now recall Mr. Campbell, or modify the instructions in conformity to which it was expected he would treat, and according to which he may indeed have treated with the republican government of Mexico; viz., that this government certainly very warmly desires and confidently hopes that it will see the foreign occupation immediately and definitively cease.

You will therefore inform the emperor's government that the president desires and sincerely hopes that the evacuation of Mexico will be accomplished in conformity with the existing arrangement, so far as the inopportune complication necessitating this despatch will permit. On this point Mr. Campbell will receive instructions. Instructions will also be sent to the military forces of the United States, which are placed in a post of observation, and are waiting the special orders of the president. And that this will be done with the confidence that the telegraph or the courier will bring us intelligence of a satisfactory resolution on the part of the emperor in reply to this note. You will assure the French government that the United States, in wishing to free Mexico, have nothing so much at heart as preserving peace and friendship with France.

The president has not the slightest doubt that this resolution was decided on in France without any mature reflection as to the embarrassment that it would produce here, and also without any mental reservation as to leaving the troops of the French expedition in Mexico beyond the total period of eighteen months, which was stipulated at first for the complete evacuation.   W. H. SEWARD.

This document proves that Mr. Bigelow was commissioned to express to the government of the Emperor of the French the wishes of President Johnson. American diplomatists, as is well known, are not in the habit of altering the purport of their instructions for the sake of mere courtesy; it is, therefore, beyond all doubt that the communication of this document to the government actually took place. The telegraphic despatch from Compiègne of December 13, after the Tuileries had been informed of the contents of the American despatch, shows that henceforth all relations with Mexico were broken off without any qualifications whatever.

On the other hand, it can be thoroughly understood that after this increase of harsh measures on the part of the French emperor, the Mexican government assumed a more hostile attitude. After he quitted La Jalapilla, the young emperor went up by easy stages to Puebla; he travelled slowly, for, under the influence of the prejudicial regimen he was following, his health had become still more impaired. The sad news received from Paris and Miramar brought no relief to his sorrow. On the other hand, until the evacuation was quite decided upon, he was not very anxious to meet the French authorities at Mexico. He stopped at the country-house of the Archbishop of Puebla, situated at the edge of the valley leading down from Amozoc. General Castelnau and the French minister, without informing the marshal, came from Mexico and obtained an interview with the sovereign. The conversation which took place was curious enough to induce the Emperor of Mexico to express in writing that he purposed to publish an account of it in Europe; but it had the effect of only strengthening the resolutions of the crown. Maximilian returned to Mexico;

but giving up the palace of Chapultepec, he took up his quarters in a modest *hacienda* adjacent to the capital, called La Teja; it was the spot where our squadrons of the Chasseurs d'Afrique had encamped the day the French entered Mexico.

CHAPTER XX.

French Pecuniary Claims enforced—Forcible Proceedings at Vera Cruz—Customhouse Difficulties in the City of Mexico—Arbitrary Conduct of the French—The Mexican Minister's Protest—Discord in the French Camp—Marshal Bazaine's Painful Position—French Intrigues with the Rebels—Decisive Telegram to General Castelnau—Maximilian's Difficulties increase—His Generous Resolve as to Foreign Soldiers—Letter from the Empress Eugénie—The Clerical Plans fail—Imperial Disasters—Maximilian's Interview with Marshal Bazaine—Plain Statement by the Latter—The Junta in Mexico—Marshal Bazaine attends it—The Marshal's Declaration—The Junta decides for the Empire—Sale of the French Cavalry Horses—Exchange of Prisoners—Honourable Conduct of the Liberals—Appeals to French Honour—The Austrian Farewell.

THE Mexican government, as may be well imagined, felt but little disposed to exhaust its treasury, poor enough already, to satisfy the requirements of the convention of July 30. The recall of the legion had definitively torn up all the conventions which bound the two parties; and, in our opinion, Maximilian was justified in seeking to free himself from the French claims. The very evening Maximilian arrived at Orizaba, our head-quarters had begged him to give orders to the customs' authorities at Vera Cruz, as a notification made on this subject by M. Dano before the court left Mexico had not met with a reply. The emperor replied by telegraph that he would see to the matter without delay. On November 1, the day on which the convention was to come into force, no measures had yet been taken; the ministers were seeking to gain time, and required that the convention which had already been approved of should now be ratified. M. Dano directed the financial agents at

Vera Cruz to enter upon their duties and to draw up an official statement of the customs' accounts agreed upon. On November 20, matters were made worse in consequence of the refusal of the Mexican officials to allow the stipulated reductions to be made. The French agent, in virtue of orders received from Paris, threatened to employ force in order to obtain satisfaction. The emperor when informed of it sent a despatch to Marshal Bazaine to induce him to put a stop to these measures.

The Emperor to Marshal Bazaine.

Orizaba, November 21, 1866.

I can in no way consent to the proceedings adopted by M. X——, towards the custom-house officials at Vera Cruz, in doing which he has made use of your authority; the question is as to funds which the minister of the *haciendas* has disposed of with my authority during the months of September and October. I now inform you that M. X—— threatens to prevent by force the duties carried on at the custom-house. I hope that you will put a stop to this illegal step. MAXIMILIAN.

Was it not truly sad to witness the spectacle of a sovereign complaining that his word was doubted? By the terms of the convention we were strictly in the right, according to the enquiry which was made without delay by an inspector of finance. But without noticing the unwillingness of the ministry, was it generous thus to deprive the monarch of his last resources when our government had itself chosen to forget its formal engagements? When the inquiry was finished, the marshal sent to Maximilian the reply of M. de Maintenant, who relied literally on the provisions of the convention of July 30:—

Mexico, November 29, 1866.

Sire,—I have the honour of transmitting to your majesty a copy of the reply that the inspector-general of finances has made to the demand for explanation which I hastened to send him. It is not my business to discuss the arguments which M. de Maintenant has brought forward; your majesty cannot be ignorant that my action in questions which specially concern financial matters is very limited. The instructions directing them emanate immediately from the French minister of finance. With the deepest respect, sire, &c.,

BAZAINE.

The same sort of scandal as that which had become public at the port of Vera Cruz was also the cause of violent measures being adopted at Mexico. The Mexican government refused to deliver up to certain merchants of the capital some merchandise which had arrived at the custom-house at Mexico, although these imported goods had already paid the duty at the port of landing. This state of things caused very great loss to commerce, especially on the eve of January 1, 1867. At the end of a meeting, in which the marshal, the French minister, General Castelnau, and the Inspector-General de Maintenant took a part, it was decided that willingly or unwillingly the goods detained should be given up to the parties interested. In spite of the opposition of M. de Pereda, under-secretary of state for foreign affairs, the affair was proceeded with, and an official notice was inserted in the 'New Era' to inform the merchants of the arrangements which had been made. These acts suggested to M. de Pereda the following solemn protest:—*

Mexico, January 6, 1867.

Monsieur le Ministre,—I have had the honour of receiving your excellency's note of yesterday's date in reply to mine of

---

* As our Government showed itself so particular just at last, when the stoppage of these small sums would but little improve the fortunes of our countrymen and our treasury, why was it allowed that twelve millions should be paid Jecker, the Swiss, who had been naturalised as a Frenchman only yesterday as it were? Why was it allowed that this claim should take precedence over the interests of all our *true* countrymen?

the 2nd instant, relative to the publication by M. de Maintenant of a notice inserted in the 'New Era;' I have also received the copy of a new official communication agreed upon between your excellency, Marshal Bazaine, General Castelnau, and the inspector-general of finance, insisting on the surrender of the goods detained in the custom-house of this capital, notwithstanding the contrary orders of the government, and going so far as to announce that an agent will be placed at the said custom-house to ensure the execution of that which has been agreed upon. I have communicated all this to the emperor, and in reply his majesty directs me to state that he observes with grief and deep dissatisfaction the course of conduct which the French authorities have followed in this business; for even if the convention of July 30 had been legally in force, it does not give authority, in letter or spirit, either that acts of jurisdiction should be exercised in the empire, or that the sovereignty of the government should be attacked.

Consequently, his majesty has ordered that I should once more protest, as I now protest solemnly and formally in his name, against proceedings as irregular as they are hostile to the rights of the nation and the supremacy of the sovereign, rendering the representatives of France responsible from the present time before France, before their own government, and before all civilised nations, for the collision produced by these proceedings and all the consequences which may result therefrom.

The new provisions made by the representatives of France have placed the imperial government under the necessity of issuing another proclamation for the just defence of the rights of the empire, couched in the terms which your excellency will see in the copy annexed. DE PEREDA.

Under-Secretary of State.

The notice to commerce published officially was thus worded:—

Notice to Commerce.

We are authorised to acquaint the merchants who are owners of goods now detained in the custom-house of this capital which have been sent forward from Vera Cruz with documents not in conformity with the laws of the empire, that the representatives of France have no authority to place agents at the said custom-house to assist the transfer of the said goods; for even supposing that the convention of July 30 was in force in all its rigour, the action of the said representatives would be confined to the port of landing, and could not extend to the custom-houses of the interior; on the other hand, if the said goods should be withdrawn without a previous settlement with the administration of the Mexican revenue, the owners will be subject to all that will be necessary to be done in conformity with the fiscal laws now in force.

It will hardly astonish when we say that perfect harmony did not prevail in the camp of the French authorities, and if we are to believe in the indiscreet things which, either purposely or not, followed the secret conferences held at the head-quarters at Buenavista, we cannot doubt that discord on a certain point had broken out amongst our representatives, the echo of which had spread as far as Washington. Now, this capital was always kept well informed by Romero, Juarez's minister, and it was well known there that Maximilian's prolonged stay was a source of irritation both to the imperial aide-de-camp and to M. Dano. Energetic measures even were spoken of such as circumstances dictated. Now it was that the marshal felt all the difficulty and painfulness of the task which he had consented to go through with. He was more than once compelled (we defy contradiction in this), to bitterly express his regret that he had not demanded his recall from Mexico. What must his feelings have been in contemplating the daily decay of the monarchy which he had as it were nursed in its cradle, and the frail existence of which he had for three years done his best to prolong?

After all, Maximilian (who had declared 'that he would not go back to Europe in the baggage-waggon of our army') could not be compelled to take a step which even the French cabinet in a moment of sincerity had themselves stigmatised. On December 31, 1866, they wrote, ' It is not easy for Maximilian to make any retreat which will not be a stain on his political life; and all must wish that it could be otherwise. But will he have the energy necessary for opening a new campaign?' Maximilian had at his own risk made use of the personal right he undoubtedly possessed, and had thrown himself back into the *melée*. But he forgot that his ambition was so far culpable that it kept on the civil war. When he entered on the career which M. Eloïn opened out before his eyes, he ought to have descried on the horizon a battle-field where he might have found the merited death which fortune has in reserve for conquerors disappointed in arms.

The marshal, however, could not help being repugnant to being the means of precipitating Maximilian's fall by entering into negotiations with the liberal chiefs, negotiations too which seemed inopportune, as the expeditionary corps was about to retire, leaving behind it a sovereign unwilling to abdicate. Thus, the military and political conduct of the French representatives must have appeared suspicious, and with good reason, since it was suggested by instructions from the Tuileries which were always vague and indefinite, opening the door to every kind of compromise. Outside head-quarters the intrigues with the rebels were still going on. As to the marshal, ever faithful to his duty and to his written orders, he informed the liberal chiefs that, although he was forbidden by his government to undertake any fresh expeditions against them, he was at any rate directed to fire upon them if they approached the places occupied by our arms, any nearer than two days' march. This was the language used to Porfirio Diaz, to Ruis and to Riva Palacios.

After a mature examination of all the contradictory documents, we are fully persuaded that the French government had wrongly thought that they should find in the marshal a docile instrument of its policy, and that he would be prompt in comprehending mere desires, and be ready of his own accord to ensure their success. In this ambiguous path, which seems authorised in modern diplomacy, military honour runs a risk of being led astray. There is no doubt that his position was a false one; but the marshal was preserved by his soldier-like honesty of purpose, and always held himself harmless behind his written instructions. If we wish to be further convinced of this, it will be sufficient if we examine the despatch from Napoleon III. which arrived by the American route, addressed to General Castelnau. The emperor, since the arrival of his aide-de-camp in Mexico, no longer communicated directly with the marshal.

The Emperor to General Castelnau.

Paris, January 10, 1867.

Received despatch of December 7th. Do not force the emperor to abdicate; but do not delay the departure of the troops. Send home all who do not wish to stay.

What fresh event could have called forth this explicit despatch? Certainly it must have been the refusal of the commander-in-chief to take a part in violent measures against the sovereign whom he was commissioned to defend. General Castelnau was, it is true, armed with full powers; but this despatch seems to prove that he was *not* provided with *written* instructions, which would perhaps have been too compromising to the French policy. The compliance of the marshal must have been reckoned on at some given moment. But, at the time when Maximilian's refusal to abdicate forced General Castelnau to assume the hostile attitude which had been tacitly foreseen at Paris, the latter, being only able to avail himself of *verbal* instructions, must have come in collision with the opposition of the head-quarters' authorities, resolved as they were to allow no alteration in the nature of their express orders, without formal directions from the government. A demand for orders addressed to the palace of the Tuileries must evidently have been the result of this collision. Hence, the imperial despatch of January 10; the French government had shrunk back at the last moment. If the marshal had been courtier enough to keep himself informed from Paris of the real line of policy which the cabinet of the Tuileries had for a long time suggested in regard to Mexico, of which it wished to wash its hands at any price, he would have been enlightened beforehand as to the course of conduct which events would be likely to impose upon him, and he would have retired in good time. Two thousand leagues away, how could he divine the wind that blew in the exalted regions of a court so variable as that of France? It would have been of service to him if he had constantly trimmed his sails, like the pilot who scans the horizon, that he may not be taken by surprise.

Since his return to Mexico, Maximilian began to perceive the inextricable complication of difficulties into which, urged on by Father Fischer, he had plunged himself body and soul. His hope of surmounting them became less every day. The unexpected recall of the foreign legion had disorganised the auxiliary contingents and the Mexican army; for the French volunteers refused to remain in the ranks of the latter after the departure of the Europeans. The Emperor of Mexico, who certainly cannot be reproached with a want of generosity, had decidedly resolved that his fellow-countrymen should not participate in the chances of his fortune, and had liberated them from their engagements. This action is an honour to the memory of the sovereign. The marshal had been waiting for this spontaneous movement on the part of the crown, in order to ask for his decision relative to our countrymen also. Maximilian replied that he gave them also their liberty; the following was his last letter to the French head-quarters:—

Hacienda de la Teja, January 7, 1867.

" My dear Marshal,—I have received the letter in which you ask if I offer any obstacle to the arrangement by which the officers and soldiers of French origin who are at present serving in our army, should return to their country (those at least who desire to do so), according to the instructions which you have received from your government. I hasten to acquaint you that our minister of war has received the order to grant to all soldiers of the French nation who have entered the Mexican service the same advantages which the Austrians and Belgians have received.

Receive the assurance of the entire friendship of your very affectionate, MAXIMILIAN.

Maximilian was still deluded as to the state of public opinion in France, and could not help recalling continually to his mind the former promises which he had received at Paris; he still therefore retained a secret hope that the court of the Tuileries would relax in the severity of its measures. A private letter from the Empress Eugénie, for whose character he professed a sympathetic admiration, had not a little contributed to cherish these illusions in the mind of the young emperor. He seemed to take a pleasure in saying that this letter, the aim of which was to heal the wound which had been made by the interview of Saint Cloud, *had much comforted him.* But the last despatch from Compiègne had put an end to these deceptions. Domestic questions, too, now began to add their part to the causes for discouragement.

The clergy fulfilled but badly their promises of co-operation; Miramon was certainly preparing for his campaign in the North, but the vacancies in the ranks of the Mexican army caused by the numerous desertions were no better filled up than the deficiency in the treasury. The spectre of bankruptcy was always menacing them. The rebels were gaining ground every day. As the state capitals were evacuated by the expeditionary corps, the transfer of each place into the hands of the imperial guards was carried out, as regularly as it would have been in Europe, by the means of our artillery and engineer officers. Duly signed official statements prove that not a single Mexican town was delivered up to the rebels by the French, and that Maximilian's troops were left in possession of all the fortified places, which also had been put in an efficient state of defence. It is true enough that a few days after, often even the very next day, the imperial commissioners repeatedly directed the abandonment of places, without even firing a shot.

The programme traced out for Maximilian by M. Eloïn had therefore the immediate effect of placing him in a fresh *cul-de-sac*, an exit from which his honour rendered difficult. How could the sovereign have flattered himself even for a moment that he should be able to assemble a congress? Was not the continual increase in the insurrection an insuperable barrier in the way of the 'notables' of distant provinces who might have consented to venture across a country disturbed by enemies, in order to come to a deliberation at Mexico? Did not this immense 'raising of bucklers' indicate that his appeal to the people was doomed beforehand to frustration? For the citizens, who rose *en masse* under the republican banner, induced either by conviction or by political necessity, had already given their votes. The lot of the monarchy was, therefore, settled without chance of appeal. But, then, would the Mexicans take up arms to elect an Austrian archduke as president of the republic, in preference to a liberal—a son, too, of the nation? This idea of a congress was an unhappy dream, which Maximilian obstinately pursued, circumvented as he was by the passions of his partisans. It was this chimera which led the unfortunate prince to his funeral pall at Queretaro.

Yet the stern reality betrayed itself too stringently to escape Maximilian's observation. Under the influence of the gloomy thoughts which were called forth, he sent for the marshal to come to the Hacienda de la Teja. There a long and friendly conversation took place; they spoke first of the health of the Empress Charlotte, then of Miramon's campaign, and at last of MM. Castelnau and Dano's visit to Puebla, the details of which the Emperor well recollected. The marshal, on being asked his opinion as to the position and future prospects of the monarchy, replied that, after the recall of the foreign legion (which deprived Maximilian of any chance of retreat in case of reverses), and the withdrawal of our soldiers, there would be nothing but danger, to be encountered without glory. 'From the moment,' he added, 'that the United States boldly pronounced their *veto* against the imperial system, your throne was nothing but a bubble, even if your majesty had obtained the help of a hundred thousand Frenchmen. Supposing even that the Americans had observed neutrality during the continuance of the intervention, the monarchy itself had no spirit of vitality. A federal combination would have been the only system to be attempted in the face of the Union, who would no doubt have acceded to it, if the South had been recognised by France at the proper time. My advice is that your majesty should voluntarily retire.' Just as they were separating, Maximilian remarked to the marshal: 'I put the greatest confidence in you, and I beg that you will be present at a Junta that I am going to convoke on Monday, January 14, at the palace at Mexico. I shall myself be present, and there you must repeat all that you think. If the majority entertain your opinion, I shall leave; if they desire that I should remain, the matter is settled. I shall remain, because I do not wish to look like a soldier who throws away his musket to run away the faster from the battle-field.'

This manly language was well worthy of the race of Hapsburg. The next day the marshal received a summons, which was sent to him by the president of the council of ministers:—

Mexico, January 11, 1867.

Marshal,—His majesty the emperor desiring to learn, confidentially and amicably, the opinion of your excellency and of other persons on a matter of deep importance, desires me to address your excellency, and to beg that you will be good enough to be present at the meeting which will take place at the Government Palace on Monday next, the 4th instant, at 2 o'clock in the afternoon.

LARÈS,
President of the council of ministers.

Maximilian's strength of will was unable to carry out his resolution. When the marshal proceeded to the palace at Mexico, at the time appointed for the meeting, he was received by an assembly of forty persons. But he was informed that the Emperor had relinquished the idea of being present at the Junta.

There is no doubt that his advisers, dreading the decision to which the crown would be impelled by the public declaration of the commander-in-chief, the nature of which had been foreseen, had objected to the sovereign being present. The marshal, astonished, was on the point of retiring; but, on reflection, he thought that it would be more expedient that he should state boldly his way of looking at the state of things—especially just now, when the French flag was on the point of leaving Mexico:—

Declaration of Marshal Bazaine to the Junta.

Mexico, January 14, 1867.

The fact that the imperial Mexican garrisons have evacuated, without firing a shot, places that were well fortified and sufficiently armed, in consequence of demonstrations made by an enemy of less strength than the above garrisons, has clearly shown the small amount of confidence which is inspired by the military protection which the empire can promise to the inhabitants. The latter have, at the present date, fully expressed their opinions. Every state has again taken its place in the federation. The elections, which have taken place on the basis of the constitution of 1857, have replaced the larger portion of the federal authorities, who have been *de facto* established since the departure of the imperial *employés*. The federal system is consequently re-established over the greatest part of the territory.

What is there to be gained by making military efforts, and incurring immense expenses, in order to go back and conquer the territory which is lost?—Nothing!

From the experience I have gained during the last two years, I gather that the population, generally, has very little disposition to support the empire; and even could it be supported by columns sent into the interior, the latter, gradually imbibing as they proceeded the republican influence, would sooner or later pronounce in its favour; and, on the other hand, they would be weakened by the garrisons which they would be compelled to leave in the great centres of population. The enemy, as is even now the case, would harass them, and keep them in a state of blockade, and all communication would be cut off between them and the central government. It would follow, as the immediate consequence, that commerce would be completely paralysed, as well as all agricultural and manufacturing labour; this would produce a state of deep dissatisfaction among the population, and an absolute want of resources, requisite to keep the troops to their duty.

The federal organisation seems as if it would save the country from any hostile attempt on the part of the United States; and this consideration appears to exercise a great influence over the minds of the people, who (rightly enough) fear lest any other form of government should prompt their northern neighbours to come down upon them as conquerors.

1. In a military point of view, I do not think that the imperial forces can maintain the country in a state of such tranquillity that the government of the emperor could be fully carried on. The military operations will be only isolated conflicts without decided results; the civil war will be kept on, with the arbitrary measures which these operations necessarily bring with them; and the demoralisation and ruin of the country will result as an infallible consequence.

2. In a financial point of view, as the administration of the country cannot be regularly carried on, the necessary means will not be produced for the maintenance of the central imperial government, and its agents will be obliged to impose heavy taxes, thus increasing the dissatisfaction of the population.

3. In a political point of view, the opinion of the majority of the nation appears, at the present time, to be far more inclined to a federal republic than to an empire; I may be allowed to doubt whether an appeal to the nation would result favourably to the present system, and perhaps, indeed, it would not respond at all to the summons addressed to it.

In short, it appears to me to be impossible that his majesty can continue to govern the country under any conditions which would be honourable for his sovereignty, without, in fact, lowering himself to the rank of a partisan chief; and that it would be preferable, both for his glory and his safety, that his majesty should surrender his authority to the nation.

This loyal declaration well deserved to reach the steps of the throne. The marshal immediately sent a copy of it to the emperor :—

Sire,—Your majesty invited me, through the medium of the president of the council of ministers, to state, in a candid and friendly way, my opinion as to the present state of things.

I have now the honour of sending to your majesty the statement which I read at the meeting held to-day, which is the sincere expression of the views I entertain.

With the deepest respect, Sire, &c.,
BAZAINE.

After they had heard the commander-in-chief's statement, the Junta proceeded to the ballot. Unanimously, with the exception of four voices, it was decided that the monarchy was to continue to struggle on. The die was cast. This vote, which closed the door to any combinations of republican reorganisation on the part of France, and irretrievably swept away the guarantee of the French claims and loans, (which might have been stipulated for with a new republican president,) decisively put a stop to General Castelnau's mission, and the attempts which were making by our diplomatists among the disaffected leaders.

The Junta likewise declared, ' that any other appeal was unnecessary, notwithstanding the express desire of the emperor to refer the matter to a national congress.'

The ministers of war and of finance asserted that they possessed—the one 250,000 piastres in cash, the other 11,000,000 piastres, of which 8,000,000 piastres were at his immediate disposal.

The French occupation was approaching its close. After the Emperor Napoleon's last despatch, directing that complete freedom of action should be left to Maximilian, one task only remained to the commander-in-chief—that of sending home the 28,000 men constituting the expeditionary corps. French honour also required that all the places which we still held should be made over to Maximilian in a good state of defence, with stores sufficient for the garrisons directed to occupy them. A just feeling of delicacy also dictated to our government that our unfortunate ally should profit by all the resources sent out from Europe for the use of the expeditionary corps, and warehoused by our commissaries at Mexico and at Vera Cruz.

All these questions had been foreseen at Paris. It must be acknowledged that they had not been settled under any very generous inspiration as regarded Maximilian. They were dated September 15, 1866, and enjoined the commander-in-chief 'only to bring to France the best of the horses, the value of which had been ascertained to be greater than the considerable cost of freight.' All the other animals were to be sold (*no matter at what price*) either in Mexico or in the Havannah. It was recommended that the rest should be conveyed for sale to our colonies of Martinique or Guadeloupe. 'You must not,' added the despatch to our head-quarters, 'leave your artillery stores in Mexico.'

This order was just and necessary, as regarded the artillery itself; for cannon marked with the arms of France are almost like standards, which must never be relinquished to foreign hands unless dearly sold. As to the horses—in the ranks of which were reckoned some old servants from the Crimea, Algeria, and Italy, which were worn out by old age and this last campaign—it would have been better to have presented them to the Emperor. Through this not being done, they helped to increase the squadrons of the Liberal cavalry, who thereby acquired the actual supericrity, which we had so often availed ourselves of in the numerous encounters in which we had gained the day by our greater speed. It was well known at Paris that the treasury of the monarchy was wretchedly poor, and the offer which was made to buy them for ready money was necessarily rejected as illusive.

What was to become of them? Our regiments being forced to go down to Vera Cruz with their horses, and our batteries being drawn by their draught-horses and mules as far as the railway at La Soledad, they were there compelled to get rid of a considerable quantity of animals, which could not be sold except at a miserable price. The Remounting Board published and printed notices, announcing that as the various columns reached Paso-del-Macho, the terminus of the railway, a miserable village situated between La Soledad and the Chiquihuite, successive public sales would take place. But the Mexicans, who knew beforehand that these horses were condemned to remain in the country, rightly enough cared but little to give four or five hundred piastres each (a price which they would readily have produced on the high plateaus) for Arabian horses that they knew they would be able to obtain ultimately at a miserable price.

The embarkation had commenced. Each of our regiments, entering the *Terres Chaudes* in the morning, reached the port the very same evening. The delicate operation of shipping a *corps d'armée* and a vast amount of stores in the roadstead of Vera Cruz, at a time when the blast of the *norte* and the attacks of the *vomito* are always to be dreaded, stringently required that the concentration of ships in the port should last as short a time as possible. Some of the troops, therefore, passed direct from Cordova to the sea. The *hacendados*, as well as the guerillas, whose costume in no way betrayed their real character, watched the arrival of the detachments. The former, wishing to cross their stock with Arab blood, pushed their biddings up to a certain sum, the average of which did not exceed a hundred francs; the latter rode away proudly, on our poor dumb companions in arms; tears dimmed the eyes of many an old trooper, when he heard the last neigh of his faithful charger. The men would have felt less regret at this separation (which in any case must be a sad one) if they had known that these faithful servants were going back to die under Maximilian's banner, for which we and they had fought for the last five years. Politics went for nothing in these sad adieus; sympathy for the deserted prince was the only thing that spoke. Rather than have witnessed this dispiriting spectacle—which really had much resemblance to the rout of an army—our soldiers would willingly have repaid to the imperial treasury the small sum that this lamentable proceeding could have brought in.

The feeling that prevailed in Paris was, however, a more kindly one, when they bethought themselves of our poor colonies of Martinique and Guadeloupe, nowadays so cast off by the mother-country that they are gradually withering away, despite their bright tropical sun, and, in order that they may exist, are asking that they may become either English or Russian dependencies. Admiral La Roncière le Noury conveyed into our possessions in the Antilles 400 of the best horses of the expeditionary corps; these, at least, will find their graves in soil belonging to their country.

Up to the last hour of the occupation, the Mexican treasury was drawn upon, although it became more impoverished every day. This was following a course of action which was hardly worthy of France; but M. Dano was forced to obey the instructions of our minister for foreign affairs, as is shown by the two following documents:—

Mexico, January 21, 1867.

Monsieur le Maréchal,—The opposition offered by the government of the Emperor Maximilian to the execution of the convention of July 30 being more active than ever, and new difficulties necessarily being the consequence, I have the honour of transmitting (enclosed) to your excellency the last instructions which have been given to me on this subject by the emperor's minister of foreign affairs.

DANO,
Minister of France.

Paris, December 15, 1866.

Sir,—By your letter of November 9 (No. 99), you inform me that, without allowing yourself to be stopped by the objections which M. de Pereda has endeavoured to introduce, you have proceeded to put into execution the convention relative to the assignment which was to begin on November 1, and you also send me an official statement of agreed accounts of the custom-house at Vera Cruz, which has been drawn up by our agents on their entering upon their duties.

You have done right, relying on the precise stipulations of article 7, in replying to the Mexican under-secretary of state for foreign affairs, that the deed of July 30 needed no other formality before it was put in force. I can only fully approve what you have done, and must impress upon you to maintain the same course of action if our rights are again questioned.

DE MOUSTIER.

Surely there had been a want of foresight when, under the pretext of recovering a few millions for our countrymen, more than six hundred millions were buried in the Mexican abyss: just now, on the other hand, there was a want of generosity in extorting from Maximilian his last financial resources.

In a military point of view, there was still one important question to be resolved. It was impossible that our army could withdraw, leaving behind them

French prisoners in the hands of the enemy. The head-quarters authorities, through the official medium of its military cabinet, were compelled to enter into treaty with the liberal chiefs at several different points, to settle the exchange of our countrymen for rebel Mexicans. Murphy, the minister of war, had begged the commander-in-chief, in Maximilian's name, to treat for the liberty of the imperialists who had fallen into the power of the Juarists. The Austrian chargé-d'affaires had also had recourse to the French authorities for the freedom of the soldiers of the Austro-Belgian legion, who had capitulated in the actions at Miahuatlan, La Carbonera, and Oajaca.

Baron Lago had even begged the marshal to intervene personally, a thing he had not done in any former negotiations with Juarez's lieutenants:—

Mexico, January 29, 1867.

Monsieur le Maréchal,—The members of the corps of Austrian volunteers having, by the dissolution of this force, ceased to be Mexican soldiers, I take the liberty of appealing to the kindness of your excellency, and beg that you will be good enough to use all your influence and all your efforts to obtain the freedom, as soon as possible, of the Austrian volunteers who are now in the hands of the rebels, especially those at Oajaca. *I would, at the same time, beg that your excellency will not allow yourself to be stopped for an instant in this noble task, by any remonstrances or observations that might be made against your personal intervention in the matter above named.*

BARON DE LAGO,
Austrian Chargé d'Affaires.

The republican generals, however, well understood that it would be highly imprudent in them, for the sake of their own cause, to delay the evacuation of the French army by any threatening demonstration, or even by firing a single shot. From the first, they had shown that they were disposed towards giving up their prisoners, whom, moreover, they had always treated honourably and humanely, in consequence of regulations which emanated from Juarez, and would have done honour to an European army.

At Pachuca, Joaquim Martinez offered to hold intercourse with us for this purpose. At Oajaca, a person named Thiele, Porfirio Diaz' private secretary, had presented himself, in November 1866, at our outposts at Tehuacan.* This person was of French origin, and had been in the police-force which was sent out from Paris by M. Hirvoix, head of the police there, for the security of the sovereigns of Mexico; subsequently he had entered Maximilian's service, and had proceeded as agent of colonisation to the coast of Oajaca. Thence he had gone over to the enemy, to avoid the persecutions of a high Mexican functionary. He had offered his services to Porfirio Diaz, from whom he now brought an answer to a note from General Aymard. This note, which opened negotiations with the liberals, was sent with a view of claiming those of our countrymen who had been surprised in Oajaca after the death of the commandant, Testard. We had seventy prisoners in Porfirio's hands (nineteen of whom were officers of the *cazadores*); on January 22, the latter handed them over to us, safe and sound, at Buenavista. This delicate operation, which had lasted more than two months, is explained in the following letter, addressed to the head of the military cabinet of our head-quarters, who had to deal with all these questions:—

* The young emperor, hoping (though very mistakenly) to bring over to his side General Porfirio, the devoted friend and countryman of Juarez, had secretly sent for the secretary Thiele to come to the city of Mexico (through the medium of our head-quarters), and had entrusted him with a confidential mission to the hostile chief, which however totally failed.

Oajaca, January 12, 1867.

Colonel,—M. Thiele has handed me the letter which you sent me. I approve of the convention entered into for the exchange of prisoners, and this very day they are on their way to the city of Tehuacan.

Colonel Milicua, chief of my staff, and my secretary M. Thiele, are appointed to officially arrange the exchange. They have full powers to deal with any incidents which may arise up to the close of the negotiations.

As to the French soldiers, taken prisoners at La Baranca Seca, they shall be placed at your disposal. I do not know where they are, and I cannot ensure that they shall be given up on any fixed day; but I can assure you that all the measures are taken to arrive at an early result. The Mexican soldiers who are prisoners in your hands are to be sent to Tlacotalpan to General Rafael Benavidez, the military commander of that district. Receive, &c.

PORFIRIO DIAZ.

In Michoacan, Vincente Riva Palacios' loyalty went so far that, over the whole extent of his command, small detachments of wounded or convalescent French soldiers making their way to Mexico from the shores of the Pacific met with every respect; he also took care that they were not troubled by the undisciplined guerillas:—

Republican Army of the Centre.

To the Colonel, Head of the Military Cabinet.

Head Quarters of Tenancingo, January 19, 1867.

I have received your letter of January 14, with the enclosures, which I have forwarded to the French officers. You can assure the marshal, in my name, that his countrymen, who are travelling over the roads from Morelia to Mexico, will meet with entire respect, both as to person and property, over the whole line of road under my command, and I am giving orders to prevent any *contretemps* whatever.

VINCENTE RIVA PALACIOS.

The conduct of these liberal chiefs was a last and striking homage rendered to the humanity of the French commanders, who, during the whole of this fierce campaign, had been able to make a just distinction between soldiers and banditti. In spite of the war—in which, however, they knew that we had but little sympathy—they felt confidence in the French flag, and they had no fear in asking protection from us against the excesses of their own countrymen :—

Republican Army of the Centre.

El Salitre, November 4, 1866.

Marshal,—Just as I was marching with my forces against the town of Toluca, being convinced that the place was not able to resist me, and desirous of sparing the town all the sad consequences of an assault, I sent Colonel J. Lalanne, with a flag of truce, to obtain an interview with the Mexican commander of the place, and to propose to them honourable terms of surrender.

My envoy was made prisoner on his road, and has been taken to the city of Mexico. This is a violation of the usages of war, which doubtless is only caused by an excess of zeal in those who took him prisoner.

I have always been aware of your honourable feelings, and I reckon on them in hoping that you will immediately have the matter set right.   VINCENTE RIVA PALACIOS.

The above request was granted, as well as the following :—

Apam, January 27, 1867.

To the French head-quarters.

The youth, Antonio Mendez, has been arrested in the capital in an arbitrary manner. He is serving under my orders. His father being dead, I allowed him leave of absence for private affairs. He was therefore separated from the republican forces, and his imprisonment is as unjust as it is shameful. I feel sure that you will not allow that such an abuse of authority should take place in the name of the French. I allowed Mendez to proceed to Mexico, because he was going under the shadow of the French flag. If I had known that it was the clerical party which he would have to deal with, I should not have permitted him to go away.

I hope that you will be good enough to see that Mendez is set at liberty. Receive, &c.,

FLORENTINO MERCADO.

The rebels, whose right to resist invasion we have the honour of being the first in France to defend, never fell into the error of mixing our army up with our policy. The following letter from Porfirio Diaz' chief of the staff shows that in the liberal camp they knew how to attribute due honour to the courage of their enemies:—

Republican Army.

Oajaca, December 29, 1866.

To the Chief of the Staff in the French Expeditionary Corps.

I have the honour of sending you, by the hands of M. Ch. Thiele, the sword worn by the Commandant Testard, who was killed in the action at Miahuatlan.

I should be glad, M. le Colonel, for this weapon to be transmitted to his family; and it will be a proof to them of the esteem which we, although enemies, feel for M. Testard, whose courage and self-devotion we admired on the field of battle which was so fatal to him. ESPINOZA,

Chief of the Staff to the Commander-in-Chief
of the Army of the East.

The time had now arrived for the Austrians to quit the soil which they had watered with their blood. Before they withdrew, they thought that it was right to bid farewell to their companions in arms, who had not forgotten their heroic resistance in the plains of Lombardy. They, too, had paid dearly for the honour of defending the throne of the prince who had sprung from the royal race of their own country:—

Orizaba, January 27, 1867.

Monsieur le Maréchal de France,—Now, as we are about to quit the soil of Mexico to return to Austria, I have the honour of expressing to your excellency our extreme gratitude for your kind protection, without which the lot of the Austrian corps would have been but a sad one.

It will ever be for us a glorious reminiscence, that we have fought under the orders of your excellency, and by the side of the French expeditionary corps.

God grant that a time may arrive when we may be permitted to offer proofs of our devotion to your excellency and of our gratitude towards France, which has protected us in Mexico, and has overwhelmed us with benefits!

I beg, &c.
For the Austrian corps,
Lieutenant-Colonel POLAK.

CHAPTER XXI.

Withdrawal of French Troops from the Capital—Position of the Rebels—Dissatisfaction of M. Larès at the passive Attitude of the French Army—Marshal Bazaine's vindicatory Letter—Maximilian's final Rupture with the French Authorities—Proposition as to the 'Cross of Guadeloupe'—Interference of Abbé Fischer—His Reproval by the French Authorities—Orders for immediate Embarcation—French Measures for the Protection of the Capital—Destruction of French Munitions of War—Maximilian's Mistrust and Visit to the Citadel—French Flag struck in the City of Mexico—Characters of Mejia and Miramon—General Castelnau's Return—Marshal Bazain's last Appeal to Maximilian—Its Failure—Marshal Bazaine fortifies Vera Cruz—Marshal Bazaine's Letter to the French Admiral—Final Departure from Vera Cruz of the French Troops—The Marshal's bad Reception in France—Its Cause and its Injustice.

AT the end of January, 1867, the bayonets of the French army, in full retreat, stretched out like a ribbon of steel along the dusty road from Mexico to Vera Cruz.

The Austro-Belgian corps went down to the sea, flanked by our troops, to embark the first, in virtue of the promise made to Maximilian. In a few days nothing but a rearguard would be left in the city of Mexico. The environs of the capital were, therefore, already invaded by the insurrection, which came on like the rising tide. The time for fighting was now over for our soldiers. The rebels took care to keep at a long distance off, and out of sight of our outposts, which were, however, well prepared to meet any attack. Could more be required from the Juarists? Ought we to have begun another campaign, to wrest from them the towns which the imperialists had given up without resistance? Such a proceeding as this would only have been an act of folly. For, not only would it have been incurring danger without any useful end, but it would have delayed the evacuation, and provoked reprisals against the inhabitants of these places, and, subsequently, would have made it worse for our own countrymen, whose position was already bad enough. Besides, the orders of the French government were expressly opposed to it; and wisely so. The president of the council, dissatisfied with the passive attitude of our troops, drew up a letter which was insulting to our good faith, and called for a complaint addressed to Maximilian himself; it also caused a rupture with the minister.

Mexico, January 28, 1867.

Sire,—I have the honour of sending to your majesty a copy of an extract of a letter, dated the 25th of this month, and forwarded to me by the president of the council of ministers.

He states in this letter:—' The marshal and General Castelnau, in their communication of the 7th of last November, declared that so long as the French troops were in Mexico they would protect as before the authorities and the inhabitants, and, in short, would maintain order in the districts which they occupy, but that they would not undertake any distant expedition.

'An attack has recently taken place at Texcoco.

'Your excellency has not deemed it expedient to give any assistance according to the request of the general of our second division. The government would be glad to know what attitude the French troops in the capital would assume if, before their withdrawal, they were besieged by the rebels, or if the enemy attacked them on any point, or made any other kind of aggression.'

The impropriety of the above language will not fail to strike your majesty, who has never done me the injustice of supposing for a single instant that the loyalty of the French army could ever be called in question.

By pointing out to his majesty the Emperor of Mexico the conduct which his ministers are pursuing towards me in his name, I believe I am performing a last act of confidence and loyalty.

I believe that I am still rendering a service to the emperor in trying to enlighten him on the tendencies and perfidious insinuations of a faction which meets with but very little sympathy, the leaders of which are misusing the ascendancy which they believe they possess and the confidence they are able to inspire, to prepare for your majesty and Mexico an era of sanguinary reprisals, of grievous catastrophes, of complete ruin and anarchy, and of humiliations without number.

I have the honour of informing your majesty that, more than ever desirous of preserving the esteem and friendship with which you have been pleased to favour me, I have acquainted the president of the council that, looking at the language of the aforesaid letter, I do not wish for the future to hold any direct communication with the administration of which he is the president.

I must add, sire, that the officers appointed by General Marquez are in daily communication with the commanders of the engineers and artillery of the French army in order to make themselves conversant with the state of the fortifications, defences, and the provision of stores, arms, and munitions in the city.

Your majesty having signified your desire to know beforehand the date at which I shall leave Mexico, I have the honour of informing you that my departure, with the last contingents of the expeditionary corps, will take place in the first half of the month of February.

Up to the last moment, sire, I shall be always ready to comply with any wish that your majesty may be pleased to express, and I shall always feel disposed to make my efforts coincide with your desires. BAZAINE.

This despatch was the last official communication addressed to the crown from our head-quarters.

The evening before, the marshal had written to the president of the council as follows:—

RUPTURE WITH THE FRENCH AUTHORITIES.

To M. Larès, President of the Council of Ministers.

Mexico, January 27, 1867.

I have received your letter of the 25th instant. I might well confine myself to merely acknowledging the receipt of it, because I do not admit that you can address me at your will, and next because your letter treats of matters which have been already settled, both in writing and also by former conferences.

In my replies to you or to the various under-secretaries of state, your excellency will find the explanations you desire.

You appear to accuse the French army of want of energy—have not I a much greater right to exclaim against the arbitrary acts and deeds of violence which have been daily committed for some weeks past, and does not our presence in Mexico appear to render the flag of France an accomplice in these proceedings? For this reason, sir, and because the wording of your letter betrays a feeling of mistrust undoubtedly based upon calumnies which affect our honour, I consider it necessary to state to you that I do not wish to have any further communication with your ministry.

The emperor, ill-advised by Father Fischer, sent no reply; and the commander-in-chief never saw his majesty again. The rupture was complete. The imperial confessor had been the originator of it, by urging on the minister to insult the dignity of a commander-in-chief whom he knew to be a slave to precise instructions. Another incident occurred to crown the matter. At the moment of leaving, for the sake of the French officers and soldiers who had deserved well of Maximilian, and belonged to the regiments which had been always fighting for him, our head-quarters' authorities, in spite of their own causes of complaint, were not afraid to remind the emperor of the proposal that he had made long back, to present them with the Cross of Guadeloupe. Abbé Fischer intercepting this despatch, wrote to General Osmont, the former minister, as follows:—

Private and confidential.

Mexico, February 1, 1867.

My dear General,—You are not ignorant that the line of conduct pursued during the last few days by Marshal Bazaine has had this final result—that his majesty has determined, much to his regret, to break off all intercourse with the marshal.

On account of this lamentable incident, I have thought it my duty to abstain from submitting for his majesty's approbation the list and proposition that you sent me the day before yesterday; for I consider that the only effect would be to increase the emperor's displeasure.

The respect which is due to you, and my high esteem for your merits, induce me to speak thus candidly.

Desirous, however, not to leave without its well-earned recompense the good services of the deserving body of soldiers comprised in this list, I now submit to your choice two methods which, in my opinion, would be likely to succeed. Either ask the emperor yourself, not in the marshal's name, but in your own; or send to me a private letter of the same import; in the latter case, I shall feel great satisfaction in promoting his majesty's approval of the same. AUGUSTIN FISCHER,

Secretary to the emperor.

In 1867 the clergy played the last part in the French intervention, as in 1861 they had played the first. The head of the military cabinet was directed to reply to the abbé as follows:—

Mexico, February 2, 1867.

Monsieur l'Abbé,—H. E. Marshal Bazaine, to whom General Osmont has communicated your private and confidential letter of the 1st of February, has intrusted me with the honour of replying to it.

Your ignorance of military usages has induced you to address to General Osmont a twofold proposition which evinces the desire you feel that brave officers should not be deprived of a recompense on which they set a value. You add that you do not think it right to submit the proposed lists to H. M. the Emperor of Mexico, on account of the lamentable incident which has taken place during the last few days.

It is in fact to be regretted that the proposed lists made long back should have been sent in under such unfavourable circumstances, but, Monsieur l'Abbé, it cannot be conceded that the private wish which you express of being courteous to General Osmont should authorise this general officer to break through the rules of etiquette which, in the military as in the clerical order, constitute the basis of discipline.

With regard to the incident which you appeal to, you cannot be ignorant who was the cause of it, and methodising the facts, you will perhaps perceive that a feeling that his honour was mistrusted and his feelings and dignity offended, have rendered necessary on the marshal's part this first rupture, the burden of which will be on the conscience of your political friends only.

Receive, &c.,
The Colonel, Head of the Military Cabinet.

Our head-quarters' authorities must have rejoiced that, in spite of the tendencies of General Castelnau, they had not the least departed from their written instructions, for our government wrote to them on the 15th of January that the movement of concentration and withdrawal ought to have been terminated; that it was necessary they should at once assemble the troops, to be ready for embarkation, and that the Transatlantic Company's vessels were to anchor in the roadstead at Vera Cruz in the latter part of the month of February.

Only one thing was now thought of in Paris, and this was to leave as soon as possible this land of destroyed illusions and bitter sacrifices.

' . . . . You have duties to fulfil;' they wrote to the marshal, 'the responsibility, whatever may happen, will rest upon you; but the responsibility should be a light one if you proceed, as you always do, straight to the end to which you have to attain,—the sending home of your troops without loss of time.' In this great shipwreck everything was swallowed up, the regeneration of the Latin race, as well as the hopes of the monarchy, the interests of our countrymen (which had been the pretext for the war), as well as the two French loans, which had only served to bring it to this disastrous conclusion. The only thing which swam safe upon the surface was the claim of Jecker, the Swiss, who had obtained his twelve millions.

In the early part of February our head-quarters were still at Mexico, and were employed in giving up the city to the Mexican authorities. Our commissaries offered to the imperial ministry our waggons, vehicles, and military clothing. Too poor to pay for all these things, the latter only purchased the clothing, to re-attire their troops, which were almost naked. Mexico, which was formerly an almost unfortified town, was now protected by a wall all round it, armed with numerous pieces of artillery, each furnished with ammunition enough for three hundred shots. There were three magazines, containing a very considerable quantity of cartridges, and the arsenal was full of muskets in good condition. Fearing that the enemy might attack the town suddenly, the marshal, in order to protect it from any such surprise, had *chevaux-de frise* placed in front of all the embankments abutting on the gates. As is usually done in any fortified place which is given up, the field-pieces, brought in from a certain extent of country, were taken into the court of the citadel, counted, examined, and made over to the officers of the imperial artillery, who also received the keys of the warehouses, where the various equipments and tools were deposited. Official receipts, duly signed, were handed in exchange to our staff. This operation had a twofold object. In case of any sudden attack on the part of the Liberals, the guns of light calibre would have been easy to carry off; but in the court of the citadel they were in a place of safety. With regard to the siege-guns left on the ramparts, their great weight was a sufficient protection against any sudden removal.

The instructions of our minister-of-war had directed that all our artillery should be brought away.

The projectiles, both hollow and solid, which would have cost too much to convey to France were destroyed; they were absolutely useless to the Mexicans, whose smooth-bore cannon could not be loaded with the rifled shot.

As to the powder belonging to the expeditionary corps, General Castelnau ordered it to be thrown into the Sequia. Mexico was now in so complete a state of defence, and so thoroughly provided with stores and provisions, that it was in a position to stand a long siege by a force more powerful than its own garrison. In fact, the death of Maximilian was the real cause of the capitulation of the place.

At the moment when we were breaking up our projectiles, two Mexicans, dressed in civil costume, presented themselves at the gate of the citadel, which was still occupied by our soldiers; notwithstanding the opposition of the sentinel, who forbade the entry of these unknown intruders, they made their way in. These two strangers were the Emperor and General Marquez. This was the first visit during his whole reign which Maximilian had paid to the fortress, notwithstanding the repeated offers of the commander-in-chief. This mysterious visit (the marshal complained that he was not advised of it, for his proper place was by the side of the sovereign) was an act of mistrust.

On the morning of the 8th of February, the tri-coloured flag, which floated over the head-quarters at Buena-Vista, was lowered, and Mexico city was now freed from the French occupation. The marshal, who knew by experience that the Mexicans would but badly discharge the executive duties of the place, left the city with his troops. To give time for the necessary organization he encamped on the road of La Piedad, about a cannon shot from the city, where he remained a day and a night. The marshal still entertained a hope that Maximilian would resolve to join him. However, he kept on his guard; for it was not impossible that the ministry, under the influence of irritation, would commit some act of hostility, in the hope of forcing our troops to return to the capital. The next day the sheen of the French bayonets disappeared on the horizon.

General Castelnau's mission was now over. The imperial aide-de-camp proceeded at once to Vera Cruz, to embark in the transatlantic steamer, sailing the 15th of February. He went down by *diligence* from Mexico as far as the *Terres Chaudes*. He went, doubtless, to give his sovereign an account of the events which he had witnessed, and of the state of the country generally. It is, however, difficult to understand how he could have been able to enlighten the court of the Tuileries to any useful purpose as to the real spirit of the people; for, excepting his short journey to Puebla, he had not once quitted the capital. General Castelnau is too clear-sighted not to have been struck, at the time he left Mexico, with the hostile feeling manifested by all parties, and especially by the clerical faction, who, impelled by the ministry, endeavoured to incite a demonstration against our flag; the advisers of the crown hoped by this means, either to induce their fellow-countrymen to forget their past alliance with the intervention, or to retard our withdrawal, which, in spite of all that had happened, they looked upon with sorrow; for they felt that the reign of reaction was drawing to its close.

Larès and Marquez were even now urging Maximilian to leave for Queretaro, knowing well that the sovereign would be powerless away from the capital, where they reckoned upon becoming the sole 'masters of the situation,' after the probable downfall or death of Maximilian. Mejia, up to the time of his execution, certainly stands out as the grandest military personification during this period of Mexican history, in which he shone out by his immutable loyalty and devotion both to the clerical cause and to Maximilian; but the impartiality of history will never be able to ennoble Miramon's head with a similar martyr-like halo of glory. Our government is generally too well informed of all that goes on at Paris not to have known that the former president of the republic used often to say in certain *salons*, that he was only returning to Mexico to reascend the presidential chair, after the downfall of the monarchy. If he had been successful in his northern campaign, it is a matter of certainty that he would have turned his arms against his sovereign.

Considering all the untoward symptoms which, at the beginning of February 1867, were already beginning to show themselves, one cannot help feeling surprised at the placidity which prevails in the final despatch addressed by General Castelnau to the Emperor Napoleon, dated Vera Cruz, the 14th of February, and conveyed to the telegraph station at New Orleans by the *Bouvet* advice-boat of our squadron.

General Castelnau to the Emperor Napoleon III.

The evacuation of Mexico took place on the 5th, and excited *sympathetic manifestations* only. The withdrawal was effected in perfect order, without firing a shot. The emperor remains at Mexico city, *where all is quiet*, . . . returns to-day to France.

On his return to Europe, General Castelnau was promoted to the rank of general of division, as a recompense for his services.

The formal mission of the imperial aide-de-camp had not solved all the difficulties of the evacuation which fell upon the marshal.

The last French column went slowly down to Puebla, so as to be able to give a helping hand to Maximilian, if necessary. With this intention, the marshal remained five days in the latter town. To protect the entry of the Mexican detachments into the place, he sent out his cavalry towards Oajaca.

The Emperor of Mexico gave no sign of life. Just at this time the news of Miramon's disaster reached the bivouac. The commander-in-chief wrote immediately to Maximilian, beseeching him to return. He informed him also that General de Castagny would remain in the rear, in order to protect him. This final attempt failed; M. Dano had to make known the emperor's decision:—

M. Dano to the Marshal.

Mexico, February 16, 1867.

General de Castagny has written me that your excellency, still being in a position to give a helping-hand to the Emperor Maximilian to enable him to retire, would be glad to know the intentions of his Majesty after the check given to General Miramon. In a few days this chance will be out of the question.

The Mexican ministers assert that you have written in the same tenour to their sovereign.

The young emperor is less inclined than ever to accept this offer. I regret bitterly that he has decided to attempt any further hazards. It will be very grievous if any misfortune happen to him. But no one is able to check him, and we least of all.

A success, which in reality is but insignificant, has taken place, which is much boasted of. To make up for it, there is a report that the rebels have entered Queretaro without firing a shot, the imperialists having evacuated the town. This news, however, is not at all certain. It is feared that the road to Mexico will now be closed for Maximilian.

As the French retired, they solidly strengthened the whole road which might serve as a line of retreat for the emperor if a moment of danger arrived. The town of Puebla (which, a month after, fell into Porfirio's power) was so well organised for defence that the 'general orders' of the 7th of April, addressed by the conqueror to his troops, ended thus :—

. . . . With the muskets taken from the enemy, this place—not without reason entitled impregnable, as the first soldiers in the world were not able to take it by assault—has yielded to the first effort of our overpowering valour. The entire garrison,* and the immense *matériel* of war collected together by the enemy, are the trophies of our victory. PORFIRIO DIAZ.

The marshal, on his arrival at Vera Cruz, in order to prepare and ensure a retreat for Maximilian, caused the fortifications of the port to be at once completed; he himself inspected the forts. At the request of M. Bureau, the imperial commissioner, he made over to the Mexicans a considerable store of cartridges, a hundred muskets, and thirty hundred-weights of powder taken from our fleet.

At one time there was an idea that the emperor had left the city of Mexico to come down to the sea. The marshal, who, in defiance of the *vomito*, had prolonged his stay at Vera Cruz, went up in great haste to La Soledad with some officers, intending to rely for pro-

---

* Puebla was commanded and yielded up by General Noriega, a friend of Marquez, who ran away before the enemy from Jalapa in 1863, but was thanked by General Forey, and reinstated by the ministry.

tection on the rear-guard and the Egyptian battalion stationed in the *Terres Chaudes*. A report was spread among the guerillas that he was about to re-open the campaign, in order to clear the road. But he was compelled to retrace his steps to Vera Cruz without the emperor. Maximilian had already reached Queretaro.

The following note, emanating from the head of the French artillery, gives an exact idea of the means of defence left to the monarchy:—

The manufacture of cartridges and percussion caps under the care of the French artillery, and by the use of French powder, was continued, for the help of the Mexican government, up to the month of January, 1867, when the above government ceased, notwithstanding repeated demands, to furnish the funds necessary for the work.

At the request of the marshal commanding-in-chief, considerable quantities of cartridges and 20,000 kilograms of gunpowder had been sent out from France for the use of the Mexican army and people. From the official documents, provided with the written acknowledgment of the parties receiving them, it appears that the number of cartridges delivered was 3,228,226, and the quantity of gunpowder reached 21,437 kilograms.

In short, when the French army quitted the city of Mexico, it left it provided with 34,741 projectiles of all calibres with charges sufficient to fire 300 shot from each cannon, and a reserve of 500,000 cartridges (without reckoning those belonging to the Austro-Belgian legion). No kind of munitions of war belonging to Mexico were destroyed or taken away from the magazines, and Mexican officers, appointed for the purpose, gave an acknowledgment for them, and certified to their being duly handed over. The same formalities were observed in all the places in the interior occupied by the army, as they were evacuated.

Up to the middle of January, 1867, that is, fifteen days before it left the city of Mexico, the French artillery continued to contribute by its own labour and by the resources which it derived from its own stores, to augmenting the means of action which it left in the hands of the Mexican government.

THE DIRECTOR OF THE ARTILLERY.

Before embarking, the marshal entrusted to the care of M. Bureau, the imperial commissioner, a final message for the unhappy prince.

To the Admiral commanding the squadron.

Vera Cruz, March 7, 1867.

Monsieur l'Amiral,—I have handed over to the Mexican military authorities in the capital, at Puebla and at Orizaba, all the arsenals and the military establishments in a perfect state of repair, with the cannon and a full complement of ammunition; the fortifications also, and the detached works, all in the best possible state of defence, everything being understood to be the property of Mexico.

So much for the capital and the places situated on my line of retreat.

My intention was to act in the same way at Vera Cruz, and to make no additions to the resources of the garrison. Nevertheless, as H. E. the minister of France has concluded a new arrangement with the Mexican government, modifying the convention of July 30th, 1866, by which the Mexican government engages to pay monthly to France a sum of 50,000 piastres (250,000 francs), I have been obliged to look to securing for the longest possible time the payment of this sum, which cannot be a matter of indifference to the French treasury; and, in fact, represents the interest of a considerable portion of the Mexican loans.

For this reason I have thought it right to give to M. Bureau, the imperial commissioner, everything that I had at my disposal in the way of arms, munition of war, harness, articles for encamping, &c. &c. It is, in fact, to our interest to enable this official to hold the city after the departure of the expeditionary corps.

Another reason, also, has prompted this resolution; this is the propriety, in my opinion, of ensuring to H.M. the Emperor Maximilian, without in any way binding the policy of our country, a place of refuge where he may find an asylum and the means of embarkation, should circumstances reduce him to it. In order to increase the strength of the place and to give the garrison greater confidence, I have wished to increase their resources in munitions of war, and especially in powder. I also think that it would be well to place at the disposal of the Mexican authority a small steamer which could protect the city from the attempts of armed bands from the neighbouring rebel population.

Following out the ideas explained above, I beg you, *monsieur l'amiral*, to let me know if you could spare 40 to 50 hundred-weights of powder from the stores of the fleet; and if, among the gun-boats now in the roadstead, one might not be found which could be made over to the Mexican government by the use of certain formalities, which would have the effect of doing away with any interpretation compromising to our policy. The gun-boat might, for instance, be denationalised and sold as unfit for service, and as not being worth sending back to France.

The gun-boat *La Tourmente* has been pointed out to me as one fulfilling these conditions.

I again repeat that I see in these measures a means of ensuring to our country the payment of an important sum; next, of protecting our countrymen for a more prolonged period, and strengthening the position and influence of our consul; and, finally, of enabling the young emperor, who is, at this time, running all the hazards of a conflict which may probably go against him, to find a point strong enough to cover his retreat and embarkation.

In acting as I have done, I have the full consciousness that I have fulfilled the wishes of my sovereign; and I should be glad to find that it would be possible for you to second me without exceeding the limits of your instructions which must principally guide your decision. BAZAINE.

On the 11th of March, 1867, at eight o'clock in the morning, the French commandant at Vera Cruz handed over the place, as well as the Mexican artillery and stores, to General Perez Gomez, who assumed the charge of both in the name of his emperor.

This general had just directed the abandonment of the towns of Cordova and Orizaba, in order to concentrate his forces at Vera Cruz. A few days after, the last French regiments crowded on board our ships, and bade adieu to the shores of Mexico and to their brave comrades who lay buried in that distant land.

Six weeks after, the 'Souverain' anchored in the roadstead of Toulon. Immediately on its arrival, the maritime prefect and the commandant of the subdivision proceeded on board the vessel which conveyed Marshal Bazaine. They announced to him, in the names of their respective ministers, that an order had been given not to pay him the accustomed honours. The inhabitants, already informed of these arrangements by the *Gazette du Midi*, which had not been contradicted by the authorities, crowded upon the quay; his reception was a hostile one. The marshal had to make his way through the crowd, carrying his head high, but with a wounded heart; when he set his foot on his native soil he had the consciousness of having thoroughly done his duty as a French soldier.

Our government, usually so jealous of the honour of the meanest of its functionaries, knows well how to restrain the press, and to prohibit the admission of foreign newspapers, when they deviate from certain principles. Three months before the commander-in-chief returned to Europe, pamphlets of American origin, and others of a similar character, were allowed to inundate our country, thus holding up to common shame the name of a marshal of France, and, in fact, misleading public opinion. It was soon forgotten that a marshal was bound to silence by his sense of military discipline, and that the government, being the guardian of the honour of its high dignitaries as well as of its own, alone had the right to speak. But this right is also an indefeasible duty, which allows of no reserve whatever, and dictates that, after public inquiry, the general who has violated his positive orders, and has failed in delicacy and honour, should be degraded; or else it should be publicly declared, after having been strict to all, that he has deserved well of his country. Our army, France, and Europe are now anxiously awaiting this final verdict!

CHAPTER XXII.

Termination of the French Intervention in Mexico—Reflections on the Fate of Maximilian—His Illusions and Errors—Retrospect and Final Considerations.

THE history of the French intervention in Mexico terminates here. The events which happened during the last three months of Maximilian's life belong to the province of Mexican history. The elect of French policy knew how to die with all the pride which befitted a descendant of Charles the Fifth. But one cannot help regretting that he had not sought a soldier's death at Queretaro, sword in hand. A conqueror, vanquished by fortune, falls with more dignity by the hand of an enemy on the field of battle, than under the sentence of a court-martial. We cannot help thinking that Maximilian, led on to his death by a guilty faction, never ceased to hope for a peaceful issue. It was a fixed idea with him to give up the authority with which he thought he was invested into the hands of Juarez, whom he had invited to a solemn compact; this testifies how far his illusions carried him. It would be difficult in any other way to explain the conduct of the young sovereign. If he had intended to plunge into the contest, and strike a last blow for the monarchy, he would hardly have quitted the capital, which was prepared to resist any attack, and have secluded himself in an unfortified town, commanded by strong positions all round it. He would hardly have left behind him at Mexico 500 faithful Hungarians, whose bodies would have been a rampart round him in the day of battle—whose sabres would have cleared a safe passage for him down to the sea. Notwithstanding his state of prostration from grief and fever, he should have resolutely grasped the sword of the Hapsburgs which in his youth he had so longed to wield. He capitulated, because his chivalrous character induced him to believe in the magnanimity of others. He forgot, at this supreme moment, when these faithful Austrians were preparing to die for his sake, that he had to answer, and justly so, for all the blood that had been shed for his cause. Ambition is a noble quality when its aim is the happiness of a nation. A prince may be momentarily deceived as to the sincerity of the vote of a nation which, yielding to constraint or to some transient influence, entrusts him with its destinies. But the matter is soon brought to a test. When, after the lapse of two years, conflicting parties are still tearing one another to pieces in every part of the territory, the ambition which still persists in its aim becomes as guilty as the hand which is lifted against the liberty of a people; the responsibility of the convulsions of the country is then to be traced back to rulers, who, though they may evade the judgment of men, cannot escape the strictures of history.

As we finish the sad investigation of this long drama, we feel a consciousness that we have vindicated the truth only, without having either undertaken or accepted any exculpatory office. Fresh documents, which for the truth of criticism it is material should be produced, wherever they may come from, may perhaps seem inconsistent with, but cannot destroy, the authentic writings on which our narrative is based. The future only will be able to reconstruct the past, aided by all the truthful materials which every day is adding to the historical records of the second French empire. At all events, from the facts already known, one great lesson is evolved—that the policy of a government cannot with impunity venture to run indefinite risks without giving a shock to its power and damaging the prestige of its dignity, at home as well as abroad. Rulers ought not to forget that human passions play their part in the most elevated regions of the community, just as in its lowest recesses, and that it is their province to submit all their actions to the salutary and restrictive control of those they govern, if they would not lay them open to the stern censures of posterity.

APPENDIX.

DOCUMENTARY PROOFS AND ILLUSTRATIONS.

PAGE 12.

It will not be without interest to add this letter written by General Prim; it needs no comment.

To M. José Gonzalez Echavarria, Mexico.

Madrid, May 11, 1863.

My most esteemed Uncle and Friend,—I have received your letter of January, and am thinking over the state of things in your country, deplorable enough no doubt, but yet tending to acquaint the world that Mexico is still a nation, and its sons are not the objectless and degraded race that some try to make them out. You are certainly the worthy sons of those who have astonished the universe by their exploits. What will that humbug M. Billault say to justify his words:—'that the perjured government of Juarez will fall before the breath of France?' In France, there is an unutterable anxiety and uneasiness caused by the war in Mexico, and to those who ask me anything about it, I reply, that the war in Mexico will become a catastrophe for France; and it is nothing but the truth. Only imagine, if Forey's army should break down before Puebla! *Ave Maria Sanctissima!* God only knows what would happen then.

We are impatiently waiting for the couriers, to get news of you and of the country. I see that Mr. Wyke, the English minister, has left for Europe, and I am afraid he went away before the courier arrived by whom, through his medium, I wrote to you as well as to my uncle Michel, and sent to you and others some copies of my speech in the Senate. This speech will be approved of, I have no doubt, not only in your country, but over all the continent of America.

Here there has been a change in the cabinet. O'Donell has fallen, and we were on the point of seeing the progressive party get the upper hand. In the end, Miraflores and Concha have come into power; both of them taking the French side in the Mexican question. But wherever and whenever you hear it said that the Spanish are coming back to Mexico to help the French, deny it at once. That which is done is done, and no one can undo it. PRIM.

The following despatch, dated in July, and addressed to President Juarez by Ramon Diaz, a Mexican, and agent to his government at Havannah, may throw a certain light on General Prim's letter.

Despatch from Ramon Diaz to Benito Juarez, President of the Republic at Mexico.

Havannah, July 19, 1863.

Very dear Sir and Friend,—Being still impressed with the repulses which we have just met with, at a time when we least expected them, and our success seemed almost beyond doubt, I write these lines to inform you that I am forming a subscription in this island, which affords satisfactory results, for the purpose of buying a portion of the arms which I mentioned to you in my last letter. For I suppose that you are unable at present to send me the funds necessary for this purchase.

I am working with great activity, and it is probable that, about the middle of next month, I shall have finished the business I am so occupied with. I therefore hope that you will give me the order to send you this parcel of arms as soon as possible. I can easily send it to Tunpan by steam with tolerable security. Tell me, therefore, if this point will suit you, or acquaint me with some other safe place for landing them. As this is a rather delicate business, I shall entrust it to no one, and shall myself accompany the arms in question. If you do not make any other arrangements, I hope that you will send me the necessary license for entering the republic.

It is probable that Napoleon will withdraw his troops as soon as the trumpery government is formed in the capital of the republic. Events in Poland are becoming more complicated, and the Confederates have just experienced some terrible reverses.

In Spain, things are much in the same state as they were. It is said now that O'Donell is going to join the ministry; but this is not credible. There is no news in this island. I have nothing more to add to-day, and I repeat that I am your devoted friend

RAMON S. DIAZ.

The Juarist agent was playing his part. But how are we to understand the attitude of the authorities at Havannah, a Spanish colony, with respect to this Juarist subscription which was intended to arm the republican troops? What a sudden contrast! From this very port, only a few months before, the Spanish squadron had set sail for Vera Cruz, to raise the flag of her Catholic Majesty by the side of the banner of France. Would not the baffled ambition of General Prim (who had perhaps dreamt of a Mexican crown for his own head) explain this violation of neutrality to which the captain-general of the colony must have been privy? Yet we were their allies but a short time before!

PAGE 29.

Looking at the following document, which derives its importance from the name of the signer, no doubt can be entertained as to the active part taken by the cabinet of the Tuileries in the creation of the Mexican throne. This transoceanic enterprise was intended to act on European politics, as we may notice that this letter, addressed to an English member of Parliament, alludes to the Venetian question, which was being discussed both at Paris and at Vienna.

To an English Member of Parliament.

Paris, December 30, 1863.

My dear Sir,— . . . . Although it may be said that the archduke has neither altered nor rescinded any of his intentions, this is very far from being the case. You may consider it as certain that he will leave next March, the date when the result of the *general* (but not *universal*) vote of the nation will become known in Europe; this is the only condition which he now imposes, and his departure is considered by us as an assured fact.

It must be remarked (and this tends to set our minds at rest), that the Mexican question is a matter altogether apart from the general political movements in Europe. It is an affair *exclusively confined to the Emperor Napoleon and the archduke, with the approbation of the emperor, his brother,* as head of the family, but without the slightest interference on the part of the Austrian government.

This state of things is favourable to Austria, *inasmuch as it puts Venetia or any other compensation out of the question*; it is also favourable to the Mexican question, by leaving it isolated and standing alone on its own special ground. France is already in Mexico, and has no other solution before her but the throne of the archduke, whether there is a war in Europe or not.

The Austrian vessel which will convey the Prince to Mexico will not be detained by England (who will probably be Austria's ally in the complications foreseen) or by France, who is conducting him thither.

It appears to me that illusion has no share in these thoroughly practical consi͏̈ rations.

I beg th⟨⟩ ⟨⟩ will always believe me your affectionate and faithful   J. M. GUTIERREZ DE ESTRADA.

PAGE 84.

We had considered that it would not be very generous to give publicity to the following document, emanating from the military cabinet of the Emperor Maximilian and referring to the decree of October the 3rd. But we no longer hesitate to do it, looking at the absolute necessity of giving to this history its real character. The following imperial order, sent to Marshal Bazaine, clearly proves that the decree of October the 3rd was not wrung from the Emperor Maximilian by the French commander-in-chief. The emperor, we repeat it, generous as he was by nature and ordinarily most merciful, had nothing else in view but the punishment of brigands.

Military Cabinet of the Emperor,
Mexico, December 16, 1865.

Monsieur le Maréchal,—His Majesty directs me to acquaint your excellency that, in case Vicente Riva Palacios should be captured, he wishes that he should be brought to Mexico. *This exception is for special reasons, and is the only one the emperor intends to make to the decree of the 3rd of October*, and he desires that your Excellency will give positive instructions that, if he is taken, Riva Palacios should not be put to death.

The Chief of the Military Cabinet of the Emperor.

Page 252.

End of Maximilian's reply :—

My sole duty consists in nominating a provisional regency until the nation can be appealed to, and in taking the proper proceedings for convoking it; and, finally, in seeking protection for the imperialists, but without mixing myself up with anything beyond.

MAXIMILIAN.

www.ingramcontent.com/pod-product-compliance
Lightning Source LLC
Chambersburg PA
CBHW031901220426
43663CB00006B/713